the **Heart**
of the
Restoration

God's
holy
fire

the nature
and function
of Scripture

Kenneth L. Cukrowski
Mark W. Hamilton
James W. Thompson

A·C·U
PRESS

God's Holy Fire:
The Nature and Function of Scripture

The Heart of the Restoration, Volume 2
Douglas A. Foster, series editor

ACU Box 29138
Abilene, TX 79699
www.acu.edu/acupress

Cover: Sarah Bales
Typesetting and book design: William Rankin
This book is composed in ITC Garamond
Body text is Garamond 10.5/13

All translations of Scripture are the authors' own unless otherwise
indicated.

Printed in the United States of America

ISBN 0-89112-037-8

Library of Congress Card Number 2001099781

1,2,3,4,5

To Philip Thompson & Eleanor Bryant

To James & Carlanna Hamilton

In memory of Arthur & Ruth McFaul

Contents

Preface to the Series

From its beginning in 1906, Abilene Christian University has existed as an institution of higher education to serve the fellowship of the Churches of Christ. While we welcome students and supporters from a variety of Christian traditions who are sympathetic with our Christ-centered focus, we know who our primary constituents are. ACU's Bible Department, now the College of Biblical Studies, has for almost a century been a guiding light for our fellowship through its contributions in Christian scholarship and ministry. Thousands of missionaries, ministers, elders, teachers, and Christian servants have come under the positive influence of these godly professors. They have steadfastly upheld the lordship of Christ, the authority of the Scriptures, and the necessity of living a life of Christian service through the church.

Abilene Christian University, in conjunction with its ACU Press, launched the *Heart of the Restoration* series with *The Crux of the Matter* in 2001, and now continues it with *God's Holy Fire*. We pray that this series will help stimulate discussion and make a meaningful contribution to the fellowship of the Churches of Christ and beyond. This volume deals with the nature and function of Scripture. Subsequent volumes will address topics such as the Church, worship, and Christology. The authors are all faculty members in ACU's College of Biblical Studies. In these volumes, they will model a biblical spirit of unity in Christ, with individual perspectives on the details of the Gospel message. Above all, they are committed to the lordship of Jesus Christ and to his church, and they are committed to restoring the spirit of the Christian faith "once for all delivered to the saints."

My special thanks go to Dr. Jack Reese who shared the dream of this series with me from the beginning. Dr. Doug Foster, as the editor of the series, has made the dream into a reality. My thanks go also to our benefactors, who believed that the project would result in a clearer articulation of our faith and identity in Churches of Christ at the dawning of a new century.

> Now to him who is able to do immeasurably more than all we ask or imagine, according to his power that is at work within us, to him be glory in the church and in Christ Jesus throughout all generations, for ever and ever! Amen.

—Royce Money
President
Abilene Christian University

Introduction

*"O sages standing in God's holy fire
As in the gold mosaic of a wall"*
—William Butler Yeats
"Sailing to Byzantium"

The title of this volume, *God's Holy Fire*, is taken from William Butler Yeats' poem, "Sailing to Byzantium." The poem speaks of a yearning for a place of truth and beauty that is beyond our daily routines. Like the poet, we desire to live in such a place. The image of fire also evokes the words of Jeremiah 20:9, "Is not my word like fire?" Fire has the awesome power to consume and renew life. Jeremiah speaks of a "fire in [his] bones" so overpowering that he can no longer hold it within himself (20:9). The image indicates that the Bible contains potent words for any age.

In the previous volume of this series, *The Crux of the Matter*, our colleagues observed that the Churches of Christ are now in a time of unprecedented change and uncertainty about the future. They described both the central place of the Bible in the history of Churches of Christ and the changing cultural situation that has led to the decreasing use of the Bible and the decline of biblical literacy. We write this book because we are convinced that this decline in biblical literacy will result in the loss of the church's memory—a devastating form of amnesia. Therefore, we challenge Christians to rediscover the Word that has sustained God's people for generations. We hope to encourage the love of Scripture, to lead the church toward the knowledge of Scripture, to equip the church for the proper use of Scripture, and to clear away misunderstandings of Scripture. Because the Bible has the power to speak to our most urgent questions, we are writing to encourage Christians to reclaim the central place of the Bible in their lives.

We recognize that we are among numerous voices in the Stone-Campbell Restoration Movement that are now responding to this changed situation with proposals for future directions. We hope that our contribution will be a part of a healthy dialogue within Churches of Christ that will result in the continuing faithfulness of God's people to the mission to which God has called them. Each of the authors has strong ties to Churches of Christ and deep love for God's Word.

James Thompson grew up in Tyler, Texas, where he first learned the Bible from both his home and extended family. His maternal grandfather, Newton Holland, was a model of serious Bible study. James began preaching in East Texas, and then graduated from Abilene Christian University (B.A., M.A.). He preached for the Queens Church of Christ in New York while completing the B.D. at Union Theological Seminary (1970). Since receiving the doctorate from Vanderbilt University in 1974, he has combined his scholarship with service to the church, having written several books for adult teachers.

Ken Cukrowski grew up in the South Whittier Church of Christ in southern California. Bible reading and study were a vital part of the spiritual heritage he received from his parents and grandparents. After attending Abilene Christian University, Ken completed his M.Div. and his doctoral work in New Testament at Yale University. He has served as an associate minister, education minister, and youth minister. Now teaching courses in New Testament and Greek, he thinks he has the best job imaginable.

Mark Hamilton grew up in the Rena Road Church of Christ in western Arkansas. His family has been part of Churches of Christ since the 1800s and has produced several generations of men and women of faith. After attending Freed-Hardeman University (B.A.) and Abilene Christian University (M.Div., M.A.), he ministered for several years in New England, eventually completing doctoral work in Old Testament at Harvard University. He enjoys living in both the church and the academy and seeks to help each enrich the other.

This book is the collaborative work of three authors. The reader will note that the authors sometimes speak in the first person singular of their own experiences, while in other instances they speak in the first person plural. We have worked together in the process of planning, writing, and discussing the content of each chapter. James Thompson is the primary author of Chapters 1, 2, and 4. Mark Hamilton is the primary author of Chapters 3, 5, 6, and 10. Ken Cukrowski is the primary author of Chapters 7, 8, and 9.

In Chapter 1, we assess the contemporary situation and call for the rediscovery of the Word of God in the church. We discuss the importance of memory and the consequences of amnesia, arguing that a knowledge of God's Word is essential to the future of the church. In Chapter 2, we explore what it means to be a people under the Word. Because many people are confused by the numerous attempts to define more precisely how the Bible is the Word of God, we reconsider the meaning of the words "all Scripture is inspired."

The inspired Scripture described in 2 Timothy 3:16 was the Old Testament, a section of Scripture often ignored in Christian teaching. Chapter 3 argues that a rediscovery of the whole of Scripture is vital to the life of the church. Eliminating the Old Testament from the Bible deprives Christians of an understanding of the character and activities of God. In Chapter 3, we maintain that the Old Testament remains the Word of God and that it continues to speak to the church.

Many people have read the Bible more as a reference work to consult than as a book that actually has transforming power. In Chapter 4, we demonstrate that the Bible is a compelling story with a beginning, a middle, and an end. This compelling narrative contains many smaller narratives about real people who struggle to be faithful to God. In the lives of these people, readers discover something about themselves.

Although the Bible forms one continuous story that begins with creation and ends with God's people awaiting the last act in the drama, it contains a gorgeous mosaic of prophetic writings, law, poetry, and letters that interpret the grand narrative. Chapters 5 and 6 describe how the various parts of Scripture shape Christian practice.

Chapter 7 both describes a process for studying and interpreting Scripture and analyzes some of the challenges connected with the process of interpretation. Attempting to connect Scripture and theology, Chapter 8 identifies ways to move from Scripture to a message for today, and then examines how to go from the challenges of real life to a response shaped by Scripture. Finally, Chapter 9 proposes ways that Scripture can be used in worship, in Bible classes, and in personal devotions.

Just as the reading of Scripture is an activity for a community, many people participated in reading earlier drafts of this book. Thanks are due to a number of friends and colleagues who agreed to read all or parts of our manuscript. We were challenged, corrected, and encouraged. Sometimes we resisted their advice. More often, we listened, and the book now benefits from those changes. For your time and wise counsel, we gratefully offer this brief recognition. This volume's readers include Frederick Aquino, Brent Ballard, Ken Berry, Jeff Childers, Paul Clark, Karen Cukrowski, Jack English, Doug Foster, Pam Hadfield, Katie Hays, Samjung Kang-Hamilton, Mark Love, Bill Rankin, Sherry Rankin, Jack Reese, Jack Riehl, Tim Sensing, Kris Southward, and Philip Stambaugh. Special thanks go to the general editor of this series, Doug Foster, and to Jack Reese for their leadership on this project, and to President Money for his support of the *Heart of the Restoration* series.

Writing this book in the midst of other pressing demands has brought the authors closer together as friends and colleagues. None of us can imagine working as closely and amicably with anyone else as we have with each other. We have grown in our appreciation of each other. Our gratitude goes also to our wives, Karen, Samjung, and Carolyn, and our children, Katie and Krista, Nathan and Hannah, for allowing us to write one last draft, one more paragraph when we should have been talking or playing with them. This book belongs to all of them as much as to us. Most of all, we offer our gratitude and praise to God for offering us transforming grace in the words of Scripture and in the Spirit-led lives of our fellow Christians.

> —*Ken Cukrowski*
> *Mark Hamilton*
> *James Thompson*
> December 2001

1
Rediscovering the Word of God

Because memory is one of our most precious possessions, allowing us to recall people and pivotal moments of the past, nothing is more devastating than the amnesia that takes this treasure away. Communities have memories also, and corporate amnesia is no less destructive. The importance of memory for the survival of communities is graphically illustrated by an analogy Stanley Hauerwas draws from Richard Adams's *Watership Down*.[1]

Although Adams describes a world of rabbits who live by the memory of their stories, the reader can easily see that this is a story about human communities. In *Watership Down*, the rabbits know that they inhabit a dangerous world where they must devote their energies to survival. A warren of rabbits senses danger in its habitat and begins a pilgrimage to find a secure place. Along the way, the rabbits survive by the stories that place them in the larger texture of the world and describe their destiny. Indeed, the story that helps them make sense of their lives is the "Blessing of El-ahrairah," the account of Frith, the god who allocated gifts to each of the species.

On a specific day, Frith called the animals to a meeting to which the rabbits' ancestor came late. By the time that El-ahrairah, the rabbits' ancestor, arrived, Frith had given sharp teeth to the fox and the weasel, and silent feet and eyes to see in the dark to the cat. All that was left for the rabbit were strong hind legs that gave strength and speed. From this point on, the world would be the rabbits' enemy, but the rabbit would survive by its ability to recognize danger and to run. The story explained the world and helped the rabbits survive.

In one episode of *Watership Down*, the rabbits approach a warren unlike any they have ever seen. Because they are exhausted by their journey, they want to accept the invitation to join the rabbits who are residents there. But something is very different about this warren. The area is spacious, but the rabbit population is thin. The residents grow large, but they are slow and do not possess the normal rabbit strength. Food is so plentiful that they no longer must struggle to find it. Here the rabbits live a life of leisure, each one doing as it pleases. The rabbits of *Watership Down* recognize how strange this seemingly idyllic warren is one evening when they tell one of their stories to the residents. After the story, one of the residents says, "Very nice," adding that they no longer tell stories in this warren. They are a community without traditions. They have *no story* that holds them together.

In fact, as the rabbits of *Watership Down* soon discover, this apparent haven is the creation of the farmer who recognizes that he does not need to build a rabbit hutch if he can fatten the rabbits and snare only a few at a time. He can leave the remaining rabbits to look out only for themselves and to forget the ways of wild rabbits. Here they could forget the old stories and do as they please. But those who had no stories were doomed to die, a point well noted by Hauerwas.

Hauerwas's analogy from *Watership Down* attempts to make an important point—people live by stories that locate their lives in the larger picture of the world. Stories express a way of viewing reality. From these stories, we can discover how to answer our most basic questions: who are we, where are we, what is wrong, and what is the solution? Stories help us find our place.[2] A community without a narrative explaining where it came from and where it is going will lose its purpose and die.

The Christian Story

Christianity is a religion with a story—a story that is known only from the Bible. These are not just fictional stories like *Watership Down*, of course. They are about real people, real places, and real events. The tourist and the archaeologist can still travel to Israel, Turkey, and Greece to see where the events of the Bible actually happened. The remarkable fact is that, not only do our children learn the same stories that we learned as children, but people continue to tell the story of Abraham, Isaac, Jacob, and their descendants after more than 3,000 years.

This fact is especially noteworthy when one recalls the incredible number of empires that have come and gone over the past three millennia. Indeed, Israel was only a tiny kingdom the size of Massachusetts, far smaller than the empires of the Hittites, Assyrians, Babylonians, or Persians. Most people today don't know much about Canaanites or Hittites, but they know of Israel, which survived despite the loss of its temple, monarchy, and land. In the same way, the early church flourished when no casual observer could have predicted that it would meet the challenge offered by the competition. Without the survival of Israel and the early church, Christians would not now be telling the ancient story.

Why did Israel and the early Christians survive when the powerful kingdoms of the ancient world are now merely objects of historical and archaeological interest? Israel had a memory that no one could take away. The Israelites survived Babylonian captivity and returned to rebuild their devastated land because of a memory, which later was gathered into a book. James Sanders, a leading Old Testament scholar, used to say that the miracle was that the Bible came out of the ashes of two temples.

One would have thought that the destruction of the temples would be the end of the story. But the Israelites had a portable faith that could survive the loss of everything. One might say that the children of Abraham had a better education program than the competition's! They had a story, and they put the story down in books for future generations. They took their story and their books into captivity, and they recited them there. That same story kept them going until they returned from captivity. No one could rob them of their memory of God's redeeming acts in the past.

In *The Closing of the American Mind*, Alan Bloom asked what might happen to a civilization that lost its memory. Part of the educational process of any civilization is to educate the people in the story that becomes their shared narrative. For most people, a cornerstone of family life consists of the stories that only their family appreciates. When newcomers enter the family, whether through marriage or birth, a part of their introduction to the family involves initiation into the family's stories. In the same way, a civilization is defined by its stories. The schools not only teach courses in mathematics, science, and language. Through their courses in literature and history, they initiate the students into the nation's story and provide a common memory.

In 1973, I made my first trip through the eerie barrier between east and west into Communist East Berlin. The wall, erected in 1961 to prevent the people of the East from fleeing into the greater prosperity of the West, was one of the great symbols of the Cold War.

My first impression, as I went through Checkpoint Charlie into the other half of this divided city, was of the stark contrast between the lights and activity of West Berlin and the backwardness of East Berlin. The buildings were drab, and the construction was not as good as that which we saw in West Germany. Many ruins from the bombing of World War II still stood as a reminder of the horror of war and the suffering of the noncombatants of the city. But then we saw the pride of the East Germans as they told how they had rebuilt their devastated city under the worst possible circumstances.

Whereas West Germany had been the recipient of the Marshall Plan and the incredible resources of the United States, East Germany had received no Marshall Plan. Instead, it belonged to the occupation zone of the Soviet Union; and Stalin had taken everything of value as reparations. Under these conditions, the East Germans had had no choice but to rebuild their buildings out of the rubble.

Despite their economic ruin, what no one could take away was the memory of architects, engineers, and other educated people who

*turned rubble into buildings and reopened
schools and universities. The devastation of
war and the oppression that followed made
life difficult for the citizens, but the memory of
those who had learned mathematics, physics,
and engineering became the resource for the
rebuilding of communities. The ravages of
war and its aftermath could destroy a people's
economy, but nothing could take away the
memory that sustained the people.*

—James

Because a civilization cannot survive the loss of
a common memory of science and literature, the
future of education is always at the center of any
national debate. Just as a civilization cannot survive
the loss of its memory, the consequences of this loss
for the people of God would also be catastrophic. A
church with amnesia might survive for a time, but
it would forfeit the reason for its existence. Because
the Bible mediates this memory from generation
to generation, we write this book in an attempt to
reclaim its place in the church.

The Irony: Rediscovering What Has Not Been Lost

To speak of rediscovering the Bible is to assume
what may not appear to be self-evident to many readers:
that the Bible has lost its central place in the church.
In fact, one might point to evidence to the contrary.
For example, the Bible is available with more helps
than ever before, and many Christians rightly take
advantage of those opportunities. The Bible is available
in countless translations. Publishers report that the sale
of Bibles in the past decade has broken all previous
records. The computer has opened up entirely new

means of studying the Bible. 91% of Americans own at least one Bible, and 58% believe that the Bible is accurate in all that it teaches (*USA Today,* May 27, 1998). Many Christians have multiple copies of the Bible in every conceivable translation and paraphrase in their homes. Such youth activities as Bible Bowl provide lessons in the Bible that will be valuable for life. Many Christians participate in informal Bible studies during the week with neighbors and business associates, while others are involved in structured programs such as the increasingly popular Bible Study Fellowship. These activities indicate, at least to some extent, that the Bible has not been forgotten.

The signs are not entirely positive, however. As previously stated, booming sales of Bibles and the presence of the Bible in multiple translations in Christian homes do not mean that people actually *read* it; many people treat the Bible more as an icon or classic collectible than a book to be read. Signs that the Bible is losing its place among Christians are evident in a variety of places. Professors in Christian universities report a continued decline of basic Bible knowledge among university students. Since students are increasingly less familiar with the names and phrases from the Bible, this lack of familiarity with the Bible reflects trends in their churches and homes.

Furthermore, the public reading of Scripture is rare; we learned recently of one congregation where those who preside at the Lord's Supper have been asked *not* to read Scripture! Sunday schools frequently follow the path of evangelical bookstores, where the educational diet is composed of self-help books and popular entertainment with a thin veneer of verses from the Bible. Serious Bible study is also often absent from many youth programs. Many people treat Bible study as an onerous chore or a bitter medicine given to resistant patients.

A friend recently recalled a young family's visit to his home congregation. The family had just moved to town, and they were looking for a church. Since one can find numerous options when looking for a congregation in this metropolitan area, our friend was enthusiastic that the family had come to visit; he was hopeful that they might become members of this congregation. As the visitor explained his family's needs, he said that he and his wife were looking for a place where they could really study the Bible. The visitor then asked the tough, unexpected question: "Where can one find a good adult Bible class?" Then he added, "I mean a class where they really study the Bible." Our friend was prepared to tell the visitor about the many benefits and ministries of the congregation: "We have a caring fellowship," "You should see our great youth program," and "We've been blessed with state-of-the-art facilities." But, although they had many classes, he could not think of a single one in which they *actually studied the Bible* in a serious way.

Reasons for the Decline of Biblical Literacy

If the Bible has lost its place in our churches, then there are reasons. First, past experiences in classes may have immunized people from serious Bible study. Sunday School classes often fail to demonstrate the relevance of the Bible for our lives. Many people have memories of Bible study that consisted of mind-numbing, fill-in-the-blank questions. They remember the tedium of plowing through passages one verse at a time, passages that they could never connect to their lives. Biblical material was reduced to a kind of trivia, even before trivia was a game: "Which of the judges was left-handed?" "Name the kings of the Northern Kingdom—in order." "Name all of the cities of Paul's third missionary journey." Many people wondered what significance this information had for their lives.

In the second place, the church now faces a culture that communicates only in sound bites. The world of television and the Internet has replaced the culture of the printing press, with the result that most people are accustomed to reading brief messages and looking at visual images, but they are not used to following a writer's linear reasoning on the printed page. As one person explained why he did not read the Bible, "I read 300 email messages a day." After looking at the computer screen all day, no wonder he was not eager to read anything that was not brief and direct. He was not prepared to face the Bible's difficult passages.

> **Reasons for the decline of Bible study:**
>
> • Past experiences have immunized people.
> • Reading for many is limited to sound bites.
> • Bible study can be a daunting task.

The unfamiliar language of Scripture makes Bible study a daunting task. Anyone who reads the Bible encounters unfamiliar language. Readers who encounter unfamiliar forms of literature, such as Revelation, can easily be overwhelmed by the prospect of understanding the Bible. Even those who read from modern translations face the challenge of reading about people and customs from the distant past; they often need experts in language and ancient culture to help them understand the world of the Bible. For example, in Paul's rules for the proper attire for men and women in 1 Corinthians 11:2-16, the reader faces the difficulty of knowing precisely *what* Paul is demanding of his readers. Did he expect the women to wear veils? Or is long hair the covering he had in mind? Is he requiring that the entire membership adopt a Jewish custom? Or a Greek custom? Anyone who asks how this passage speaks to a congregation in the 21st century realizes the additional challenge of determining how a book written to an ancient culture actually addresses modern congregations. Therefore, despite the claim that anyone can understand the Bible, many readers soon discover that the Bible can be a difficult book. Under these circumstances, many are tempted to leave Bible study to the experts who have the time and the skills to pursue these hard questions.

What Difference Does It Make?

Does it really matter if the Bible is left to the experts and loses its central place in the life of the church? On the surface, one might argue that it does not. In fact, one might even fear that the demands of rigorous Bible study place obstacles in the way of many Christians and inhibit the growth of the church. Although no one can give statistical evidence for an immediate connection between church growth and rigorous Bible study, the evidence from the past is clear: in the long run, the Bible is indispensable to the continued health of the church. Without the Bible's role in sustaining the people of God for many centuries, there would be no living faith today.

For thousands of years, the people of God have recognized accountability to a voice other than their own, and they have found that voice in the Bible. Christians have scarcely any knowledge of Jesus Christ apart from the Bible. Therefore, just as Christians have inherited a legacy from those who told the story of God in the past, the church will pass on its legacy only by listening to the Word of God. Consequently, we face a critical moment in the life of the church. The absence of the Bible from our collective consciousness is ultimately disastrous for the church.

Thinking With the Words of Scripture

The words to Timothy in 2 Timothy 3:15-17 speak directly to the question, "What difference does it make?" The writer describes the threats to the church that come from destructive forms of education (2 Tim. 3:1-9); the church is threatened by some who are "ever learning and never coming to a knowledge of the truth." False teachers go from house to house with dangerous teachings that undermine the fabric of the church. In this context, Paul recalls the source of appropriate instruction, reminding Timothy that from infancy he had learned the sacred Scriptures (2 Tim. 3:15) that alone are able to "make [Timothy] wise to salvation." That is, in the marketplace of ideas, the Bible is the primary resource for shaping the individual.

In the reference to Timothy's education "from infancy," Paul points to the formative role of his mother and grandmother (2 Tim. 1:5) as they taught him the Bible. Undoubtedly, the home and the local community of faith had been instrumental in equipping Timothy for the tasks ahead of him. Clearly, Bible study was not the exclusive domain of experts. Without education in the sacred Scriptures, Timothy would not have been equipped for the task ahead. Scripture—the Old Testament—had been his curriculum.

A remarkable phrase in Hebrews 11:32 reinforces the vital importance of Scriptural memory. Near the conclusion of a series of Bible stories about the major characters of the Bible, the author says, "Time would fail me to tell about Gideon, Barak, Samson, Jephthah, David and Samuel, and the prophets." Then the author summarizes their mighty works. These people "conquered kingdoms, established righteousness [...] stopped the mouths of lions, survived the fire, and [...] became mighty in war." Why doesn't the author retell these stories? Because he *assumes* that his audience will recall them. To a community facing discouragement, the author recalls the faithful people of the past who overcame greater obstacles than his readers now face. The knowledge of those stories was vital for their Christian lives, for these stories gave the listeners the means to interpret their own situation.

Knowledge of the Bible is not a matter of trivia; it is the core memory that we share, reminding us of *who we are*. We need to learn the stories—to have Enoch, Noah, Abraham, Moses, Deborah, Amos, and Paul become the people we know. A reference to Enoch, who "walked with God" (Gen. 5:22), or to Joseph and his brothers will shape one's understanding of what God calls his people to be. To speak of Babel, Pentecost, Sinai, or Zion should evoke memories from the Bible to help us interpret the present situation. To lose this knowledge of the Bible is to lose the memory that holds people together and to suffer spiritual amnesia.

Like Timothy, many of us have learned the sacred Scriptures "from infancy," and we continue to learn. Our grandparents, parents, and Sunday School teachers introduced us to the world of the Bible, and Abraham, Isaac, and Jacob have been our companions since childhood. We began to learn, as Timothy did, "from infancy," and we continue to discover the depth of Scripture. Timothy's educa-

> "I have been reminded of your sincere faith, which first lived in your grandmother Lois and in your mother Eunice and, I am persuaded, now lives in you."
> —*2 Tim. 1:5 NIV*

tion in the home and congregation made a difference for the challenges ahead. Many people have learned from their own "Eunices" and "Loises," who formed them by providing Scripture as a constant companion. Although our grasp of many parts of Scripture was undoubtedly limited, often leaving us puzzled about statements in the Bible, we learned the biblical faith from our own mentors who had been so shaped by the biblical story that their speech was filled with references to Scripture.

We echo the language of the Bible in our speech. My grandfather often said disapprovingly of someone, "He pitched his tent toward Sodom." In other instances, one might speak of someone's bad choice as "selling his birthright for a pottage of lentils." We might respond to an inquiry about another with the words, "Am I my brother's keeper?" In moments of discouragement, someone might say, "There are seven thousand who have not bowed the knee to Baal." Scripture became the lens through which we interpreted our lives. We spoke the language of Scripture because it was part of our constant discourse.

Having grown up surrounded by the language of the Bible, I have memories of its formative power. I still recall the flannelgraph presentation of Jacob wrestling with the angel, the Israelites marching around Jericho, and the story of Jesus welcoming the little children.

Sometimes the stories had power in ways that our teachers never imagined. I'll never forget my first encounter with the story of the Good Samaritan. This parable confronted me for the first time with questions about the separation of the races and the denial of basic rights to people because of their ethnic

13

*background. The story, which undoubtedly
spoke with power to Jesus' original listeners,
continued to speak to me about a parallel
situation. The despised Samaritan, rather
than the priest and the Levite, became the
model for all of us as we considered what it
meant to love our neighbor. When I learned
how, against all the customs and traditions
of his period, Jesus spoke to the Samaritan
woman, I could not resist making parallels
to the customs of our own time.*

—James

Fred Craddock, one of America's most respected
preachers, recalls an occasion during his days in
graduate school in Nashville when he recognized the
evocative power of Scripture and the consequences
for the church when people lose that memory. He
describes an incident when he was sitting in his favorite
coffee shop preparing for his next class while near
him a black man was being ignored and humiliated by
the proprietor of the place. Craddock could think of
nothing other than his next class, so he said nothing.
Later, in a sermon, he recalled the incident, but then
he added that he felt ashamed of himself after he had
left the coffee shop. He had failed to say or do anything.
He added, "I thought I heard the cock crow." After the
sermon, someone came to him and said, "I enjoyed your
story, but I didn't understand the part about the rooster."
The listener had missed a vital image from Scripture. In
the story of Peter's denial of Jesus, Craddock *had seen
himself,* for the story of Peter had given him a means
of interpreting what was happening around him—an
insight lost on some of his "story-less" listeners.

Such failures to communicate signal the loss of a
vitally important memory of *who we are.* To recognize

the phrase "he pitched his tent toward Sodom" is to acknowledge the power of the ancient stories for our lives and to invite comparisons between Lot's story and our own. In his move toward Sodom, Lot came closer to the corrupt world that this ancient city represented. To know the origin of "I heard the cock crow" is to acknowledge the evocative power of the story of Peter's denial and to know that the stories shape our identity as we see ourselves in this unflattering picture of Simon Peter. To hear these stories is to look into a mirror that reflects our own struggles and temptations. To lose contact with the biblical story is therefore to lose our own identity.

Useful for Teaching, Rebuking, Correcting, & Training

The words of 2 Timothy 3:15-17 demonstrate the impact of the knowledge of Scripture shaping our identity. This passage, the only passage in which the word "inspired" actually appears in the Bible, has played an important role in biblical instruction within Churches of Christ. While the passage is important for its claim about the nature of the Bible (see Chapter 2), one should not lose sight of the context and original emphasis of the passage. When Paul comments on the nature of Scripture, he declares: "All Scripture is inspired and *useful* for teaching, rebuking, correcting and training in righteousness" (emphasis added). Chapter 2 examines the significance of the term "inspired." Here we simply wish to observe that Paul's comments focus on the fact that the inspired Scripture is *useful*. The passage answers our question: what difference does Scripture make? Scripture was *useful* to the Christian and indispensable for his or her life. Scripture alone formed the curriculum for Timothy's spiritual growth, useful as his means of defending

15

the church against destructive ideas. This passage
in 2 Timothy 3:16–17 provides a framework for the
importance of Scripture to the life of the church.

First, Scripture is *useful for teaching*. It provides a
knowledge of God that we can gain in no other way.
Because biblical faith requires instruction, from the
most ancient times, Israel emphasized the passing
on of a tradition:

> Only be careful, and watch yourselves closely,
> so that you do not forget the things your eyes
> have seen or let them slip from your heart as
> long as you live. Teach them to your children and
> to their children after them. Remember the day
> you stood before the Lord your God at Horeb,
> when he said to me, "Assemble the people before
> me to hear my words so that they may learn to
> revere me as long as they live in the land and
> may teach them to their children."
>
> —Deuteronomy 4:9–10 NIV

The Bible is also *useful for teaching* because it introduces
us to a strange new world that shapes our imagination
and challenges the values of our own culture. We believe
that God is working out his will in the world—that God
created the world and that he will bring it to completion.
God comes to the aid of the downtrodden; thus, his
coming to the aid of defenseless slaves in Egypt becomes
a permanent reminder for every generation that God's
people may look to him for redemption.

From God's special concern for the poor and powerless, Christians discover models for their own lives. In
the story of King David, we recognize both the good
news that God has provided a leader and the tragedy
associated with that leader's life. In the story of David's
sin with Bathsheba (2 Sam. 11–12), we learn that even
kings are subject to God and that no one has the right to

destroy those who stand in his way. In Israel's captivity and return to the promised land, both the consequences of sin and God's unfailing commitment to his people become evident. In Jesus Christ, Christians recognize the extent of God's love as it pursues a rebellious sinner. In a culture that looks with despair to the future, faithful people know from the Bible that the resurrection of Christ ensures the hopeful future that God has ordained. The Bible is thus *useful for teaching* as it tells us about God's deeds on our behalf, our own resistance, and the demands that God makes on our lives, shaping how God's people see the world.

The Bible is *useful for teaching* also as a suitable protection from half-truths that endanger the church. One can see many of these problems in popular religious literature. Here one finds numerous attempts to give a thin veneer of biblical teaching to a perspective that is contrary to the larger message of the Bible. In some popular literature, we discover that the Bible can be used as a cloak for greed, disguised under the promise of a gospel of health and wealth. Verses from the Bible, removed from their ancient contexts, become the basis for the view that God promises wealth and peace of mind to those who commit their resources to him. Other books cite the Bible to advocate a philosophy of self-improvement based more on pop psychology than on the Bible. Although these texts cite biblical passages for support, they are in fact not based on an understanding of the whole of Scripture.

In the bestselling book of 2001, *The Prayer of Jabez*, Bruce Wilkinson appeals to the brief account of Jabez in 1 Chronicles 4:10 in order to claim that God stands ready to answer every kind of request. Just as God responded to Jabez's request that God would enlarge his territory, according to Wilkinson,

God will bless all who ask. Whether one asks for success in one's ministry or in one's business, God answers with incredible blessings to those who ask. God's response is "your life will become marked by miracles," according to the author. Such miracles are a "guaranteed by-product of sincerely seeking His blessing." One can understand why the book has sold twelve million copies (so far!): it responds to a basic need, and its message has an element of truth. A fundamental conviction of Christians *is* that God answers prayer. The problem of the book is that a half-truth actually can become a distortion; sometimes God's answer is a resounding no!

The careful student of the Bible will recall the psalms of lament and recognize words from the psalmist that hardly fit *The Prayer of Jabez*. The psalmist cries, "O my God, I cry out by day, but you do not answer, by night, and am not silent" (Psalm 22:2). One who reads the entire Bible also encounters the prayer of Jesus in Gethsemane ("Abba, Father, everything is possible for you. Take this cup from me" Mark 14:35) and Paul's prayer for relief from his thorn in the flesh (2 Cor. 12:8). The knowledge of the *entire* Bible is a protection against dangerous half-truths and Scriptures taken out of context.

Second, Scripture is also *useful for rebuking and correcting.* Here is a voice to challenge all of us, a voice that one would prefer not to hear. One of my former professors reminded his students regularly that the churches that received Paul's letters often weren't happy with the word that they received from the apostle, who confronted them with their shortcomings. Despite the fact that many people have misused the Bible as a weapon for the reproof and correction of others, it is useful for our own reproof and correction. Churches today are not far removed from the Corinthians and their partisanship; in the failures of the Corinthians, one may see many of the failures of the contemporary church. Nor are Paul's opponents far removed from the church of today. The Galatians who wished to limit membership in the church to those who shared their own ethnic and social background have their counterparts today. When Paul confronts Peter in Galatians 2:11–14, he confronts not only one "back then" who did not grasp the implications of the gospel for our interaction with others, but also all of us today who do not recognize that the gospel must be put into practice in concrete ways.

Third, Scripture is *useful for training in righteousness* in order that the people of God may be ready for every good work. Christians face extraordinary moral choices. In the workplace, we face difficult ethical choices. Such issues as abortion and homosexuality confront the church. Advances in technology force moral choices about issues involving the environment, medical experimentation, and our treatment of the terminally ill. While the Bible may not speak directly to every question, it shapes our values and influences our moral choices. Thus, while we may hear the clichés that "my body is my own," we readily recall the words of Scripture that "you are not your own. You have been bought with a price" (1 Cor. 6:19–20). We face a culture obsessed with material acquisition, and instead recall that a person's life does not consist of the abundance of possessions (Luke 12:15). We hear the voices of hate and racism, but we recall the God who shows no partiality. In the Bible, we read of those who sacrificed themselves for the sake of others. We learn of a God who has a special care for those who cannot help themselves, and we know that the Bible challenges us to adopt this divine perspective in a world of competing claims and clashing values. When we recognize how the Bible transforms our values, we understand the consequences of losing its influence on our lives.

A Rediscovery of the Bible

We may take comfort in the fact that this generation is not the first to live through times when "the word of the Lord was rare" (1 Sam. 3:1), and we may learn from the moments in the past when ancient Israel rediscovered the Word of God after periods when they had ignored it. One of the great moments of reform appears in 2 Chronicles 34, which describes how, in the course of repairing the temple, the workers found the book of the law of the Lord. When Hilkiah the priest read the book aloud to King Josiah, the king "tore his clothes" in dismay (2 Chron. 34:19). Then, in one of the great moments of reform, he turned to the prophetess Huldah to interpret the words of the book of the law. When the prophetess declared that God would punish Israel for its disobedience, Josiah assembled the elders of Judah and Jerusalem and read in their hearing all the words of the book of the covenant that had been found in the house of the Lord (34:30). Hearing the words of the Lord, the people of Judah committed themselves once more to the covenant. The *reading* of the law *resulted* in the renewal of Judah.

Generations later, after the Israelites had returned from exile, the restoration of the land was accompanied by the reading of the law. When Israel returned, all the people gathered together to hear Ezra read the book of the law of Moses. Ezra read to the assembled crowd from early morning until midday, "and the

ears of all were attentive to the book of the law"
(Neh. 8:3). Scripture spoke with power to Josiah and
Ezra—but only after the people of Israel had lost and
ignored it for generations.

The rediscovery of the Bible in ancient times
provides the model for the renewal of the church in
our own time. Christians who take advantage of the
many opportunities for the study of the Bible will again
discover the power of memory in our own time.

This continued power of the Bible is evident today
in the work of Alec McGowen, a Shakespearean
actor who performs the Gospel of Mark in theaters
throughout the English-speaking world. He offers a
glimpse into the way in which Scripture still comes
to life in our own time among those who know
practically nothing about it. His performances, largely
without any props and with no words other than those
of Mark (from the King James Version of the Bible),
have enthralled secular audiences, including those
with no prior familiarity with the Bible.

In the introduction to the performance, McGowen
tells of listeners who have come to him asking such
questions as "Did you write it?" and "Where can I
get a copy of the script?" To the latter question,
he responds, "In almost any hotel room!" The
response to his oral performance illustrates not only
the unfamiliarity of the modern audience to the
Bible, but also the compelling power of Scripture.
For many people, hearing the Gospel of Mark in
one sitting—less than two hours—allows them to
discover a powerful message.

The video of Alec McGowen's performance of the
Gospel of Mark demonstrates some vital principles of
the study of the Bible. Listeners recognize that the Bible
was meant to be *transmitted orally.* Ancient people had

no copies of books and could not study them privately. The oral performance makes Christians aware of the importance of hearing the text in worship. Also, by hearing the *entire* gospel, listeners recognize the power of the story itself. Finally, listeners hear the story as it was meant to be heard—all in one sitting.

Throughout the history of Christianity, moments of renewal have been preceded by the rediscovery of the Word of God. Few people doubt that the current period of secularization has confronted the church with a special challenge. The church will be tempted to respond to a general resistance to the Bible by placing Scripture at the margins of our lives. However, we are convinced that genuine renewal will come only when we rediscover the strange world of the Bible that challenges all of our values. We challenge congregations to ensure that we actually hear Scripture in our worship services and classes. We believe that, not only is preaching from the Bible vital, but we also believe that the church can be revitalized by the public hearing of Scripture, as we argue in Chapter 9. This return to the Bible is not optional for a people who believe that the Bible is the Word of God.

As we have observed in this chapter and will demonstrate in future chapters, *we turn to the Bible because we believe that it is the Word of God*, a book like no other. People have given their lives to preserve and translate the Scriptures. When we hear the Bible read publicly, we join with the Israelites who listened as Ezra read the sacred words to Israel. But in what sense can one say that the words in a book are actually God's inspired Word? Many faithful people have attempted to define inspiration. In the next chapter, we examine the Bible's own claims and attempt to clarify the meaning of this difficult concept.

2 The Bible as the Word of God

The only book on my shelves that has been in my possession since adolescence is the Bible I received from my parents on my seventeenth birthday. With its black binding and gold lettering, it looks unmistakably the way a Bible is supposed to look. It is the American Standard Version, published in 1901. Its style is the affected Elizabethan English that makes it sound much like the King James Version of 1611.

When I call up verses from memory today, I am most likely to recall the language of that ASV and its peculiar phrasing. I learned to say that love "vaunteth not itself" rather than "does not boast" (1 Cor. 13:4). According to my memory, King Agrippa said to Paul, "With but little persuasion thou wouldest fain make me a Christian" (Acts 26:28). I learned to quote Paul's words to the Philippians, "I am in a strait betwixt the two" instead of "I am torn between the two" (Phil. 1:23).

Before I received this Bible as a gift, my first experience with the Bible was the family Bible, which also had a black cover and gold lettering on the outside. This Bible was the King James Version. Like many other families, we treasured our copy of the Bible.

*It was a major investment for us, and it had
a special place of honor in our home.*

—James

Few people read the Bible today in the English
of the King James Version or even the American
Standard Version, and most people are as likely to
read from paperback or cloth bindings as from black,
leather-bound Bibles. Although the sheer number
of modern translations can be overwhelming, the
new translations have greatly benefitted our study of
the Bible, for they incorporate the latest information
that comes from new manuscript discoveries and
the continued advances in our knowledge of ancient
languages and cultures.

Nevertheless, the daunting black covers and
old-fashioned language of the earlier Bibles communicated an important truth: *the Bible is not like
other books.* On the bookshelf, this book simply
looked different from other books. One could hear
the cadences of the quotations of the archaic English
and again recognize that these words came from
the Bible. We memorized its words because of their
importance. Few doubted that this book was the
Word of God, and practically everyone treated it with
respect. My mother would not underline or write
notes in the margins of her Bible as she might with
other books—because this book was different. To
dispose of a Bible that was tattered with age also
presented a problem, for we could not bear to put
worn-out copies of the Bible in the garbage. It was a
special book that no one treated casually.

When our families explained why this book
enjoyed such a privileged place among our possessions or why it was important that the church live
in accordance with the Bible, they said simply that

it was the "Word of God" or "book of books"—that this book alone was "inspired" by God. Two passages in the Bible were important for expressing our convictions about the Bible. According to 2 Timothy 3:16, "All Scripture is given by inspiration of God, and is profitable for doctrine, for reproof, for correction, for instruction in righteousness" (KJV). The NIV renders the words even more literally: "All Scripture is God-breathed." The other familiar passage is 2 Peter 1:20-21: "Knowing this first, that no prophecy of the Scripture is of any private interpretation, for the prophecy came not in old time by the will of man; but holy men of God spake as they were moved by the Holy Ghost" (KJV). These passages articulate what Christians believe about the Bible: that it is not of human origin. Consequently, when the congregation says in the worship service, "Hear the Word of God," it expresses the conviction that God is the ultimate author of the Bible.

The fact that Christians regard the Bible as inspired is the reason for the urgency of this book. Not only is the Bible the *source* of our knowledge of God, but it is also important because it is the very Word of God. For centuries, Christians have made the remarkable claim that God actually speaks to us through a book. Therefore, whenever the church ignores the Bible, it also ignores the voice of the God who addresses the people of faith.

This remarkable claim raises the question that we will explore in this chapter: What do we mean when we say that the Bible is inspired? How does the living voice of God actually speak through a book? Christians have been engaged in a continuing debate, especially in recent years, in order to answer that question. Indeed, they have been attempting to do what the Bible does not do: to define precisely what we mean by the *Word of God* or the *inspiration* of the Scriptures. Indeed, in this "battle for the Bible" that emerged in the 1970s, people debated the appropriateness of adjectives to use in describing Scripture. Interpreters have used such words as "infallible," "inerrant," and "authoritative" to express their understandable desire to define precisely *how* the Bible is the Word of God, *how* God has spoken through his human instruments. This chapter focuses on the *meaning* of inspiration, in order to provide a greater appreciation of the way in which the Bible is a special book. This is an initial step in our attempt to rediscover the power of the Bible for the church.

A People Under the Word

With their reverence for the Word of God, Christians join the people of God of all ages. Long before they possessed bound copies of the Bible, the people of God lived under the authority of God's Word. In the Old Testament, the prophets claim clearly that they speak for God. When Miriam and Aaron rebel against Moses, the Lord speaks directly to them: "When a prophet of the Lord is among you, I reveal myself to him in visions, I speak to him in dreams. But this is not true of my servant Moses; he is faithful in all my house. With him I speak face to face, clearly and not in riddles" (Num. 12:5 NIV). According to Exodus 33:11, "The Lord would speak to Moses face to face, as a man speaks with his friend" (NIV). The Pentateuch contains frequent references to God's direct conversation with Moses. Here the "word of God" was God's immediate voice in the midst of Israel. A similar phrase appears in the prophetic literature: "The word of the Lord came to...." God speaks and the prophets listen and communicate the words they have been given to Israel. The books of Jeremiah, Hosea, Joel, Jonah, Zephaniah, Haggai, and Zechariah have at, or near, the beginning the phrase "The word of the Lord that came to..." or a similar one. During the course of the prophetic book, the prophets' words are often introduced by "Thus says the Lord." Malachi begins, "The oracle of the word of the Lord to Israel by Malachi." God's Word is the oral communication by which the prophets become divine instruments to speak to the people.

Prophetic literature speaks specifically about how the prophets become God's instruments. God both calls the prophets and places his words in their mouths. The most vivid portrayal of the power of God's Word appears in the story of Jeremiah. When the Lord calls Jeremiah, the prophet resists, saying, "I do not know how to speak" (Jer. 1:6). Then the Lord touched Jeremiah's mouth and said, "Now, I have put my words in your mouth" (Jer. 1:9). Later the prophet complains:

> O Lord, you deceived me, and I was deceived;
>> you overpowered me and prevailed.
> I am ridiculed all day long;
>> everyone mocks me.
> Whenever I speak, I cry out
>> proclaiming violence and destruction.
> So the word of the Lord has brought me
>> insult and reproach all day long.
> But if I say, "I will not mention him or speak
>> any more in his name,"
> his word is in my heart like a fire,
>> a fire shut up in my bones.
> I am weary of holding it in; indeed, I cannot.
>> —Jeremiah 20:7-9 NIV

Generations of preachers have looked back to Jeremiah as the model for the preacher who has been irresistibly captured by the Word of God.

The Word of God was not merely words on a page; it was the actual voice of God communicated by the prophet. For the prophets, God's Word is the promise of fidelity to Israel. Just as God spoke the world into existence through his Word (Gen. 1:3), God's promises are also words that will not fail. Isaiah 55:9-11 has a compelling passage about the constancy and power of God's Word:

> As the heavens are higher than the earth,
>> so are my ways higher than your ways
>> and my thoughts higher than your thoughts.
>
> As the rain and the snow
>> come down from heaven
>> and do not return to it
>> without watering the earth
>> and making it bud and flourish,
>> so that it yields seed for the sower and
>> bread for the eater,
>
> so is my word that goes out from my mouth;
> It will not return to me empty,
>> but will accomplish what I desire
>> and achieve the purpose for which I sent it.

Although God's Word is thus not limited to books or scrolls, the prophetic words are known only because they were committed to writing. According to the book of Exodus, Moses wrote down the oracles of God to ensure that later generations would remember them (Exod. 17:14; 24:3-4; 34:27). References to prophets writing down the Word of the Lord they had received are also present in the prophetic literature (Isa. 30:8; Jer. 30:2). When the psalmist speaks of meditating on God's Word "day and night" (Psalm

2:2), he undoubtedly refers to the importance of the written word in the spiritual life of Israel. The two great renewal movements in Israel were set in motion, as we pointed out in the introduction, by the discovery of the written law of the Lord. Ezra's reading of the book of the law of God (Neh. 8:9) indicates that the people of God recognized the inspiration and authority of their sacred writings. The restoration of Israel would be based on the authoritative writings.

Judaism and Christianity have always recognized the divine origin of Scripture, expressing this conviction in a variety of ways. The rabbis came to distinguish books that "defiled the hands"—those sacred books that required special handling—from other books. In the time of Jesus, the community of faith recognized that the Word of God was associated with scrolls that the community treasured. When writers say "Scripture says" (John 13:18; Romans 4:9) or "it is written" (Rom. 1:17; 3:10), they point to the sacred quality of these writings, an authority that comes from God. Similarly, writers introduce scriptures with such words as "the Scripture [...] which the Holy Spirit spoke long ago through the mouth of David" (Acts 1:16) or "the Holy Spirit says" (Heb. 3:7). Like the priests and rabbis, Christians treasure the Word of God as it is contained in a book and recognize the authority of the written Word.

The early church soon saw the New Testament as an authority alongside the Old Testament. The apostle Paul initiates this transition to the New Testament when he cites his own words as authoritative alongside the Old Testament and the words of Jesus (see 1 Cor. 15:51). Indeed, Paul describes himself in language that compares him to Jeremiah; as with Jeremiah, God knew Paul from his mother's womb, and God called him too for a special task, giving him the authority to build and to plant (see 2 Cor. 10:1-10; Jer. 24:6). The early Christians collected his writings and circulated them "along with the other Scriptures" (2 Pet. 3:16). From the earliest days, therefore, Christians regarded the writings that were later included in the New Testament as authoritative for the Christian life.

In the second century, Christians acknowledged the authority of the books that contained the story of Jesus (the Gospels) and the works of the apostles (the letters). Their adherence to the Holy Scriptures was especially evident in the second and third centuries when they faced the challenge of persecution. When the imperial police knocked at the door and demanded that the Christians surrender their sacred books, they faced a critical decision: for which books were they willing to suffer and die? In some instances, Christians surrendered books that they did not regard as sacred, hoping to preserve both themselves and their books.[1] Others actually went to their deaths rather than surrender their sacred books. Under these circumstances, they declared their fidelity to the Word of God, demonstrating their faith that the Bible could be compared to no other book.

The Bible: Human & Divine

Today Christians still believe that the Bible is the inspired Word of God, but they have very different ideas about how the actual voice of God became the printed page of our Bibles. When I first learned that the Bible was the inspired Word of God, I assumed that our English translation came directly from God without human mediation. Furthermore, I assumed that if God authored Scripture, the entire Bible must have been written in one style—human authors were only secretaries taking dictation.

This view, not very different from some of the ancient views of inspiration, imagined a process in which the writers fell into a trance and became the mouthpieces of God, losing all of their individuality. Athenagoras, one of the ancient apologists, wrote that the Spirit used the writers "as a flautist might blow into a flute" (*Plea on Behalf of the Christians* 9). Calvin wrote

> The apologists of the 2nd century gave a reasoned defense of Christianity to pagan contemporaries.

that Isaiah and Moses were "instruments of the Spirit of God" who offered nothing on their own (*24th Sermon on 2 Timothy*).[2] Some of the early Reformers even claimed that the Greek of the New Testament was pure and free from the vulgarisms of the spoken Greek of the time. Indeed, many people thought of inspiration as the mechanical dictation of every word in Scripture, concluding that, if (and since) God is the author, the Bible must speak in one style that is free from grammatical errors. My understanding as a young man is best captured by a Rembrandt painting in the Louvre, which pictures Matthew writing the gospel while the Holy Spirit whispers into his ear.

Other religions actually teach that their book came directly from God without any human element. For example, according to a story that appeared in *The Atlantic Monthly* in January 1999, the discovery of ancient manuscripts of the Koran in the Middle East has created a dilemma for orthodox Muslims because it challenges a cherished belief; according to traditional Islamic teaching, the Koran as it has reached us today is the perfect, timeless, and unchanging Word of God. To say that the Koran has a history and that the present Koran has been transmitted by copyists, subject to errors in transmission, is to threaten the Muslim understanding of their foundational document as the Word of God.

Despite obvious similarities, the road taken by Muslims is not the same as that taken by Christians. Christians have not resisted the investigation of the origin and transmission of our Bible. Christians believe that the Bible is the Word of God, but we have never really questioned the human element in the transmission of the Bible. *The Bible comes to most people only by means of translators, and God's Word is present in the translations.* However, no translation is perfect, for translators face human limitations and matters of judgment in rendering the words of the ancient text.

The human factor in inspiration...

- The Bible comes to us by means of translators.
- Our Bible is a collation of manuscripts.
- The process of determining canon is, in part, a mystery.
- Biblical writers had their own style and personality.
- Biblical writers employed sources.
- Biblical books were written to specific situations.

Furthermore, in numerous passages of the Bible, the precise meaning is not clear. For example, in 1 Corinthians 7:21, some translations interpret Paul's advice to slaves as a call to exercise their freedom, while other translations give the opposite rendering ("make use of your present condition"). This passage is but one example of the fact that passages are sometimes ambiguous, and that translators have no perfect insight into the actual intent of the author. Few would claim, as the Jews once claimed of the Greek translation of the Old Testament, that the translators were without flaws. Nevertheless, though one hears the Word of God through translations, no issue of translation is significant enough to affect our understanding of the Christian faith.

We know that our Bible is actually the collation of thousands of manuscripts that date from as early as the third century B.C. (for the Old Testament) and the second century A.D. (for the New Testament). No original autographs from the biblical authors have survived. The fact that more than five thousand manuscripts have been preserved multiplies the number of textual differences among the manuscripts. Scholars analyze the manuscript tradition, fully aware of the common mistakes of copyists, but unafraid of the consequences of examining every manuscript discovery. Biblical copyists can make, and have made, the same kinds of mistakes that humans make in copying any work. While scholars can trace the transmission of the manuscripts well enough to believe that they record the message of the biblical writers reliably, numerous footnotes in study Bibles frequently have the words "Other ancient authorities read...." These footnotes indicate that the editors of our Bibles had to choose among many variant readings of the Scriptures. The Septuagint (the Greek translation of the Old Testament) often has a different reading than the Hebrew text. These variant readings are most commonly matters of style and minor details; but they are reminders of the human element in the transmission of the Bible.

Furthermore, the process of collecting the books of the Bible into a library composed of sixty-six books is, in part, a mystery. In ancient times, when few people possessed copies of Scripture, the books of the Bible were written on scrolls. As long as the Bible was a collection of scrolls, the issue of which books belonged in the Bible remained an open question. In the time of

33

Jesus, the Bible comprised "the law, the prophets, and the psalms" (Luke 24:44). Although traditional usage had largely determined the contents of the Bible, the precise limits of the last part of the Bible had not yet even been established in all of the Jewish communities. Similarly, while the four gospels and the letters of Paul were being read in the churches as early as the second century, the earliest list of precisely the 27 books of the New Testament only dates from A.D. 367, when Athanasius wrote a letter to the churches, providing a list of the books that the churches in his native city of Alexandria regarded as authoritative. Before Athanasius, the status of individual books was a matter of debate. Some groups that were later judged to be heretical recognized additional books in their list of Scriptures. Other churches had recognized the four gospels and the letters of Paul, but had reached no consensus on the last books of the New Testament (Hebrews to Revelation); Athanasius's list of the 27 books of the New Testament was one acknowledgment of a consensus that finally emerged throughout the ancient world.

While Christians believe that God was at work in the process of preserving the words of Scripture, they also recognize that God used individuals and communities in the process. Those books finally included as the 66 books of our Bible actually emerged because they survived the test of time. The list emerged after a careful sifting process, as churches recognized those books that were useful "for doctrine, for reproof, for correction, for instruction in righteousness."

The biblical writers had their own style, personality, and level of education. Some, such as Luke and the authors of Job and Hebrews, wrote with elegant style. In each of these books, the prologue appears in a style that would appeal to an educated audience. Students of elementary Greek soon discover that some books, including the Gospel of John and the letters of John, are written with a simple vocabulary and syntax. The Hebrew of Deuteronomy sounds like the work of a lawyer, while that of Job is extraordinarily rich in poetic style; other books also have a complex syntax and an extensive vocabulary. Therefore, the human element of the Greek and Hebrew styles is undeniably present in the biblical writings.

The biblical writers consulted sources before writing. Joshua 10:13 and 2 Samuel 1:18 both quote from the "Book of Jashar." Some of the material in 1 and 2 Kings was drawn from the "Book of the Chronicles of the Kings of Israel" (1 Kings. 15:31; 16:20; 2 Kings 10:34; 13:8). Ezra consulted Persian archives (Ezra 7:1–26). Luke

> "So the sun stood still, and the moon stopped, until the nation avenged itself on its enemies, as it is written in the Book of Jashar."
> —*Joshua 10:13*

(see also chapter 5) opens his gospel with the words,

> Many have undertaken to draw up an account of the things that have been fulfilled among us, just as they were handed down to us by those who were eyewitnesses and ministers of the word. Therefore, since I myself have carefully investigated everything from the beginning, it seemed good also to me to write an orderly account for you, most excellent Theophilus, so that you may know the certainty of the things you have been taught.
> —Luke 1:1–4 NIV

The biblical writers, therefore, acknowledge that they are quoting from archives and other sources. Sometimes, as we have seen above, they identify their sources; in other cases, they do not specifically identify them.

Finally, the Bible is a library of books, each of which was written to a specific situation in the life of the people of God. For example, Paul never provides a comprehensive analysis of the Lord's Supper. His instructions on the topic are actually the response to the Corinthians' misuse of the Lord's Supper (1 Cor. 11:23-26); presumably, had the Corinthians *not* abused the Lord's Supper, Paul's thoughts on the topic would be unknown. Similarly, his teachings on justification by faith are a response to a critical issue in the life of the church. Paul's influential teaching, like that of the authors of the gospels, Revelation, and the Old Testament books, occurred in the midst of concrete situations in the life of the church.

Toward an Understanding of Inspiration

The human factor in the writing and transmission of the Bible does not diminish its power as the Word of God. Although most people no longer think of the writers as abandoning their own personalities to become passive instruments of the Holy Spirit, Christians do believe that the Bible stands alone as the Word of God. Nevertheless, the human element in Scripture challenges us to reflect on the nature of inspiration. As a result, our understanding of the nature of Scripture should be taken from Scripture itself, and we should be cautious about adding human definitions.

Two Important Passages

Although the New Testament writers frequently introduce quotations from the Old Testament with phrases indicating the divine origin of Scripture (2 Cor. 6:16), the Bible says remarkably little about itself and about the process by which it was formed. The focus of the Bible is always to point beyond itself to the activity of God. Two texts address the issue most directly.

The first passage, 2 Timothy 3:16, belongs in a context in which Paul contrasts Timothy's education with the instruction offered by the false teachers (3:1-9), as we noted in Chapter 1. Paul challenges Timothy to be strong in his faith, remembering both his childhood instruction and his good teachers. Timothy's education consists of the personal instruction that he received both from Paul (3:10-12) and from the "holy writings" (3:15), which he has known from infancy. These "holy writings" are obviously the Jewish Scriptures, inasmuch as the New Testament had not been written during Timothy's childhood. These Scriptures have sustained Timothy's faith all of his life, and they will continue to sustain him in the future. Because these Scriptures are inspired by God, they are useful for reproof, correction, and continuing instruction in righteousness. Equipped by Scripture, Timothy is prepared for the task of evangelizing.

The focus of the passage is on the *usefulness* of Scripture for transforming and equipping the person, not on the divine origin of Scripture (see Chapter 1). Nevertheless, the statement in 2 Timothy 3:16 does address the issue of the inspiration of Scripture, although the translation of the passage is uncertain. Because of the absence of "is" in the Greek text, one can render the passage either "every [or "all"] Scripture is inspired [NIV "God-breathed"] and profitable" or "every [or "all"] inspired Scripture is profitable." The word "inspired" (*theopneustos*) is used only here in the Bible, and it is rare in other ancient Greek texts as well. The literal meaning of the word, as the NIV indicates, is "God-breathed." Thus Scripture is useful precisely because it is "inspired."

37

Although the passage affirms the divine origin of Scripture, it does not give precise details on *how* the inspiration actually occurred.

The second major passage on the divine origin of Scripture appears in 2 Peter 1:19-21 in the context of assurances about the Christian hope (1:16-18) and warnings about the false teachers who threaten the church (2:1-3). The church holds to a possession that is "more sure," the prophetic word "which is a lamp shining in a dark place" (2 Pet. 1:19). This prophetic word consists of the Hebrew Scriptures, the foundation for the church's hope and the defense against the opinions of the false teachers. Prior to the warnings in 2 Peter 2:1-3, the author adds, "First of all, you must understand this, that no prophecy of scripture is a matter of one's own interpretation, because no prophecy ever came by the impulse of man, but men moved by the Holy Spirit spoke from God" (2 Pet. 1:20-21). The issue here is the private interpretation of Scripture and the subjective and destructive inroads made by false teachers. Because God is the source of the prophetic word and no prophet offers his own private opinions, the church finds its assurance and direction, not in private opinions, but in the divine Word.

These two classic passages on the divine origin of Scripture provide important insights for the church of all ages. On the one hand, both passages serve as continuing reminders of the vital importance of Scripture as the source of the community's life. Because Scripture is the Word of God, it is the source of the church's future. On the other hand, neither passage gives an elaborate definition of inspiration. These two insights provide an appropriate model for our own time. Scripture is the Word of God that can alone guide the church. At the same time, one should be cautious about adding the nonbiblical categories to define inspiration that have been at the center of the "Battle for the Bible." Because Scripture contains both the human and the divine element, it is a mystery that resists our human definitions.

Defining Inspiration

One who allows the Bible to speak for itself will be cautious about attempting to define the nature of inspiration, for our definitions easily obscure what the Scripture claims for itself. Jesus condemned the Pharisees because they, with their own traditions, silenced the Word of God. Our own definitions can easily have the same effect.

In recent years, the "Battle for the Bible" has been fought over the use of one such definition: *inerrancy*, a term that was not used in the Bible and was not in common use to define the nature of inspiration for many centuries after the writing of the New Testament. Although we appreciate the sentiments of those who insist on this term and share their desire to maintain the highest view of Scripture, for a variety of reasons this terminology is not helpful. Human definitions simply create more problems, for what constitutes an error remains unclear. One may ask whether or not the word applies to matters involving *every* statement in the Bible on cosmology, botany, and the other sciences. For example, when the Bible describes a "firmament" that separates the waters above from the waters below, one may wonder if the Bible intends to make an accurate scientific statement. When Jesus says that the mustard seed is the "smallest of the seeds of the earth," one may ask if that is a scientifically precise statement.

To ancient peoples, the firmament was a domed expanse of heavens dividing the upper and lower waters.

Additionally, one must ask whether or not inerrancy even applies to minor narrative details. For example, in numerous instances in the Bible, one finds apparent inconsistencies in the narratives. Many of these are well known. For example, in the raising of Jairus's daughter, in Mark's account the girl's father says to Jesus, "My daughter is at the point of death" (Mark 5:23), while in Matthew the father says, "My daughter has just died" (Matt. 9:18). In Mark's gospel, the messengers come while Jesus is on the way to Jairus's house to report the death of the little girl; similarly, in Mark's gospel, Jesus makes his triumphal entry into Jerusalem and then returns on the following day to curse the fig tree and cleanse the temple (Mark 11:1-19). Yet, in Matthew, the cleansing of the temple and the cursing of the fig tree follow immediately *after* Jesus' entry into Jerusalem (Matt. 21:1-22). In Matthew 27:9, although the actual citation is in Zechariah 11:13, the evangelist says of the thirty pieces of silver paid to Judas, "Then was fulfilled what had been spoken by the prophet Jeremiah."

Sometimes the narrative does not correspond to the historical record. For example, our available knowledge indicates that the census under Quirinius was held in A.D. 6, although Luke's Gospel places the census before the death of Herod the Great, who died in 4 B.C. (Luke 2:2). Similarly, Gamaliel's speech in Acts 5:33-39 refers to uprisings made by Theudas and Judas the Galilean. According to Josephus, the most important Jewish historian of the first century A.D., Judas the Galilean came before Theudas (*Antiquities of the Jews* 20.97-99). In fact, the revolt of Theudas came after the probable occasion of the speech of Gamaliel recorded in Luke.

One may ask if inerrancy involves the *sequence* of events as they are described in the stories. The order of the events in the gospels varies considerably. For example, in Luke's Gospel, Jesus' return to his home synagogue occurs at the beginning of his ministry (Luke 4:16-30), while in Matthew and Mark it occurs after some time (see Matt. 13:53-58; Mark 6:1-6). The sequence of events recorded in the Gospel of John varies radically from the sequence of events in the other gospels. In John, for example, the cleansing of the temple occurs at the beginning of Jesus' ministry (John 2:13-17), while in the Synoptic Gospels the event occurs during the last week of Jesus' life.

> Because they share a common view of the story of Jesus, Matthew, Mark, and Luke are called the Synoptic Gospels (*syn* = "same," *optic* = "view").

These problems are not insoluble. More information might actually resolve many of these difficulties or future research might clarify specific discrepancies between the biblical narrative and our knowledge of secular history. Often the answer involves the very simple matter of the genre of the writing. The ancient writers worked with standards that are not our own.

The Gospel of John declares near the end, "Jesus did many other signs that are not written in this book. These are written that you may believe; and that believing, you may have life in his name" (20:31). That is, John has written a gospel that is intended to create and sustain faith. He writes as an evangelist to elicit faith, not as an investigative journalist. For example, when John places the cleansing of the temple at the beginning of Jesus' ministry in contrast to the placement of the same story immediately prior to the arrest of Jesus in the Synoptic Gospels, one need not conclude either that the event happened twice (a contrived and improbable explanation) or that this fact undermines the credibility of John's report. The story in John serves the author's purposes.

Authors throughout history have used the sequence of events to make their points rather than to inform a future reader about a precise order of events.

Although one may find satisfactory answers to these and other problems, simple answers are not always available. People who insist on inerrancy disagree about the extent to which the Bible speaks metaphorically or literally on scientific matters. Others suggest, not that our current Bibles are inerrant, but that the original manuscripts were inerrant on matters of history and science. They assume that God ensured the precise accuracy of the original versions. Often people engage in elaborate harmonization to preserve their theories about the Bible. For example, Osiander (1496–1552), an early Reformer, argued that Jesus raised Jairus' daughter three times! Others compare the gospel narratives of Jesus' trial and suggest that Peter denied Jesus six times. These contrived answers stretch credulity and actually *create* faith problems for people. To insist on inerrancy is to apply standards for the authors that they did not claim for themselves.

In my introduction to the New Testament course, recently a student asked if he could write his research project to meet the challenges of an unbelieving relative who had pointed to discrepancies in the Bible. The relative pointed to discrepancies in the Gospel accounts as evidence of the Bible's untrustworthiness. Like many other people, this student had been taught an "all or nothing" principle, according to which any discrepancy would undermine the truth of both the Bible and the Christian faith. Therefore, he felt an urgency to find an explanation that would satisfy both himself and his unbelieving relative.

I was sympathetic with the dilemma and recalled similar challenges I had faced, both from believers who wanted answers and from unbelievers who wished to challenge the truth of Christianity. In one instance, a friend discovered the kinds of discrepancies mentioned above. He observed that Acts records the conversion of Paul three times and that the details of the narrative differ. He struggled to resolve this problem in his own mind, and while he heard numerous explanations, he found no satisfactory answer.

Having been taught that any inconsistency within the story, however insignificant, was sufficient to undermine the Christian faith, he struggled to find answers. He did not believe those who insisted that the original manuscripts were free from the inconsistencies he had found, nor was he persuaded by contrived answers that harmonized the accounts in unconvincing ways, forcing the evidence to fit preconceived theories. His faith was undermined, not by the problems he discovered, but by the definitions of inspiration that well-meaning Christians had superimposed on the Bible.

—James

Ironically, the inconsistencies that both students discovered actually had (and have) nothing to do with the point of the biblical authors. Because of preconceived definitions of inspiration and our modern concepts of accuracy and precision, their faith was challenged. In these instances, the Bible was more in danger from its friends than its enemies! In their attempts to provide absolute certainty, Christians have actually created a crisis of faith, forcing the evidence to fit the theory, always feeling a responsibility to provide an answer for every potential discrepancy. To unbelievers and to those struggling with faith, their contrived solutions often work to undermine belief.

The Power of the Bible

Despite the challenges we have seen, the power of the Bible does not depend on our ability to explain every problem. Scripture has lasted for thousands of years without our defending it, and it is not in danger today. "God's holy fire" has transformed lives throughout the centuries and continues to do so. Our task is to accept the view of inspiration that the Bible actually claims for itself. Anyone who returns to the Bible's claim for itself will observe Paul's words that the "holy Scriptures are able to make you wise to salvation" (2 Tim. 3:15) and believe his claim that the inspired Scripture is "useful for doctrine, for reproof, for correction in righteousness." That is, the Bible is not a book of history or science, but is more than sufficient for what it claims to do. In his book *Inspiration*, I. Howard Marshall has correctly said,

> The purpose of God in the composition of the Scriptures was to guide people to salvation and the associated way of life. From this statement we may surely conclude that God made the Bible all that it needs to be in order to achieve this purpose. It is in this sense that the word "infallible" is properly used when applied to the Bible; it means that it is 'in itself a true and sufficient guide, which may be trusted implicitly.' [...] We may therefore suggest that 'infallible'

means that the Bible is entirely trustworthy for the purposes for which God inspired it. (52)

The result of describing inspiration in this way is to shift the focus of the discussion from the scientific accuracy of the Bible in all of its details to its total sufficiency for what God intends it to do.

Because the Bible has come to us through human beings, our view of the divine origin of Scripture is not a matter of mathematical certainty, but ultimately an affirmation of faith. The constant temptation for Christians is to follow the path of Thomas, who said, "Unless I see [...] I will not believe" (John 20:25). However, throughout the Bible, when God reveals himself, he calls for faith rather than certainty. When Abraham answered God's call to go to the promised land, he went in faith, trusting in God's promise even when he saw no proof of the existence of the promised land. When Jesus revealed himself to the crowds, some believed—but others saw the same deeds and did not believe. Similarly, Christians trust that the Bible is God's Word—when others do not believe. Believers turn to God's Word, trusting that here alone one hears the voice of God. Christians join the people of all ages who have, in the midst of many voices, listened most intently to the voice of God revealed in the Bible.

The ultimate challenge is not then our *definition* of inspiration, but our *willingness* to hear the Word of God as it addresses God's people. To read the Bible, to treat it with reverence, to know the story of God's endless search for a relationship with humanity is far more important than our explanations. Because knowing the old story is indispensable to the life of faith, the following chapters address our efforts to reclaim the entire Bible for the church and especially to see the richness of the Bible's story. 🌿

3
The Redeeming (W)hole of Scripture

One of my earliest memories of church comes from when I was four years old. As fourth-generation members of Churches of Christ, my parents sought to pass on the faith to my brother and me. As usual, my parents had taken me to Sunday school in our rural Arkansas community. Wearing a little tie and carrying my pocket New Testament and Psalms, I entered that classroom ready to learn. But no teacher or students showed up! So, already a good member of our tradition, I stayed by myself and pretended to read (perhaps I could read, a little) the book that seemed to excite everyone I knew. The teacher and students in the next class pleaded for me to join them, but my little Bible was all I needed.

—Mark

The little boy I was then did not know what powerful influences bore down upon him at that moment. He could not have known about the hunger for the Word of God that had animated Luther and Calvin in the sixteenth century and Stone, Campbell, Errett, and Lipscomb in the nineteenth. Nor could he have known to what degree this tiny episode served as a parable of a whole movement that loved Scripture sometimes more than it loved those in whom Scripture brought to life the passion of Jesus Christ.

We could explore this tale at greater length, but for now the chief point is this: using only the final portion of the Bible spoke volumes about how a whole group of people educated itself in the things of God. Sometimes we have danced to the Bible's tunes selectively, hearing mostly only the last quarter of it, the New Testament. My carrying a New Testament and Psalms, sized just right for a child's hands, epitomizes how we sometimes operate on the assumption that all that is truly essential appears at the end of the Bible. Unlike the early church, we have not often read the Old Testament for its ability to shape our lives. It has served as background for the "real" Bible found in the New Testament. For many of our churches, a hole exists in the Bible. The time has come to fill it. We must reclaim the whole of Scripture, or rather be reclaimed by it.

This chapter seeks to make three points. First, the church's use of the Bible has changed over time—and not always for the better. While a full catalogue of these changes would require hundreds of pages, a snippet or two from history may help us understand where we have been and where we could go. Second, the shrinkage of Scripture to the New Testament profoundly limits our ability to see the full scope of God's work in history and among us. While the Bible does shed light on issues of church organization and other issues that have attracted the attention of many of us, it does not provide a constitution or pattern for church organization, focusing instead on the much more important issues of spiritual and moral life, justice, peace, and reverence before God. Scripture concerns the largest issues imaginable, some of which we have neglected in recent decades, to our detriment. Third, a fuller appreciation of, and submission to, the words of all of Scripture, Old Testament and New, will lead us closer to God and closer to each other.

A major task facing our churches is the reintegration of the Old Testament into the regular teaching, thinking, and practice of the church. *All* of Scripture must play a role in our canon. We must let the three-fourths of the Bible that we inherited from God's first people, Israel, speak to us afresh.

Throughout history, Christians have found that Scripture provides the chief means through which God nourishes and leads the church. The early church, in particular, knew that a deeper understanding of, and commitment to, the words of the prophets, sages, psalmists, and storytellers of Israel would fashion us into spiritually mature people who could love God with all our being (Deut. 6:5) and our neighbors as ourselves (Lev. 19:18). Eliminating the Old Testament from our canon severely curtails our understanding of the character and activities of God, leading to spiritual poverty. Recovering the Old Testament, conversely, could transform us more fully into what we have always sought to be—Churches of *Christ*. Considering how Christians have heard the Old Testament in church can help this recovery begin.

The Old Testament in the Church: Two Models

This chapter began with a memory of the meeting of the church together for worship because for most of the church's history, public worship was the primary place where Christians encountered the Bible. Indeed, before the printing press made books affordable for everyone, it was the *only* place. Even now, though most of us own multiple copies and translations of the Bible, hearing its words in the company of other believers fully influences how we read and reflect upon it.

As we discuss elsewhere in this book, the growth of the church in its worship and service *depends* on its ability to hear the Bible afresh, especially in the context of communal worship. Such settings profoundly shape how we think about God's work in the world. Let us consider two periods of congregational worship, the first a composite of many such services, the other a real, datable event, the first in the second century, and the second in the early twentieth. The second-century case presents the oldest full-fledged description of a Christian service that survives. The second service captures a picture of our practices in the past decade. Placing them side by side should help us see both who we are and who we could be. Comparing these two services highlights the fact that, although we have genuinely sought to make the early church's experiences a model for our own, we have gone a different way than they in what we think important in Scripture.

Scripture in the Early Church

When Christianity was born as a Jewish sect (one that eventually went its own way), the "Bible" was still solidifying as a closed, unified work. Most Jews read in synagogue the equivalent of our Old Testament (with slight variations), but Samaritans accepted only the Pentateuch, and the Qumran community (the Essenes) apparently included other books in their much larger canon.

No one, as far as we know, discussed precisely what made a book canonical. Just as there was no conspiracy to suppress some books or canonize others, so also was there no obvious test of a book's "inspiration" that could objectively demonstrate its status to all questioners. Rather, a book became Scripture in a dynamic process of reading and interpretation by and for the community of the faithful. Canonical books were those read in the synagogue and church, preached and commented upon by leaders, and remembered by believers at moments of victory and defeat in life.

We do know that some persons in the first century rejected works like Ezekiel and Ecclesiastes because they seemed doctrinally off-base, and Song of Solomon because it could lead to immorality (first-century musicians sang it in taverns as bawdy music).[1] Or rather, they believed these books to be Scripture, but wished to restrict their circulation to a few trusted, mature persons. The wide consensus existed, however, that the books that both the synagogue and church read "soiled the hands," that is, were holy texts.

In the first and second centuries, Christians often lived at the margins of society, a dangerous minority that only occasionally wormed its way into the halls of power. The Bible offered them solace in the face of persecution, guidance in the face of their culture's moral and spiritual confusion, and the language in which to describe how God was moving among them.

In Rome in the middle of the second century, one of the church's leaders was a Palestinian Gentile named Justin (called Justin Martyr after his execution for practicing this new faith). Between 151 and 155, he wrote a defense of Christianity now called his *First Apology*, in which he answered charges that Christians violated society's

> **Justin Martyr**
>
> Justin was an early Christian philosopher and teacher. His major surviving books include the *First Apology*, the *Second Apology*, and the *Dialogue with Trypho* (a Jew). Justin was born in Palestine, but spent much of his career in Rome.

moral codes by loosening traditional religious and family ties. Among other accusations, pagans often criticized the church's worship itself as secretive and possibly sexually immoral. Justin responded to these charges by describing such a service this way:

> And on the day called Sunday all who live in cities or in the country gather together in one place, and the *memoirs of the Apostles or the writings of the prophets* are read, as long as time permits. Then when the reader has finished, the Ruler [elder, bishop] in a discourse instructs and exhorts to the imitation of these good things. Then we all stand up together and offer prayers; and, as we said before, when we have finished the prayer, bread is brought and wine and water, and the Ruler likewise offers up prayers and thanksgiving to the best of his ability[…]. (emphasis added)[2]

With a few adjustments, such a worship service sounds familiar to contemporary Christians, because we also enjoy the nourishment that comes from the sharing of the Lord's Supper and the reading and preaching of the Word. Moreover, this worship form reflects first-century practice, as we can infer from Acts 20:7 and other early texts outside the New Testament, such as the *Didache*. In Justin's context, describing Christians as people who eat, study, and pray together captures the essence of who these participants in the strange new religion truly were. This characterization is still true, far more than we realize. But for now let us focus on the crucial phrase, "memoirs of the Apostles or writing of the prophets."

Who are these prophets? Throughout Justin's *Apology*, he repeatedly argues that the Old Testament Scriptures, which even pagans could respect on account of their great antiquity, confirm the truth and virtue of the church's message. The ancient writings speak of God's intervention on behalf of humanity culminating, Justin notes, in the life, death, and resurrection of Jesus of Nazareth. Because it speaks of God's promised renovation of a creation marred by sin, the Old Testament is concerned with Jesus, just as much as are the "memoirs of the apostles" (probably our Gospels). All these sacred texts provide a framework for the moral life of exemplary citizenship that Justin's pagan audience could admire. For Justin, as for the early church in general, the Old Testament anchors the life of faith because it speaks of the God who works both in Israel and in the Israelite, Jesus Christ.

Why would Justin bother to tell his pagan readers about the sometimes clandestine worship of the church? He places this description of the church's worship at the very end of his tract, as if to clinch his arguments that the church posed no danger to the Roman Empire. People who worship as modestly, thoughtfully, and lovingly as these people threaten no one, he seems to say.

Christians celebrated the Lord's Supper, cared for the poor and imprisoned, prayed for peace, and, most of all, read words that revealed to them the will of the Creator. Justin informs his readers, "We all hold this common gathering on Sunday, since it is the first day, on which God transforming darkness and matter made the Universe, and Jesus Christ our savior on the same day rose from the dead." He ties together Genesis and the Gospels, creation and redemption, Israel and the church. The wholeness of Scripture replicates the wholeness of the world as God gradually redeems it through the saving act of Jesus Christ. The early church's broad-gauge vision of Scripture offers 21st-century readers a wider vista from which to contemplate God's saving work.

Why should we care what Justin's congregation did? Partly because their activities reflected the primitive practice of the church, to which we have always appealed. But mostly because Justin recognized that worship—when it focuses on the revelation of God's grace in creation, the community of the saved, and Scripture, all woven together as one—gives the outside world its best view of the Christian faith. Scripture, in the communal worship of the church, can make us wise unto salvation. *All* the Bible does this, the prophets as well as the gospels, the Old Testament as well as the New. Justin's vision—the early church's vision—is what we wish to capture today.

Worship in the Twentieth Century

The second event for us to consider occurred in the spring of 1922 at the Ryman Auditorium in Nashville, Tennessee. It reveals to a great degree the basic attitudes and behaviors that, for better or worse, have characterized Churches of Christ for the past century. As many as 8,000 persons jammed the building to hear N. B. Hardeman set forth what he and the Churches of Christ of his era believed to be the bedrock tenets of the Christian message. Like fundamentalist preachers of many denominations of his generation, he laid the intellectual foundation for his work not with theological reflection on the nature and work of God or Jesus, but with his understanding of the nature and function of the Bible.

Hardeman's second sermon, "Rightly Dividing the Word of Truth," based on 2 Timothy 2:15, suggests that readers of the Bible must approach it systematically, just as one would a textbook. Like any good textbook, the

Bible delivers facts in a logical arrangement. To discover the relevant facts, students must look in the right part of the book. Just as one does not find a discussion of fractions in the chapter of the math book that deals with calculating

> Hardeman's basic arguments come ultimately from Alexander Campbell's 1817 "Sermon on the Law." For more on this sermon, see Everett Ferguson's "Alexander Campbell's 'Sermon on the Law': A Historical and Theological Examination" in *Restoration Quarterly* 29 (1987), 71–85.

bank interest (Hardeman's analogy), one does not find data about the Christian life in the section of the Bible devoted to Judaism. Christians must understand the basic organization of the Bible in order to make sense of it. The most notable divisions are the Old and New Testaments; for Hardeman, a sharp contrast exists between the two Testaments, which he equates with two covenants, one of law between God and Jews, and one of the Spirit "to the sons and daughters of men wherever they chance to dwell upon earth[…]." Further subdividing the Old Testament into law, prophets, and Psalms (following Luke 24:44 and, incidentally, ancient rabbinic tradition as well), Hardeman dismisses each part in turn in his "Tabernacle Sermons," the Law at length and the others more briefly:

> The prophecies simply mean the foretelling or the prediction of events not yet come to pass. They are never destroyed, wiped away, or blotted out, but can only pass in every instance when they merge into history[…].

> The Psalms constitute that part of the Old Testament written in metrical units that could be sung and accompanied by the lyre […] counted and referred to by both Christ and the Jews as a part of the law.[3]

Hardeman's sermon elegantly and succinctly summarizes the previous century's reflection on the Old Testament in at least some circles of the Restoration Movement. His statements of the views of Churches of Christ have continued to influence us significantly (through such media as the Jule Miller filmstrips, for example), even if that influence has now seriously declined.

Since Hardeman's ideas so well represent a previous broad consensus in Churches of Christ, we owe it to ourselves to ask whether he stated the issues in ways that reflect actual biblical evidence. Here, the verdict is mixed. Certainly no one should question Hardeman's love for God or commitment to teaching the Word to all. His importance as a historical figure also remains secure. His students, now respected elder statesmen and women, still speak with reverence of his work as a teacher and preacher.

On the other hand, he is clearly wrong to think that 2 Timothy 2:15 distinguishes sharply between the Old and New Testaments. Hardeman does correctly recognize that the Old Testament *Torah* addresses Jews, not Gentiles. Like Campbell before him, he apparently emphasizes this point to combat those who would cite circumcision as a model for infant baptism. Nevertheless, the sharp distinction that Hardeman draws between the Old and New Testaments *as books* does not fit the biblical evidence; to the contrary, the New Testament cites or alludes to the Old as authoritative scripture in virtually every paragraph, understanding it to equip Christians for a life of spiritual maturity (2 Tim. 3:16) and hope (Rom. 15:4).

"Whatever was written before was written for our instruction, so that through endurance and the comfort that comes from the Scriptures, we might have hope."
—*Romans 15:4*

56

So Paul, for example, can compare his church's vulnerability to temptation with Eve's (2 Cor. 11:3), or he can understand his ministry to Gentiles as fulfillment of prophecies of their election (Rom. 15:8-12), or when mentioning the collection for the poor of Judea he can allude to Isaiah 55 (2 Cor. 9:10), again underscoring his work's connections to Israel's Bible. The question for the apostolic church was not *whether* the Old Testament exercised authority over them—they had no doubt it did—but *in what precise ways* it should provide a script for their lives together. In Chapter 5, we will examine some possible answers to that question, with which the church in every generation has wrestled.

One may find other problems with Hardeman's arguments. His view that prophecy more or less equals prediction severely restricts the power of the books of Isaiah through Malachi to one small part of their actual work. His description of the Psalms, though correct as far as it goes, leaves much more unsaid. And his depiction of the law or *Torah* obscures much of importance in that part of Scripture. *In the brief form he stated it, his description of the Old Testament fails to account for most of the material in the Bible itself.* In fact, unintentionally, the view that Hardeman states so clearly robs us of basic understandings of the nature of God's enduring acts of grace among humanity.

Hardeman's highly representative sermon reveals another set of problems, his use of some biblical prooftexts that seem to support his argument. They include Galatians 3:16-19, Matthew 5:17-18, Colossians 2:14, Ephesians 2:13-22, and Romans 7:1-7. In every case, Hardeman ignores the context of Paul's or Matthew's discussion of the role of *Torah*, in effect forcing the verses to fit a preconceived notion of how the argument should proceed. He also ignores texts that would correct his position.

Perhaps the most extreme example of this widespread misunderstanding of the biblical text relates to Colossians 2:14. Notice some translations of this verse:

KJV: "...blotting out the handwriting of ordinances that was against us, which was contrary to us, and took it out of the way, nailing it to his cross."

NIV: "...having canceled the written code, with its regulations, that was against us and that stood opposed to us; he took it away, nailing it to the cross."

NRSV: "...erasing the record that stood against us with its legal demands. He set this aside, nailing it to the cross."

Hardeman equates "the handwriting of ordinances" with the Old Testament. This interpretation of the verse once dominated our discussion of the Old Testament as Scripture, and in many circles it still does (in fact, it was fairly common in the nineteenth century throughout Protestantism). Understanding the text this way grossly oversimplifies matters, however. The language of Colossians derives from the law courts, and refers simply to an indictment. At most, Colossians celebrates the fact that Christ's saving action on the cross disproves or removes the *accusation* that we have broken the law. We are found not guilty! God has thrown the case against us out of court.[4]

Certainly the Old Testament can indict us for evildoing, but it does far more than this. Equating the Old Testament with an indictment in a one-to-one way implies that most of the Bible constitutes a barrier between us and God, surely a conclusion to which neither Hardeman nor any other Christian would wish to come. This interpretation radically diminishes the authority of Scripture in the ongoing life of the church. By failing to appreciate the subtlety and complexity of the argument of Colossians, we end up sidelining much of the very Bible that we seek to understand.

Now, by this time one may wonder why we've spent so much time on a sermon from the 1920s, only to dismiss its arguments out of hand. The reason is simple and bears repeating: Hardeman's views exerted great influence over Churches of Christ for many decades. Those views did not originate with him, but his statement of them in extraordinarily eloquent, and widely reprinted, sermons before thousands rendered these ideas almost incontestable in many circles—until recently.

Clearing away such misunderstandings of basic aspects of the function of Scripture in the church seems crucial. We need a fresh look at these ancient texts that profoundly shaped the earliest Christians and can shape us today as well. We need to learn again to read the Old Testament in ways that will form us more closely to the image of the God who reveals himself in Jesus Christ. As the New Testament scholar Krister Stendahl recently put it, "I would rather use the whole set of keys supplied by the Scriptures. And the canon is the key ring."[5] *All* of Scripture, not just part of it, unlocks the door to the Christian's path to God—by modeling for us the chief ingredients of a moral life, by furnishing us the language of thanksgiving and lament, by calling us to wisdom and a balanced life, and most of all, by drawing us into the grand story of God's saving acts, from creation to exodus to Golgotha—and to our own living rooms.

What Falls into the Hole of Scripture

Granting that the early church treasured the Old Testament as part of its Bible, why should we do the same? One way to answer this is to consider what has happened when Christians have silenced the Old Testament completely.

In the second century, Christians discussed the question of the authority of Scripture and its extent. One group, called Montanists after their leader Montanus, sought the prophetic voice unmediated by written texts. Other groups, like Valentinians and other Gnostics, prized secret knowledge (sometimes in special books) unavailable to those who could read only the Bible in its unadorned simplicity. Perhaps the greatest threat to the church's seamless connection to the long story of redemption came from the followers of Marcion, a contemporary of Justin Martyr. For Marcion, the questions became, which books represent the true gospel, and how should faithful Christians interpret them? These were not idle questions, for which texts a community read would determine the behaviors and beliefs it embraced.

Marcion, a rich merchant who had moved from Asia Minor to Rome around 150 A.D., insisted that the followers of Jesus should reject the Old Testament altogether. His money and obvious talent ensured his views a hearing, and Marcionite congregations survived long after the founder's death. For him and his followers, the Old Testament did not come from God the Father of Jesus Christ, but from an evil god who had created the world, and from whom Jesus came to rescue us. Marcion's canon consisted only of the gospel of Luke and the letters of Paul (with some adjustments made to conform them to Marcion's distinctive views). Needless to say, the church fought mightily against Marcion, because his views denied the foundational Christian belief in one God and reduced creation (and therefore humanity itself) to a tragic mistake.

To what degree Marcion's activities forced Christians to clarify the content and nature of the canon remains a hard question to answer. Certainly the issues he raised were in the air even where he exerted no direct influence. Other heretical leaders, Gnostics, also disputed the legitimacy of the Old Testament in the church, although few of them went as far as Marcion did. For the faithful church, at stake was the connection of the Christian faith to the history of God's activities stretching back to creation and the delivery of Israel from Egyptian slavery. Christian morality, doctrine—life itself—hung in the balance. The church, guided by the Spirit, kept its connections to the past by means of the Scriptures of Israel. This momentous choice has profoundly shaped the course of Christian history—more than we will ever know—and we may capitalize on it to our own benefit.

Now, how does this old discussion relate to our situation today? Few people today would agree with Marcion's radical views about the nature of God. Most Christians would acknowledge that the Bible contains 66 books, not Marcion's handful. But in many congregations, the practical canon—the Scriptures in active use in sermons, classes, and the decision-making processes of leaders—has consisted chiefly of Paul, Acts, and the Gospels. Most of us can remember hearing arguments dismissed with, "Well, that's in the Old Testament after all." (In an extreme form of this notion, some have even argued that the *Gospels* themselves belong to the so-called Mosaic Dispensation and thus exercise no authority in the lives of Christians!) As a result, we have lost much of the power of Scripture in the life of our congregations.

Why the Old Testament Matters

When Marcion reduced the canon, he did more than complicate the lives of readers who could no longer make sense of the New Testament's constant practice of quoting the Old Testament. He changed his followers' perception of the very nature of God and God's redemptive purposes in the world. The same thing, though on a less drastic scale, may happen in today's congregations when the first three-fourths of the Bible become the exclusive preserve of children's Sunday school. By failing to include these texts in our canon, we compromise our ability to understand the gospel itself.

On the other hand, reintroducing these texts into the life of the contemporary church will force us to deal with hard issues we have often ignored. Taking the Old Testament as a guide to God's work today will stretch us. *An unread book cannot live as Scripture for us.* No matter how holy one thinks a book to be, if he or she does not use it, it ceases to serve as canon.

The Old Testament in Today's Church

To remedy this situation, to avoid letting Marcion win this battle posthumously, we must open our eyes and minds to the broader perspectives of all of the Bible, perspectives that do not always match our own and often challenge our most cherished assumptions. We also need to foster some basic virtues for reading all of Scripture, including humility, attentiveness, open-mindedness, and care for others. We will read together, listening for each others' insights, seeking through careful study to learn and to allow what we have learned to transform our lives.

Hearing God's voice in the words of the Old Testament depends on some simple commitments on our part. We must begin by reading! That sounds obvious, and it is. But how many of us have read and, more importantly, studied these texts? How many of our preaching ministers place them front and center in sermons and adult education? Although Churches of Christ have produced outstanding Old Testament scholars for several generations, their excellent work has too rarely reached those of us sitting in the pew. Typically, Old Testament stories have been the occupation of our children until they reach early adolescence, when we "promote" them to something else.

Let us begin to refill the hole in our Bibles by reading these texts. The next chapters offer some hints as to what we will discover when we do this.

Since the Old Testament is hardly easy to understand in many places, we urgently need our publishers to disseminate new books about it for adults, our ministers and elders to equip Sunday school teachers to teach it with skill and relevance, and our professors of Bible to write and lecture on it. Great needs demand great activity.

What will the payoff of this activity be? Recognizing that the Old Testament functions just as fully as the New in the canon of the church can effect at least three changes in our churches today: 1) broaden our horizons by connecting us to a great story of redemption that includes Israel and its descendants, Jews and Christians, and through us the world; 2) expand our understanding of, and appreciation for, Scripture as a window onto God's work in our world in every time and place; and 3) deepen our comprehension of the interactions among the Bible, the church, and the God who works in both.

Broadening Horizons

Reading the texts that we inherited from Israel and now share with Judaism will challenge the church. But spiritual growth never comes without challenges. The stories of the Old Testament introduce us to complex characters with fouled-up lives, lives that God redeems. Discovering the relevance of those ancient lives for our own poses difficulties that call for Christians to think together, to draw on their own experiences, and to submit them to the judgment of the biblical texts.

We can learn at times from how others—Jews and Christians throughout the history of the church—have understood these texts. In so doing, we will learn that our own perspectives on the texts do not exhaust their possible meanings. For example, we may read Isaiah 53 in the light of Jesus' last week, as Christians usually have, or we may also appreciate Jewish readings of this text that understand the "suffering servant" to be Israel itself. Both readings have value, and there is no reason to insist that one and only one of them can be true. Truth can only come from consideration, over time, of many factors. It comes by reading the many texts of Scripture again and again and never allowing any one of them to silence the others.

Expanding Our Understanding

Since the church's concern with the Bible does not revolve primarily around historical or literary issues—though those are important—but around Scripture's role in the life conformed to the will of God, we need to be clear about what effect the Old Testament can have on our lives together. If we as a fellowship argue as our ancestors did, that the New Testament is a constitution for the church, and the Old Testament for Israel, then we have little to discuss. However, Scripture never describes itself this way, and a legal or constitutional model for any part of the Bible (except possibly small parts of the Pentateuch) fails to account for what we actually read in the text. The obligations that Scripture imposes upon us are far more powerful, expansive, life-giving, and life-changing than any constitution could provide. Constitutions concern processes for governing. Scripture concerns commitments for living. The Bible points us to the life in the Spirit that finds God in the Cross and in the generous service, humble worship, and demanding ethics of God's people.

The Old Testament helps us capture the richness of the life of the Cross that redeems real humanity, not some phony, "churchy" humanity that religion sometimes seeks. The Old Testament abounds with the language of praise and lament, affirmation and questioning, story and counter-story. Laws function as part of a story, and stories relate directly or indirectly to laws. What we see in the pages of this book is life itself, life as seen through a mirror held in the hands of God. Readers confronting this text with utmost seriousness cannot help but experience its radical claims upon their lives as individuals and as members of communities.

Admittedly, life was simpler when we saw the New Testament as a constitution now in effect, and the Old Testament as one that had been repealed. But this model, whatever its strengths, does not adequately reflect God's work in the whole Bible for the whole church.

Deepening Our Comprehension

In shaping us in our congregations, the Bible, now complete and with its hole refilled, sets the stage for the thoughtful, prayerful, intense inquiries that healthy churches need. The canon provides limits for us, and also opportunities for fruitful disagreement.

We will never see everything the same way. Such uniformity exists only in heaven—where we will know the truth and experience God's love and grace—and in hell, or the hells on earth created by totalitarian political systems. Some of our congregations, to be blunt, seemed to have uniform thought because they had silenced or expelled everyone who disagreed with the party line. The canon of Scripture, if we allow its discussions of key issues to serve as a model for our own, will never allow us to silence views other than our own in such repressive ways.

Let us be explicit here. On such key issues as the oneness of God, ethical obligations of the powerful to the powerless, the importance of family and community, and a range of other things, the Bible speaks with one voice. But often this voice is polyphonic, to use a musical analogy. God surpasses our comprehension to such a degree that no single metaphor or idea can capture his nature. Approaching God from many directions allows the Bible to give us the clearest possible picture, one that blurs again if we ignore its full witness.

Conclusion

Too often, we in Churches of Christ have made a mistake in removing the Old Testament, for practical purposes, from our canon. The hole in Scripture has produced a hole in the practice of our faith. Without the prophets' concern for the poor, we focus on the desires of the upwardly mobile. Without the Psalms' laments, we fall victim to a theology of blessing that gives us no way to speak honestly of death, sickness, and failure. Without the stories of God's redemption of Israel, we forget that our story is not the same as the consumerist, acquisitive story of our culture.

Despite pure motives and a well-placed concern that non-Christian practices not creep into the church, we have too often dismissed from our consideration powerful texts that illuminate the nature of God and human relationships to God. In seeking to escape the tyranny of Law, we have run headlong into a legalism more galling than any the Pharisees could invent, precisely because we have failed to understand what *Torah* entails in Israel. We have robbed ourselves of the riches of praise and lament in the Psalms, of the ethical and social concerns of the prophets, and of the cool-headedness of the wise men and women of the ages. And we have thereby failed in our deepest passion, to model ourselves after the earliest Christian communities. So here we plead for a renewed attention to the whole canon of Scripture.

But Christians need something more. In this book, we are asking our fellow Christians to begin to seek a deeper, richer understanding of what the Bible itself *is*. The Bible does not save us: Jesus does. Scripture is not a rulebook covering every imaginable situation, if we only know how to decode it correctly. Reading it that way has led us deep into sectarianism. On the other hand, the Bible is not merely a love letter, offering pleasant words that sedate us into satisfaction with a relationship to a God who is as congenial and undemanding as a fishing buddy. No, Scripture ushers us into a world where those who encounter God fear for their lives, but also eagerly await a new life in this world and in the world to come. After reading Scripture with an open mind and heart, no one can return to business as usual. Its words draw us into a new world where commitments endure, relationships enrich, and the telling of the old, old story brings new life to nations yet unborn. ꙮ

Knowing Our Story

In the spring of 1999, America said good-bye to the top-rated television show *Seinfeld*. Jerry, George, Elaine, Kramer, and the other characters had engaged the attention of Americans for almost a decade, and they will continue to do so in syndication for years to come. The remarkable fact about this show was that it presented itself as "a show about nothing." The consistent theme of the story was that the characters had no story and no basic theme to give life meaning. In a format that was undoubtedly creative and with characters that were consistently interesting, the story kept the attention of millions of people. Although many television shows have been about nothing, this show actually worked hard to underscore the point. Its characters lived with no basic commitments—either to basic ideals or to people. They shrank back from love and fidelity, and they pursued sex without commitment. Whenever they came close to a deepening relationship with another person, they backed away.

One might wonder why this story of self-absorbed individuals became a cultural phenomenon. This story about nothing apparently functions the way stories commonly function: millions of viewers see something of their own lives mirrored in the meaninglessness

69

of the lives of Jerry and his gang. *Seinfeld*, like many other stories in the movies and art, speaks for a postmodern audience in which human lives no longer fit into any larger story that makes sense of their lives. The popularity of this situation comedy rests on the fact that ours is a time when people tell stories about *not* having a story. The church faces the challenge of addressing a culture that has no story to make sense of their lives or offer direction for living.

If communities of faith have been sustained by the story of the Bible for thousands of years, as we argued in Chapter 1, the contemporary church faces a special challenge, for stories have been a neglected part of the educational curriculum in Churches of Christ. In our experience, stories from the Old and New Testaments provide the basic curriculum for children through the elementary grades. Memories of Cain and Abel, Jacob and Esau, Joseph and his brothers, Moses and Aaron, and David and Bathsheba were formed in the elementary Bible class and then live on through movie portrayals. Some of us are sure that Moses looks like Charlton Heston or the animated character from DreamWorks Studios! These stories are ideal for the curriculum because they grip the imagination and hold the interest of the listener.

Something happens, however, to the congregation's involvement with stories as children reach the high school and adult years. Bible stories are relegated to the children. Adults take on "weightier" topics—either from other parts of the Bible or from our contemporary concerns. This loss of the story has serious consequences for the church, as we shall see in this chapter, for the primary mode of communication in the Bible is the story. The Bible contains numerous short stories that explain

Israel's existence as well as a grand narrative that explains God's plan for the world. Without the biblical narrative, Christians join the countless others in our culture who have no basic story that shapes their lives. Consequently, in this chapter we observe the urgency of telling the story, not only for children, but for the entire community of faith. We'll demonstrate that stories have oriented the lives of the people of God from ancient times until the present, shaping the values and answering the deepest questions of the people of God. Indeed, as we'll see, Christians themselves play a part in an unfinished drama—a story that is still unfolding.

Telling Our Story

Telling the Story in Israel

Although the Bible is a gorgeous mosaic of narrative, wisdom literature, law, prophets, epistles, and apocalypses, as we'll demonstrate in Chapters 5 and 6, the basic story provides the perspective that allows us to understand the other pieces of the mosaic. Long before the ancient Israelites owned Bibles, they knew their story. In their homes and assemblies, they retold the story of what God had done. In some instances, they told the story in great detail, while in other instances they recited the story in only a few brief sentences. When the Israelites recalled a name or a phrase out of the old story, they evoked memories of the larger story that helped them make sense of their lives. The household, for example, was one context for retelling what God had done, and the story was the anchor of the family's continued existence. In Deuteronomy, Moses instructs the people about the importance of passing on the story in the context of the home. He tells the people,

In the future, when your son asks you, "What
is the meaning of the stipulations, decrees
and laws the Lord our God has commanded
you?" tell him: "We were slaves of Pharaoh in
Egypt, but the Lord brought us out of Egypt
with a mighty hand. Before our eyes, the Lord
sent miraculous signs and wonders—great
and terrible—upon Egypt and Pharaoh and his
whole household. But he brought us out from
there to bring us in and give us the land that
he promised on oath to our forefathers."
—Deuteronomy 6:10-23 NIV

Here, in only a few lines, the father recites the
story of the exodus and conquest and explains the
family's traditions and practices. By reciting these
words regularly, the Israelites reinforced the memory
that held them together as a people and explained
their place in the world to the next generation.
Children grew up hearing the basic story in the home
and at the major festivals during the year.

The telling of the story extended beyond the
family. Israel also recited their story in the context of
worship. Deuteronomy indicates that Israel retold the
story in the context of the assembly. At the harvest
festival, for example, each responsible male in Israel
is instructed to appear before the priest with a basket
of produce and to recite the words:

My father was a wandering Aramaean, and
he went down to Egypt with a few people
and lived there and became a great nation,
powerful and numerous. But the Egyptians
mistreated us and made us suffer, putting us
to hard labor. Then we cried to the Lord, the
God of our fathers, and the Lord heard our voice
and saw our misery, toil and oppression. So

the Lord brought us out of Egypt with a mighty hand and an outstretched arm, with great terror and with miraculous signs and wonders. He brought us to this place and gave us this land, a land flowing with milk and honey.

—Deuteronomy 26:5-9 NIV

This is the basic story line of Genesis through Joshua. It collapses centuries into the brief story of the patriarchs, the exodus, and the conquest of the promised land. The center of worship is the telling of the story, which bridges the gap between the present reality, when God is hard to see, and the past, when God acted decisively on Israel's behalf. The story reminds Israel that God can act again.

In pivotal moments in Israel's history, the Israelites summarize the story. In Samuel's farewell address, for instance, the prophet speaks to the assembled gathering at a moment of transition in Israel's history. His speech consists of the story of what God has done:

Now then, stand here, because I am going to confront you with evidence before the Lord as to all the righteous acts performed by the Lord for you and your fathers. After Jacob entered Egypt, they cried to the Lord for help, and the Lord sent Moses and Aaron, who brought your forefathers out of Egypt and settled them in this place.

—1 Samuel 12:7-8

He describes the consequences of failing to remember the story, recalling that Israel's past amnesia had resulted in devastation at the hands of a foreign power (1 Sam. 12:9). Then he recalls how Israel recovered from this loss of memory and cried to the Lord, who sent the great heroes to Israel's rescue (12:9-11). In this instance, the memory of Israel's story provided a needed perspective for the community. What God had done in the past, he would also do in the future. The memory of past events guaranteed that God would also redeem Israel in the future.

The closing chapter of Joshua, also describing a pivotal moment in the history of Israel, demonstrates again the power of memory. In this farewell address to Israel, Joshua recognizes the peril facing this vulnerable group of tribes in the world of the great powers. The speech suggests that Israel's greatest need is to recall the events of the past and the story that binds the people together. Joshua relates to the assembled tribes the great moments of Israel's history, beginning with Terah the father of Abraham and concluding with the conquest of the land. He recalls the stories of Abraham's spiritual descendants, Moses and Aaron, and the many battles that resulted in the conquest of the land.

The tribes of Israel share this story, which will continue to be their possession as they live in the land. This memory becomes the basis for the challenge which Joshua lays before the people: "Now fear the Lord and serve him with all faithfulness[...]. Choose for yourselves this day whom you will serve" (Josh. 24:14). The memory of God's deeds of the past becomes the motivation for Israel to respond faithfully to the God who had redeemed them in the past. The memory of the past shapes the commitments of the people of God and challenges them to live faithfully in his service.

The recitations mentioned thus far summarize the story that ends with the conquest of the land. The story does not end here, however. Israel's hymnal tells the story that continued after the conquest of the land and culminated in David's reign as king. In Psalm 78, the psalmist recites the story in the context of the worship service, a story of "what we have heard and known, what our fathers have told us" (78:3 NIV). The account begins with Jacob and continues to tell Israel's story as the narrative of divine mercy and human rebellion. Like the other accounts of Israel's story, the psalm retells the story of God's gracious deeds at the exodus, the wilderness, and the conquest of the land. Unlike the other versions of the story, however, the theme of this account is the way in which the people of God respond to God's gifts with ingratitude. This story reaches its conclusion with God's selection of Zion as the place of God's sanctuary and of David as the king. Israel's worship reminds them not to act as some of their ancestors had.

In other instances, the telling of the story was the basis for Israel's faith that God would redeem the people from destruction. In Psalms 105-106, we observe again that Israel's hymnal contained songs that recited the story. In the context of the psalm, the people have lost Zion and the promised land. They are in captivity, waiting for God's redemption, and they are still reciting their story. The people in captivity heard once more about the promise to Abraham and drew courage from the memory of the oath of God to their ancestor, recalling that the God who was true to his promises in the past will surely be faithful to his promises again. Psalm 106 again tells Israel's story, recalling the narrative of God's mercy and human rebellion. The story concludes, not with the conquest of the land, as with the other recitations, but with the loss of the land. This telling of the story served as an explanation for Israel's captivity. The long recitation comes to a close with a prayer:

> Save us, O Lord our God,
>   and gather us from the nations,

that we may give thanks to your holy name
and glory in your praise.
                                    —Psalm 106:47

Again, reciting the story gives shape to worship and
expresses the faith that God will act in the future
to redeem Israel.

Telling the Story in the Early Church

The early church also expresses its faith with a
recitation of God's mighty deeds. When the Christians
announce the good news, they tell the next act in an
unfolding drama. Even Paul, who writes letters rather
than stories, often appeals to the Christian narrative to
reshape the values of his people. When the Corinthians'
conduct undermines the meaning of the Lord's Supper,
Paul recalls the story that he has told them at the
beginning of their Christian existence:

I received from the Lord what I also passed on
to you: The Lord Jesus, on the night he was
betrayed, took bread, and when he had given
thanks, he broke it and said, "This is my body,
which is for you; do this in remembrance of
me. In the same way, after supper he took the
cup, saying, "This cup is the new covenant in
my blood; do this, whenever you drink it, in
remembrance of me."
                                    —1 Corinthians 11:23-25

Paul recalls the account of Jesus' institution of the
Lord's Supper to correct and challenge the behavior of
the Corinthians. Christian behavior is shaped by the
memory of Jesus' death. Those who proclaim Jesus'
death each week through the reading of Scripture and
participation in the Lord's Supper will recall that their
story began with the one who gave himself for others.
This memory transforms the values of people who

now recognize conflicts between their selfish behavior and the story that they profess and believe.

Similarly, when the Corinthians doubt the resurrection, Paul recalls their story: "For what I received I passed on to you as of first importance: that Christ died for our sins according to the Scriptures, that he was buried, that he was raised on the third day according to the Scriptures[...]" (1 Cor. 15:3). Paul, like the ancient Israelites, can express his faith by summarizing a grand story in a few words. In fact, throughout his letters he returns to brief summaries of the faith in order to transform the values of his readers. In 2 Corinthians, for example, he can reduce the story to even fewer words. To those who are bewildered by his ministry of weakness and suffering, he explains himself with the words, "One died for all; therefore all died" (2 Cor. 5:14). He responds to a crisis in this church by recalling the story that brought the church into existence. When he says to the Thessalonians, "We believe that Jesus died and rose again and so we believe that God will bring with Jesus those who have fallen asleep with him" (1 Thess. 4:14), he recalls a story that the community already knows.

The culminating moment in this memory of the past was the story of Jesus of Nazareth. While Paul never actually tells stories about Jesus and rarely mentions information that appears in the four Gospels, his message constantly alludes to the memory that holds the church together. For example, when the Philippian church experiences the natural tensions that occur in every congregation, Paul instructs the congregation to "be of one mind" (Phil. 2:2). Because Paul knows the difficulty of bringing strangers together into a harmonious community, he adds the story that many people call the "Philippian hymn." He describes the mind of Christ:

Who, being in the form of God
  did not consider equality with God
  something to be grasped,
but made himself nothing,
  taking the very nature of a servant,
  being made in human likeness.
And being found in appearance as a man,
  he humbled himself
  and became obedient to death—
even death on a cross!
Therefore God exalted him to the highest place
  and gave him the name
  that is above every name,
that at the name of Jesus
  every knee should bow,
  in heaven and on earth and under the earth,
and every tongue confess that Jesus Christ is Lord
  to the glory of the Father.
                    —Philippians 2:6-11 NIV

If these words, with their beautiful rhythm, are actually
a hymn, as most scholars believe, Paul is probably
quoting words that his listeners know, appealing to
their memory of the story of Jesus. He knows that the
people will never be brought together in harmony
unless their minds are united by a common story of
the one who emptied himself. The human desire to
have one's own way destroys many communities, but
the Christian community tells a story that unites the
people in respecting the desires of others.

Although Paul never wrote a gospel or an extended
narrative, he assumes in the letters (see our Chapter 6)
that his listeners also recall the Old Testament narrative
as well as the Christian story. Even when he writes to
Gentile churches, he assumes that his readers know
about Abraham and Moses. He even speaks of the

Hebrews who left Egypt at the exodus as "our fathers" (1 Cor. 10:1). He assumes that his readers can follow his appeals to Abraham (Gal. 3:6-29), Hagar and Sarah (Gal. 4:21-31), and numerous other heroes from the past. From the very beginning of their Christian existence, the new Gentile congregations had a memory of the past.

The foundation of the church's existence was a memory of the acts of God. When evangelists preached the gospel to those who had not heard, they told a story. When they preached in the synagogue to those who were acquainted with Israel's past, they again appealed to the ancient story of Israel, declaring that Jesus Christ was the goal of the Old Testament. Unlike many of their own contemporaries, the evangelists told the story that shaped the faith, the moral conduct, and hope of the communities of faith. They knew the story, not only because they responded to it at the beginning of their Christian existence, but also because they recited it regularly when they came together in worship.

Israel and the church knew the value of summarizing the grand story and repeating it regularly in worship. With this constant repetition, every child would be able to tell the story, and the people would be able to state simply the essence of their faith. This practice of summarizing the faith in song and Scripture is an appropriate model for the contemporary church, for the regular repetition of our most basic convictions helps us to maintain our focus, express our faith, and maintain our memory. When the congregation regularly listens to the reading of the familiar passage of 1 Corinthians 11:23-26 at the Lord's Supper, for example, it recalls Jesus' words, "Do this in my memory." Like Israel at the Passover and the church at Corinth, the church participates in a reenactment of an ancient event that awakens the memory and makes the past become real for the community sharing in the meal. As the church "proclaims the Lord's death until he comes," it declares again the saving significance of the crucifixion of Christ and reaffirms the faith that unites its people.

Baptism is also a reenactment of the foundational story for Christians. When Paul writes to the Romans, he recalls what the readers already know from their past experience: "Do you not know that as many as have been baptized into Christ have been baptized into his death?" (Rom. 6:2). Then he appeals to the memory of the community: "We were buried with him through baptism into death, so that as Christ was raised from the dead through the glory of the father, we might walk in newness of life" (Rom. 6:4). The experience that all Christians share, according to Paul, is the retelling of the story of the death and resurrection of Christ. Christians live by the memory of the story that called the church into existence, and they continue to tell it through words and deeds.

Short Stories

We have seen above that the center of the faith of Israel and the early church was a grand story of the saving deeds of God, which the people of God could reduce to a "pocket size" summary and recite both in the home and in the assembly. These summaries are the outlines of the grand narrative that extends in the Old Testament from Genesis to Nehemiah and then continues to the Gospels and Acts in the New Testament (see Chapter 5). Israel also expressed its faith through the multitude of short stories that tell about the numberless ordinary men and women in whom God is at work, even if God is behind the scenes throughout the entire narrative. Where are these short stories in Scripture? Fortunately, not only does the Bible have one long narrative, as we shall see in Chapter 5, but it is filled with smaller stories that encapsulate the larger story. The short stories take on new meaning in the context of the larger story. The smaller stories become miniature versions of the larger story, describing the way God works in human lives in ways quite different from our expectations.

Consider, for example, an unusual story that appears in Genesis 38. On the surface, this story is not very edifying. It probably does not appear in many Sunday School quarterlies. The story, which appears to interrupt the narrative of Joseph and his brothers, tells of an incident in the life of Judah, one of the brothers. The plot revolves around Tamar, Judah's daughter-in-law, who is left childless by the death of her husband. In keeping with ancient practice, Judah promises Tamar his third son. However, as the plot develops, Judah does not keep his pledge. Tamar then takes matters into her own hands by disguising herself as a prostitute and enticing Judah, who unwittingly has sexual relations with his own daughter-in-law. When Judah hears that Tamar has become pregnant as a result of her sexual encounter, he is enraged until he discovers that he is actually the father of the child. Then he says, "She is more righteous than I."

The remarkable fact of the story is that the narrator never comments on the immorality of Judah or Tamar. The story does not shield us from the less-than-honorable conduct of its major characters. The focus is, instead, on the outcome of the story. Tamar gave birth to twins, Perez and Zerah (Gen. 38:29–30), and the readers of the story know that Perez was the ancestor of David, the founder of the Davidic dynasty (Ruth 4:18–22). This story, which appears to be lacking in redeeming social value, is thus actually an account of God's work behind the scenes, using ordinary people to bring about his purposes.

Similarly, the short story of Ruth, complete with its own plot, epitomizes the larger story. At first the reader wonders what this narrative teaches about God's purpose for Israel, for the focus of this story seems far removed from the promise to Abraham. Ruth is a Moabite woman married to an Israelite, who soon dies and leaves her childless. When she accompanies Naomi, her widowed mother-in-law to the land of Judah, their lives are desperate. Two widows without land or husbands appear to be in a hopeless condition until events transform their despair into hope. Through circumstances that Ruth could not have anticipated, she finds a new husband and "redeemer" in Boaz. God has been working behind the scenes to secure the future when all hope was seemingly gone. At the end of the story, Ruth gave birth to a son who became an ancestor of David, the great king. This story was never forgotten because the Israelites saw not only the story of Ruth; they saw their own story also. Here they learned that God works in impossible circumstances. The small story summarizes the larger story.

Or consider one of the stories in the gospels. In fact, the gospels are composed of shorter stories that can be seen as the gospel in miniature. One of the first stories that I recall from Sunday School was the account of the little children who were brought to Jesus so that he might lay his hands on them and pray (Matt. 19:13-15). In using the passive verb "were brought," Matthew places the emphasis on the helplessness of the little children; someone—Matthew does not say who—brought the children to Jesus. One who reads this story in the context of Matthew's gospel will notice that others "were brought" to Jesus during the course of his ministry (Matt. 4:24; 9:2, 32; 12:22; 14:35). In each case, those who were brought to Jesus were the helpless people whom others had ignored and excluded from the people of God. In this story, as in the others, Jesus welcomes those whom society excludes. This story is actually the gospel in miniature, offering good news for the helpless. Readers may easily identify with the disciples, who rebuked those who brought the children to Jesus, knowing that they themselves are constantly tempted to adopt normal human means of considering their mission. However, in the story, Jesus offers good news to all who sense that their lives are broken, and he challenges all who measure the worth of a person according to human calculations.

The stories that Jesus tells are also the gospel in miniature. The reason that the parables of Jesus have been familiar scenes in works of art is that those parables continue to live in our memories. No story has inspired artists more than Jesus' story of the Prodigal Son, which one might describe as the entire Bible in miniature. Although the story was taken directly from the customs and practices of ancient Israelites and addressed a particular situation in the life of Jesus, it continues to live. In its original context, it explained why Jesus reached out to tax collectors and other unsavory types. In the story, Jesus says to his critics, "I reach out to sinners because God is like the remarkable father in the story. He continues to respond to our own rebellion with love, even to the point of accepting the son who has disgraced the family." Readers of the story celebrate the fact that God has responded to their own rebellion with his steadfast love.

83

The Power of Stories

The Bible communicates through stories because the truth of God can be understood in no other way. The Bible could have described the lost condition of humanity without telling of Adam and Eve and their banishment from the garden, but a message on the human condition would not communicate the depth of our situation with the same force as Genesis 1-3. Jesus could have given a lecture on God's grace toward sinners rather than tell the story of the prodigal son, but the message would not have the same power. As we observed in Chapter 1, Israel's story sustained the people through the centuries, allowing them to understand their situation. The stories were not relegated to children alone, but addressed the entire community. Their experience can tell us much about the necessity of retelling the story today.

Stories are like mirrors in which we find ourselves. The story has power, for it is not merely about people of the past. In reciting the story, the Israelites see themselves. "*We* were slaves in Egypt," the father says to the son. The Israelites say, "My father was a wandering Aramaean, and *we* went down to Egypt." Those who listen to the story recognize themselves in the narrative, identifying with its characters. In the telling of the story, every generation described the ancient narrative as their own story. In the same way, when we tell the stories, we find ourselves in the narrative. These people in the stories were not always heroes; they had all the human flaws that we experience. Thus through Abraham, readers today have heard the promise and lived between trust and doubt. With Abraham, they have learned to wait when they see no evidence of God's works in the world. Nevertheless, God works out his purpose in the context of human faithlessness.

Like the ancient Israelites, Christians today continue to find themselves in the story. When listeners today hear the stories about the disciples of Jesus, they recognize themselves. They might say, "We heard Jesus' call, 'Come, follow me,' and we followed him." Or they might say, "We were in the boat with Jesus, fearing that we might be lost in the storm, but Jesus stilled the tempest." We accompany Peter as he tries and fails to walk on the water, and we are with the disciples when they cannot stay awake in the garden. Reading the story is much like looking into the mirror and seeing ourselves.

Additionally, stories are an incredible source of encouragement. The Israelites found encouragement as they told the story and applied it to new situations. For example, when Israel lived in exile, wondering if God had abandoned the people, the ancient prophet recalled Israel's story. When the people despaired of ever returning home to the promised land, the prophet said,

> Look to Abraham, your father,
>> and to Sarah, who gave you birth.
> When I called him he was but one,
>> and I blessed him and made him many.
> The Lord will surely comfort Zion,
>> and will look with compassion on all her ruins;
> he will make her deserts like Eden,
>> her wastelands like the garden of the Lord.
>> —Isaiah 51:2-3

The memory of the past interpreted the present and gave hope for the future.[1] The ancient story of Abraham came to life for the exiles in Babylon. Perhaps Paul has this experience in mind when he speaks of the "endurance and the comfort of the Scriptures" (Rom. 15:4). As readers struggle with their own faith, they recall that Abraham's long wait finally resulted in the fulfillment of the promise. When they read of Israelites in captivity, wondering if God is silent or uncaring, they discover that God answers his promises.

The Christian story transforms our values and subverts the stories of our culture. In a world that considered death on the cross the epitome of foolishness, the gospel writers told the story of Jesus, demonstrating that the shameful crucifixion was not a miscarriage of justice, but Jesus' own decision to give his life for others (Mark 10:45). When Christians tell this story, they offer an alternative to the values of a self-absorbed culture that emphasizes individual rights over the rights of others. The story of Jesus' death challenges the natural human views of power and authority and offers a different understanding of leadership from the one that is dominant in our culture. Indeed, as we saw in Paul's memory of the one who "emptied himself" (Phil. 2:7), that story transforms communities by changing their understandings of power.

Stories also serve as a warning. If the Bible is a mirror in which we see ourselves, we see accounts that confront us with our own sin and the consequences of our disobedience. When Paul describes "our forefathers" in 1 Corinthians 10:1, he points to a moment in Israel's history when disobedience led to disaster. The rebellion of the ancestors in the wilderness had resulted in their judgment. Consequently, Paul says, "This was written for our instruction" (1 Cor. 10:11). Similarly, the author of Hebrews tells the story of Israel's failure in the wilderness and concludes, "The Word of God is living and active, sharper than any two-edged sword" (Heb. 4:12). He invites his first-century readers to identify with the ancient people of Israel and to see in Israel's failure to reach the promised land their own failure and impending judgment. As the readers of Hebrews read the ancient story, the Word of God "does surgery on them" with a "two-edged sword." If we see ourselves in the ancient stories, we too will see the consequences of our failure to acknowledge God's claim on our lives.

Entering The Story

In the next chapter, we'll examine in detail how the various books of the Bible structure the story of redemption. But before moving to a more detailed survey of biblical narrative, we first should ask how to read these ancient narratives. What strategies will we use to make sense of them?

When we come to a modern story—a novel, say—we know how to read it. We know what to expect in the action to some extent, and we know how characters will be put together. We expect it to move in a more or less linear way, and when it breaks the temporal sequence, we speak of flashbacks or foreshadowing. We can speak of writing conventions that writers can either follow or break—but at least we know what the conventions are. Similarly, when we read a newspaper, we also know how to read its various pieces. We need to find out whether the words "Mighty Casey had struck out" appear on the sports page or in the personal advice column, because context makes a difference in meaning. We also know that a novel is not a newspaper and vice versa. They employ different standards of "truth."

Moreover, neither of them resembles a web site, which lacks the simple linearity of a book. To read any of these types of text, readers must acquire some competencies (we'll say more about all this in Chapters 7–9).

For now, however, note that the Bible's narratives follow their own rules. With rare exceptions, their chief qualities are economy of words and a refusal to eliminate tensions. They rarely reveal a character's motives or indulge in detailed description. Rather, biblical stories usually tell only the minimum, leaving the reader with two risks: over-interpretation and under-interpretation. That is, we may make the text say things it does not, or we may miss what it does say. We can avoid the first by asking, whenever we read the text a particular way, "Where is that in the text?" We can avoid the second by noticing where the text says more than absolutely necessary, where it repeats itself, and often where it allows us to experience, however briefly, the innermost thought of the characters. We may not find foolproof ways of reading these texts, because they deliberately preserve tensions that would allow for different ways of understanding them. Some of these tensions arise from the complexities of reality itself and some from the fact that the biblical books were for the most part not written all at once, but over long stretches of time.

As a result of this economy of style, biblical stories strikingly often refuse to state explicitly a moral judgment on the characters. Good storytellers often do this; but more is involved here than just skillful storytelling. The text does lay out a moral and spiritual vision, but only as one learns to read it as a whole, seeing the wide patterns of cause and effect that befall the various characters in the text. We must wrestle with the texts in order to enter into their vision—God's vision—of a broken but redeemable humankind. We read one episode after another, letting the layers of the overall story build in our consciousness until we begin to think in terms of the story about our own experiences. The story locates us in the world and in the world to come.

The End of the Story

The Bible begins with the declaration that "in the beginning God created the heavens and the earth" and then proceeds to describe the alienation of the world from its creator. The center of the Bible for Christians is the declaration that in Jesus Christ God has reconciled the world to himself (2 Cor. 5:19). With its depiction of a "new heaven and a new earth" and the restoration of the tree of life, Revelation makes a fitting conclusion to a drama that began with human rebellion, the loss of the garden, and the alienation of the nations from one another. In telling this story, we affirm that God has a story of the universe and we tell that story each week in order to remind the whole community of our destiny. God is at work in the world, and our lives make sense when we conform our personal stories to God's story.

As we pointed out in the beginning of this chapter, we live in a culture that has lost its story, leaving individuals without orientation for their lives. Our situation has many similarities to that which the earliest Christians faced, for early Christianity also encountered a world dominated by chaos. The power of Christianity was that it confronted the chaos with a coherent story of the world's beginning, middle, and end. People who had no narrative to provide direction for their lives found that narrative in the Christian message that God created the world and

89

would bring it to completion. Our task today is to tell God's story to a culture that has lost its story.[2]

The biblical story gives us a new way of looking at the world. Instead of seeing an ending full of chaos, we see the biblical world in which God is not yet finished with us. Like the early Christians, we tell a story that is not yet completed. In the last book of the Bible, the people continue to cry "How long?" and to await God's creation of a new heaven and a new earth. In the meantime, the powers of evil and death have not yet been destroyed. We live in the midst of famine, persecution, and sword, knowing only that "nothing will separate us from the love of God in Christ Jesus our Lord" and that God will ultimately destroy death. Thus in the concluding page of the Bible, the faithful people wait for the end of the story. It is as if the book closes at the end of Act Four of a five-act play. The people of God continue to live faithfully until the end.

At the end of Hebrews 11, the author brings his list of heroes to an end with the words, "apart from us they would not be made perfect." The author challenges his readers to recognize that *they* are the next chapter in the story; the great heroes of faith are now counting on them! In the same way, we too play our role in the final act of the drama. We can play the role well, however, only if we *know* the first four acts of the drama. Like generations before us, we identify with Abraham as he waits on God to fulfill his promise; we wait with the Israelites in exile to see if God's promises will ever come true; and we join the earliest Christians in trusting that God has reconciled the world through Jesus Christ. Next we will see how the Bible, through its very arrangement of narratives and other types of texts, ushers us into the company of the men and women of faith who inhabit its pages.

5

The Gorgeous Mosaic of Scripture

To speak of the life-giving story of Scripture is also to recognize that we live in a world in which death and its companions, fear and hate, stalk us all. David Weiss Halivni tells of his life as a fifteen-year-old Jewish boy in Auschwitz. For years before the Nazis imprisoned him and gassed his family, he had studied Talmud in his East European village. He had found life in the ancient words—and ultimately in the still more ancient ones in the Bible. Now, in the camps, he and his fellow Jews lived under the cruelest circumstances that modern science, politics, and economics could devise.

One night, he writes, he walked as usual out of the tunnel in which he and thousands of others were building a munitions plant that would be safe from Allied bombers. He passed, as often before, a guard eating a sandwich. This time, he happened to notice that the guard held the sandwich in a greasy piece of paper on which Hebrew letters appeared. Halivni recognized the leaf as a page from a famous medieval commentary on the Talmud, the *Shulchan Aruch*. He says, "Upon seeing this wrapper, I instinctively fell at the feet of the guard, without even realizing why; the mere letters propelled me. With tears in my eyes, I implored him to give me this [...] page." The guard first reached for his revolver, but then, recognizing that the Jewish boy could not harm him, gave him the sheet, which he carried back to his fellow prisoners. One of them took responsibility for hiding the page, for, had the guards discovered it, they would almost unfailingly have punished its owner. On their few days off, the prisoners could study this page. This one greasy piece of paper became, Halivni says, "a visible symbol of a connection between the camp and the activities of Jews throughout history."[1]

A single page, part of a commentary on a commentary on Scripture. So remote, so irrelevant. Yet, a flicker of life. Amid the comfort of our churches, we may easily forget what sort of career the texts of faith have had. Under the smoke of the crematorium, a boy in Auschwitz finds a connection to a larger, sounder, happier world.

This story reminds us that in our lifetimes or those of our parents, humans have faced stark evil, by turns brutal or banal. We may do so again. Christians in Sudan and Afghanistan do so as I write these words. Even if we do not face something of the magnitude of the 1930s and 40s, we nevertheless do confront a world in search of wholeness and meaning deeper than that provided by a swollen bank account or a magnificent house in the suburbs. We look for depth, for something real. We can find it in the words of Scripture.

How do we reach the depths of Scripture? In this and the next chapter, we will argue that to do this, Christians must understand both *what* the Bible does and *how* it does it. Its ancient texts, stained with the grease of sandwiches or the blood of martyrs, record and reflect upon Israel's and the church's ongoing experiences with God. These texts form the society of readers who can live in faith with the God of Israel and Jesus Christ. Scripture draws us to new horizons of moral, spiritual, and communal growth by transporting us from our immediate experiences and prejudices to new places of the Spirit.

However, understanding the Bible is not always easy. A friend of mine who is studying Isaiah recently asked me, "I read a chapter and it promises Israel they'll never suffer again. Then the next chapter says they will. When do the promises finally stick?" She asks a good question. To answer it, one needs to know how to read a prophetic book. We could say the same for the rest of the Bible. We need to know *how* to read it.

As Chapter 7 will work out in more detail, reading a biblical text requires opening our eyes and ears to its logical flow, its literary rhythms and figures, its large arguments. We ask ourselves *why* it says what it says in its historical setting. Is it persuading readers to think and act differently than they now do (as often in Paul's letters or the prophets)? Or is it reminding readers of what they already know but have forgotten? We also ask about each biblical book's historical background and content, not as an act of fact collection, but as a way of retrieving the text's message. Although the text is not about us, it is relevant to us.

> *The texts of Scripture have enjoyed spectacular careers in the most difficult places. They have inspired human creativity in all its forms and media. Several years ago, I visited a church just outside Jerusalem, near the traditional site of the Garden of Gethsemane, the Church of All Nations. Atop its columned entry sits a gold-hued mosaic, depicting the sleepy apostles and mourning women looking expectantly to God, who is about to raise Jesus from the dead. Inside, mosaic scenes of the Bible, from Eden to Golgotha,*

cover the walls. This modern building, paid for by believers around the world, points us to the savior of "all the nations." The old art form of the mosaic, which goes back thousands of years, still carries a message that speaks to modern people.

—Mark

We can think of the Bible as a mosaic, the most gorgeous of all. Its many small pieces are stones of many colors and textures arranged by the Spirit living in Israel and the church to portray the destiny that awaits us all in the arms of God. To speak more plainly, the Bible contains various types of literature. Each contributes something to the overall dialogue of the Spirit that the canon of Scripture preserves and carries forward. Narratives provide the cement, binding the stones together, offering us the basic story of who we are and how we came to be. Laws frame the picture, giving readers the boundaries they need to make sense of the narratives of ancient times—and their own narrative of faith.

Other types of literature fill out the mosaic, sometimes with luminous colors, sometimes with dim. Together, they capture the rich complexity of the life of faith. Letters reveal how churches may work out processes of discovering the implications of the gospel in their own ever-changing situations. Psalms offer a language for praise and lament, by both individuals and the church as a whole. Wisdom literature shows us the limits of religion, or rather, how true religion never remains content with pat answers, but always seeks new depths of understanding from the humble search for God.

Learning how Scripture works demands, then, that we gaze intently upon the text, so that it can also work upon us. Chapter 7 will offer some hints as to how to do that. The diligent reader of the Bible finds that it contains jewels of many colors and materials that fit together into a dazzling mosaic. Now let us examine the various kinds of texts we find in Scripture and determine what role they play in revealing to us God's work and will.

This and the following chapter will examine in turn narrative, law, prophets, psalms, wisdom literature, apocalypses, and epistles. We begin with story in order to highlight the fact that Scripture arose in the interactions between God and a specific people with a particular past, one that we who are grafted into Israel now share.

Reading Biblical Narrative

Someone coming to the Bible for the first time might well expect it to contain mostly divine speeches about various topics, glowing depictions of angelic mysteries, or heartwarming stories of lives transformed. Commands, examples, and necessary inferences would also be nice, but they too are surprisingly hard to come by. Instead, Scripture opens with powerful stories—about the beginning of the world and the turbulent lives of a certain family of humanity ancestral to Jews, and thus to Jesus Christ.

The story of redemption runs throughout the canon: in the Pentateuch; the Deuteronomistic History (Joshua to 2 Kings without Ruth); Ezra, Nehemiah, and Chronicles; Ruth and Esther; the Gospels; and the Acts of the Apostles. Together these books of the Bible furnish a superstructure on which the remainder of the canon rests. Abraham, David, Jesus, and a host of other characters grace the pages of this grand, sweeping story.

This story concerns not merely long-dead heroes. Rather, its main character is none other than the true and living God, who still constructs humanity's story out of the raw material of flawed, yet redeemed lives.

The Pentateuch: Genesis to Deuteronomy

The Pentateuch recounts stories of primeval times when culture began (Gen. 1-11), and of patriarchal times when God worked with a strange assortment of ne'er-do-wells like Jacob, and men and women struggling with faith like Abraham and Sarah (Gen. 12-50). Then Exodus opens with the account of Israel's first holocaust, in Egypt, and their subsequent deliverance from the "house of slaves." Next, the book escorts Israel to Sinai, where the Israelites receive the Law (Hebrew: *Torah*—more on this later) and the abiding presence of God in the Tabernacle. Following that, we find Israel wandering through the desert (Numbers to Deuteronomy) and finally reaching the Promised Land outside the pages of the Pentateuch, in Joshua and Judges.

An outline of the Pentateuch as a whole might look something like this:
1. The Creation of the World and Human Ways of Life (Gen. 1-11);
2. God's Choice of the Patriarchs (Gen. 12-50);
3. The Liberation from Egypt (Exod. 1-18);
4. The Formation of Israel Through the *Torah* at Sinai (Exod. 19-Lev. 26);
5. The Formation of Israel Through Wandering in the Desert with Further Instructions (Num. 1-36);
6. The Formation of Israel on the Plains of Moab (Deut. 1-30);
7. Concluding Blessings and Transitions (Deut. 31-34).[2]

This story peaks with the election of the Patriarchs, the exodus, the giving of the Law at Mount Sinai, and the preparation to enter the Promised Land, each climax more dramatic than the previous one. Spanning several centuries, the narrative introduces us to the story of the wandering and settled people of God.

The Christian reader of these texts may wonder how to extract systematically from them moral or religious insights. Biblical narrative does reveal a profound moral vision, but it does not usually do so in a way that we can pick up quickly when we meet some crisis in our lives. Say, for example, you read Genesis for advice on marriage and child rearing. First you find Cain killing Abel, then Abraham twice tries to fob his wife off as his sister, and Isaac tries the same trick. Rebecca helps her son Jacob lie to his poor, blind father and swindle his brother out of his inheritance. Not to be outdone, Joseph the braggart finds himself at the bottom of a cistern where his jealous brothers throw him just before they sell him to traders who happen to pass by. Suddenly my family crises don't seem so bad!

On the other hand, Genesis does note that sometimes one's actions predictably lead to ruin (Jacob being cheated by Laban) or to success (Joseph meeting Pharaoh through the butler's good offices). And sometimes grace trumps the rules of the world and lets a Jacob see his grandchildren and give them, still in his own tricky way, a blessing. Even the most dysfunctional families can be places of grace in a world in which the God of Israel lives and works. As Chapter 4 notes, each small story of the Bible can tell the Big Story as well.

In Genesis 12, God calls Abraham and Sarah for some undiscovered reason to leave Ur and head for parts unknown, where they will receive a child and a land, and where they will somehow become a blessing to all humanity. Then, after many delays and false starts, Abraham and Sarah produce the heir, only to hear God demand him as a sacrifice. Genesis 22:1 describes this command as a test, and the story eventually emphasizes God's gracious provision to a man who would trust his maker so implicitly.

Still, we ask questions. Why choose Abraham? Why delay the giving of the heir? Why test this aged father through the grisly practice, albeit common in the ancient world, of human sacrifice? And, for that matter, why is Abraham so accepting? Why did he, who had protested God's impending destruction of Sodom a few chapters back, acquiesce apparently uncomplainingly to the potential retraction of God's promise that Isaac's death would have meant? The text answers none of these questions, despite the fact that they have been obvious to readers for over two thousand years. But by placing the claim "The Lord will provide" at the exact center of the story, Genesis does emphasize God's promise and the fact that its fulfillment does not depend upon human actions, thus sending us back to the promise in Genesis 12 and reminding us that the Lord does indeed live up to his commitments. God will do what God will do, and people of faith will try to conform their lives to that sovereign will. The subtleties of this story, one example among many, worm their way into our consciousness until their meaning shakes us to our core. By asking questions of the story (like those above) and refusing to settle for simpleminded answers, Christians can discover new truths that refashion how we think about the world.

Genesis continues with God's promise and human failure. Jacob is the go-getter who cheats Esau out of the birthright. Joseph is the spoiled child of his father, and his brothers react with rage to his boasting by selling their brother into slavery. At the end of all this intrigue, Genesis ends with Joseph's statement, "Don't be afraid. Am I in the place of God? You intended to harm me, but God intended it for good to accomplish what is now being done, the saving of many lives" (Gen. 50:20).

As Exodus begins, Abraham's descendants are further from the promise than ever. Now they are slaves in Egypt and far away from the promise of a place, their own place. Then, as all of the recitals of God's mighty acts indicate, the story reaches its climax in God's great act of redemption. This dramatic rescue under the leadership of Moses formed the initial climax of the story, providing the people of God with the vocabulary for describing God's deeds in future generations. Just as God "redeemed" and "ransomed" slaves from Egypt, future generations would recall that event as they looked forward to God's ultimate moment of redemption.

The event that most fully reveals God's place at the center of the human story is the exodus from Egypt. Here God hears the cry of wretched slaves, remembers the promises to their ancestors, and acts through the unlikely hero Moses to deliver them. Today's readers may ask certain "modern" questions that may not help us arrive at the theological message of the text. We ask, what really happened? Why do Egyptian records contain little or no mention of the plagues or the escape of slaves? When did the exodus occur? Did natural phenomena (volcanic eruptions, red tides) cause the plagues? How many people left Egypt, millions or thousands? Was their settlement in the land gradual, as Judges and the archaeological record imply, or more sudden, as one might infer from Joshua? All of these are legitimate questions for historians, and scholars, Christian or not, come down in different places on them.

But what is crucial for the church today is not the raw data of the *history* of the exodus and subsequent events, but the meaning of the *story* of exodus that Jews and Christians repeated over and again to their children (Exod. 12:24–27). In this story, we glimpse a vision of God's sovereignty over other gods and political powers, God's concern for the oppressed, and God's willingness to enter into covenant. It is not accidental that later biblical texts appeal to the exodus as typical of the modus operandi of God and can call him to act again as before (for example, 1 Kings 8:51–54; Isa. 40; Jer. 31:1–22). Deliverance from Egypt creates the people who understand their place in the world on the story's terms, not the world's. The story does not remain locked in a distant past, but comes alive daily as Israel lives under the covenant. As Jews repeat at Passover each year, "*We* were slaves in Egypt, and God delivered *us*[...]." Israel keeps the Sabbath and allows even slaves and animals to rest because they were "a slave in the land of Egypt, and the Lord your God brought you out from there with an outstretched arm[...]" (Deut. 5:15). The story, as part of the greater Story, leads to morality, to spirituality, to life.

The Deuteronomistic History: Joshua to 2 Kings

Continuing the Pentateuch's story of Israel's redemption, Joshua, Judges, 1 & 2 Samuel, and 1 & 2 Kings form part of what scholars often call the Deuteronomistic History. Using many sources of varying dates, the person or persons who put together this narrative placed on it the stamp of a single religious outlook and agenda. This large work wears this name today because it understands Israelite history in terms of the main ideas of

Deuteronomy, especially that book's emphasis on how gracious God's gift of the *Torah* is, and what a responsibility for ethical living it places on those in covenant with this benevolent God. Deuteronomy's preoccupation with worship of God alone influences how these books interpret Israel's history. Thus the cycle of sin → punishment → repentance → deliverance that one sees in the book, especially in Joshua and Judges, is a theological understanding applied to events. The Bible would not agree with *Dragnet*'s Sergeant Friday: "Just the facts, ma'am." In its pages, the facts of history work in the service of religious reflection. The telling of the story allows the reader to place himself or herself within it, to be shaped by it into something new and better. The text tries to understand the theological relationship between human

> **Main ideas of Deuteronomy & the Deuteronomistic History**
>
> Deuteronomy and its accompanying historical texts (Joshua, Judges, 1 & 2 Samuel, 1 & 2 Kings) emphasize the following key themes:
>
> - God has chosen Israel to be a special people, bearers of divine grace;
> - This choice leads to the giving of the covenant in the *Torah*;
> - The *Torah* leads to life (see Deut. 30:19-20);
> - Sacrifice to God must occur in only one place: Jerusalem;
> - Ethics and worship go hand-in-hand;
> - Sinful behavior of the people leads to divine punishment;
> - Repentance of the people leads to divine forgiveness;
> - God does not abandon Israel—even when they sin—but calls them to repentance and restoration;
> - God raises up leaders (judges, then kings) to bring about restoration and to demonstrate grace;
> - The prophets call rulers and subjects to be faithful to the covenant.

agency and the sufferings of Israel, thus allowing also for a broad moral vision in which human beings, especially powerful ones, must answer for their actions.

Far from a mere pile of names and events for children to memorize, the Deuteronomistic History actually reflects on theology. As Chapter 4 noted, the

Bible uses story to tell about God's activities in the world precisely because stories are the most intimate ways humans talk to each other. Behind the stories of Samuel to Kings lie several major religious teachings.

First, the Deuteronomistic History emphasizes prophets (Huldah and many others) and their role in revealing the will of the sovereign God who acts in accordance with the covenant and alerts Israel to that effect.

Second, the keeping of *Torah* matters to the Deuteronomists. The faithfulness of those in power is particularly important. God holds accountable officials who permit, much less participate in, the oppression of the poor.

Third, unfaithfulness and injustice can have consequences beyond the life of the individual perpetrator.

Fourth, and most importantly, the Lord keeps covenant with the community of faith, the chosen people, even when they do not reciprocate. Generations pass away, but the covenant and the covenant people remain forever. God's willingness to enter into the untidiness of human history, to proclaim a Word that remains forever (Isa. 40:8), defines the ability of biblical faith to adapt to, and transform, our troubled world.

This attempt at transformation begins with Israel's entry into Canaan, an event in which the promise to Abraham finally appears to be realized. However, the people of God are still threatened by enemies and wonder why, if Israel was liberated from Egypt and placed in its own land, is everything not now perfect? In the judges, they catch momentary glimpses of God's redemption through great leaders, but the redemption never lasts. Israel continues to look forward to God's ultimate salvation. In the story that culminates in the anointing of the king, Israel's hopes for the fulfillment of the promise reach a new climactic moment. David was the new Abraham, the new Moses, through whom God would complete what was begun earlier.

Their hopes rest on the monarchy, but once again Israel squanders the time of divine favor. Even David is deeply flawed, and his sin with Bathsheba sets in motion a disastrous history of intrigue and violence. David's successors disappoint God, their subjects, and all future readers of their stories. Consequently, the kingdom is soon divided. The kings do not heed the prophets, and both Israel and Judah ultimately go into exile. The curtain of this sad narrative goes down with the return from exile of a few of those who have gone into exile. Hopes are high for the restoration of Israel and the fulfillment of God's promise of the land. But once again, the survivors must face the reality that the Davidic monarchy will not be reestablished, and Israel is not a mighty kingdom. At the end of this narrative, Israel has returned from exile and lives in hope that God will repeat in the future the great deeds of the past. Israel looks for a new Moses, a new exodus, a new David, and a new creation.

These books tell the story of the settlement in the land against great opposition, the gradual development from tribal culture to statehood, and the eventual fall of the state owing to the unfaithfulness of both rulers and subjects. 2 Kings ends by holding out the faint hope of return, which was to be realized sometime later.

It is tempting to think of these books as merely recounting the events of a distant past, perhaps with a few moral admonitions thrown in for good measure. Certainly the stories of kings and commoners all serve to model faithful and unfaithful behavior for the reader. But in combining these stories, the Deuteronomistic

History also makes larger claims about the sovereignty of Israel's God and God's refusal to allow this people to sink into a sinfulness that would render them unfit for their calling to bless the nations, as the covenant with Abraham in Genesis 12 puts it.

In dealing with the messiness of human history, the Deuteronomists sometimes focus on particular heroes, who, despite imperfections, exemplify faithfulness to God and generosity to human beings. A good example is King Josiah, who lived when the Deuteronomic movement began to flower. 2 Kings 22-23 tells of his reform of Judah's worship. After the discovery of the book of the *Torah* (probably Deuteronomy or some version thereof) and the confirmation of its validity by the prophetess Huldah (2 Kings 22:14-20), Josiah rid the land of idols and practitioners of illicit religion. He also celebrated Passover in an unprecedented way (2 Kings 23:21-23). On account of all this, the Deuteronomistic historian tells us, Josiah was the model ruler, greater than any before—including David!—or after (2 Kings 23:24-25).

Despite the piety of this model king of Judah, his Egyptian overlord, Pharaoh Necho, unexpectedly executed him. The death of the great hero caused a huge problem for the Deuteronomists, who finally argued that this turn of events was owed to the sins of Josiah's grandfather Manasseh (2 Kings 23:26-27; 24:3). Sin has consequences "unto the third and fourth generations."

2 Kings ends, then, during the time of the Babylonian Exile, when hope flickered but dimly. For the Deuteronomistic Historian, the lessons of Israel's history consisted of missed opportunities. But it also revealed the faithfulness of God, who might act graciously to deliver again in the future, just as in the past.

Chronicles, Ezra, & Nehemiah

On the other side of the Exile lie these four books. Parallel to the Deuteronomistic History, and extending it a century or so further, are 1 & 2 Chronicles, Ezra, and Nehemiah. An extensively rewritten version of Genesis to Kings, Chronicles retells the story of Israel's past from Adam to the return from Babylonian Exile at the behest of the Persian ruler Cyrus after 538 B.C. The book covers much of the same ground as the older historical works. So, readers may ask, why does it exist at all?

Again, remember that the Bible values diversity. Chronicles emphasizes how Israel can enjoy the presence of God in worship in the Temple. Also, whereas the older histories underscore the precariousness of Israel's faith, Chronicles singles out those moments when faith triumphed and God blessed Israel. For the Deuteronomists, the glass was half empty; for the Chronicler, it was half full. The first history spoke to people choked on their own pride, while the second bolstered those depressed by their ancestors' failure.

To be sure, Chronicles presents its own challenges. Modern readers often find the first chapters of 1 Chronicles especially boring. One usually finds lists of names only in telephone books! But Chronicles lists them for a purpose: to remind the Israelites returning from Babylon that they have a history, that it stretches back to the beginning of humanity, and that it continues. So, the list includes not only ancient figures, but the names of those families living in the restored community around Jerusalem.

But the book does not end there. Rather, it reworks the stories of rulers, notably David and Solomon, to explore the significance of Israel's rise and fall from a particular point of view. Chronicles airbrushes their stories, removing blemishes that the Deuteronomist emphasizes. That is, this book, like the Deuteronomistic History, uses history to make first and foremost a theological argument. Like the laws in the Pentateuch and like Ezekiel, both of which we will talk about a little later, the Chronicler underscores the importance of the Temple and its worship as symbols of God's abiding presence in Israel. The cult reminds us of God's abiding justice.

> **The cult...**
>
> Scholars do not often use the term "cult" in the popular sense of a religious group tightly controlled by a powerful leader. The more technical meaning refers to worship in the form of sacrifice of animals and other items, probably led by a priest, usually in a temple or other holy site. "Cult" in this book bears this second, technical definition.

The books of Ezra and Nehemiah, which are closely related to Chronicles at the literary level and may even stem from the same group of writers, continue the theme. The Persian imperial government repatriated citizens of Judah (soon to be called "Jews") from Mesopotamia, where Nebuchadnezzar had deported them, back to their ancestral land. This return fulfilled the promises of Jeremiah (Jer. 31) and other prophets, who had announced God's future restoration of Israel. Ezra and Nehemiah tell of their struggles to rebuild Jerusalem and its Temple (see also Haggai and Zechariah) and thus to reclaim their identity as worshipers of the true and living God. As we noted previously, it was probably also during this period that the shift from an oral to a written *Torah* became pronounced.

Ruth & Esther

These two short stories—some scholars call them historical novellas—tell the stories of remarkable women whose spunk and creativity led, respectively, to the continuance of the Davidic dynasty and the survival of Jews living far from home. Esther has the added distinction of being the only book in the Bible that does not mention God by name.

These books offer us snapshots of the lives of persons outside the main flow of the narrative—women with connections to Gentiles. Ruth speaks directly of God's care for a Moabite woman in distress, and of how she becomes not only a member of the covenant people, but the ancestor of its greatest king. Esther offers a vigorous critique of the powerful when it lampoons the mighty Ahasuerus, who can rule the world but not himself. It certainly emphasizes the bravery of the young Esther and her formidable uncle Mordecai. Both of these stories, written in the period after Israel's Exile in Babylon, remind us of the scope of God's concern for human beings. Perhaps they both—especially Ruth—also remind the readers of Ezra and Nehemiah not to overemphasize their unique claim on God. God rules all nations, not just Israel.

The Gospels

Building on the stories in the Old Testament are those in the gospels. Significantly, Matthew opens by connecting Jesus' genealogy back to Abraham via various ancient figures. All the gospels quote the Old Testament repeatedly and allow its words and ideas to influence how the life of the Lord is told. Now let us address three questions: what is a gospel, why are there four, and how should we read them?

Luke opens his work by noting that:

> Many have undertaken to draw up an account of the things that have been fulfilled among us, just as they were handed down to us by those who from the first were eyewitnesses and servants of the word.

—Luke 1:1-2

Three points are crucial for our purposes: 1) Luke had predecessors in the business of writing gospels; 2) the gospel story (as opposed to the literary genre, *gospel*) originated with eyewitnesses who passed it down to others, eventually reaching Luke; 3) the content of what was handed down concerned things "fulfilled," that is, somehow carried forward the theme set forth in the past, in Scripture, and now realized fully in the gospel story.

The gospels do not purport to be direct eyewitness accounts of Jesus' life. Rather, they trace back to oral and written stories about Jesus remembered by his disciples and shape those accounts in light of the ongoing needs of the church, guided by the Spirit, to understand Jesus' life, death, and resurrection.

The choice and ordering of stories and sayings, which varies from gospel to gospel, corresponds to a theological need to which each work responds. As John 20:30-31 puts it:

> Therefore, many other signs did Jesus indeed do before the disciples, which are not written in this book. But these are written that you [plural] may believe that Jesus is the Christ, the son of God, and in believing, you might have life in his name.

The gospel writers emphasize the commitments and beliefs of the faithful community that the written gospel can stimulate and sustain (notice that the verb "believe" or "have faith" is plural in Greek).

Gospels are thus not biographies in the modern sense. They tell little about Jesus' early life (Mark and John tell nothing at all). They do not explore his psyche, explain his motives, nor line out the connections he made to other people. They offer no political, sociological, or personal explanations for his actions or those of his disciples. They do, however, focus so singlemindedly on the last week in his life that one could almost say that the Passion week is the starting point of the story, with the rest of Jesus' life simply a prelude to the decisive events surrounding Easter. That is, the gospels call attention to the core gospel story of divine grace manifested at Golgotha.

The earliest gospel is probably Mark, from which both Matthew and Luke drew material. As Chapter 2 pointed out, these three are called the Synoptics owing to their close resemblance to one another; John reflects a different perspective on the story of Jesus—again reflecting God's apparent love of diversity. Matthew and Luke follow Mark's basic outline, though they smooth out his rough-and-ready Greek, compress his episodes, and fill in some of the blanks he leaves. Notably, they add the stories of Jesus' early years. They also clarify the story of the resurrection, which Mark does not spell out in detail, perhaps because he thought it was better told orally in the sermons of the church (Mark 16:9–20 is a later addition not present in the earliest Greek manuscripts).

Matthew and Luke also share much material, especially sayings, that are not in Mark. Scholars often call this group of sayings "Q" from the German word for "source." Whatever the precise origins of this material, the gospel writers combined them into a coherent whole that bears witness to the power of the gospel in the ongoing life of the church.

When we turn to a gospel, we look for how its structure and its choice of sayings and miracles work together to set forth a theological message. Take Matthew, for example. The book is organized in alternating bands of narratives (often of miracles) and discourses:

A. Introducing Jesus (chapters 1-4);
B. Speech 1: The Sermon on the Mount (chapters 5-7);
A. Miracles (chapters 8-9);
B. Speech 2: The Charge to the Disciples (9:35-11:1);
A. Controversy Stories (11:2-12:50);
B. Speech 3: Seven Parables (chapter 13);
A. Jesus' Travels (chapters 14-17);
B. Speech 4: Discourse on the Church (18:1-19:1);
A. Traveling to Jerusalem (19:2-23:39);
B. Speech 5: Speech on the End of Time (chapters 24-25);
A. The Passion Week (chapters 26-28).

This pattern of five long speeches seems to imitate the five books of the Pentateuch, with the aim of portraying Jesus as the Messiah giving the new *Torah*, like Moses. This is why Jesus speaks on a mountain like Sinai (chapters 5-7) and why Matthew recounts his trip to and from Egypt (reminiscent of Israel itself, as Matthew 2:14 makes clear by its quotation of Hosea 11:1—"Out of Egypt have I called my son"). Matthew employs this image of Jesus because it spoke to the experiences and understandings of the gospel's church audience, Jews and Gentiles deeply influenced by the Old Testament.

Other gospels present the life of Jesus in different ways, sometimes even presenting the same event at different points in the story (as when Luke 4 places Jesus' provocative sermon in Nazareth at the beginning of his ministry, and Matthew 13 and Mark 6 place it later). Again, chronological order was not of primary importance to the Evangelists. They aimed instead to explore the multiple dimensions of the person and work of Jesus and their implications for the church that called him Lord.

Here we have emphasized the origins of the gospels, albeit briefly. Even more important than their origins are surely their major theological claims. Jesus, they all agree, has come in the flesh to die, and in dying and rising from the dead has bridged the gap between God and humankind. Jesus, born of Israel and thus part of the ongoing story of faith that goes back to Abraham, introduces God to all the world. Jesus thus fulfills the ancient promises, not by undoing them or radically altering their meaning, but by carrying them forward to their full extent. He saves Israel and through Israel, the world!

Acts of the Apostles

This theme of salvation is the subject of the final narrative we will consider here, found in the sequel to Luke's gospel—Acts. Luke extends the gospel model provided by Mark into the time of the church, following the center of time that is the life and passion of Jesus. His heroes, Peter and Paul, imitate Jesus by doing miracles and proclaiming the good news. For his Gentile audience, Luke portrays the first generation of Christians as something like the already familiar philosophical schools (Acts 24:5, 14; 28:22). But he also emphasizes that Christians are followers of the Messiah longingly awaited by Israel.

In our congregations, although Acts has received an enormous amount of attention, we still may have missed key aspects of its theology. Too often, we have read it as a manual on evangelism or a rulebook for organizing churches. Certainly evangelism does play a major role in Luke's story, but no single method commends his approval—unless it is converting entire households after a miracle! Similarly, we have emphasized baptism based on this text, although not every example of conversion mentions baptism. These omissions do not diminish the importance of baptism, which all early Christians unquestionably practiced. But they do indicate that Luke did not set out to write a defense of baptism, but rather to tell the story of God's work among the baptized.

To use Luke's language, Acts recounts the movement of the Holy Spirit in the church from "Jerusalem, Judea, and Samaria, to the uttermost parts of the world" (Acts 1:8). By paralleling the lives of Peter and Paul, apostles to Jews and Gentiles respectively (though each ministers to both), Luke presents the story of the church, which he sees as the true Israel, including both Jews and now Gentiles, as it moves to the very center of the known world. Thus the faith of Israel becomes not the property of a people in a backwater province, but of men and women in every place and station of life.

The Story as a Whole

To read Old and New Testament narrative, then, is to find a grand story spanning millennia and drawing the reader into a world wherein God gets involved in the blessed chaos of human actions. All the rest is detail. We need not read the story in an absolutely literal way as mere facts to be believed (as we used to say), but we can find in it profound examinations of the largest issues of human life amid the swirling movements of history. Though never as neat as we would like, the real world in all its complexity provides the stage on which the promises of God become reality. Now let us turn to the other parts of Scripture that ornament this narrative superstructure.

Reading Old Testament Law

Embedded within the narrative of the Pentateuch is the Law. Actually, we might do well to use the Hebrew term *Torah* (as this chapter does), because for many of us "law" conjures up the deadening notion of rules to which one must adhere simply out of fear of divine wrath. This view of Law comes in part from an exaggeration of the Reformation's legitimate repudiation of contrived rules to define who was and who was not a Christian (a problem that was not unique to the medieval church, by the way). However, this view of a dead Law could not be further from the biblical concept of *Torah*.

> **Torah:**
>
> The Hebrew word meaning "instruction," often translated "law."
>
> **Nomos:**
>
> The Greek word that Greek-speaking Jews, including Paul, used to translate the Hebrew word *Torah*.

To illustrate Scripture's consistently high view of *Torah*, note a few texts, from both Old and New Testaments:

> [God is] the one who announces his words to Jacob, and his legal decisions to Israel. He has not done so for any other nation, and they do not know.
>
> —Psalm 147:19–20
>
> Blessed are the ones who stay perfectly on the road, those walking in the *Torah* of Yahweh.
>
> —Psalm 119:1
>
> How I love your *Torah*: all day long it is my object of study.
>
> —Psalm 119:97
>
> The Law [*nomos*] is holy and the command is holy and righteous and good[...]. For we know that the Law is spiritual.
>
> —Romans 7:12, 14

The verses from Psalm 119, the longest chapter in the Bible, also grab our attention. An alphabetic acrostic extolling the life shaped by *Torah*, Psalm 119 describes how, in the words of one recent commentator, *Torah* "has become for the psalmist much more than the laws by which Israel should live, as given in the Pentateuch[.... It] has become a personal way to God."[3]

The last quotation hints at the attitude of Paul, who held up a vision of salvation for Jews and Gentiles in which all kept the Law of faith through Jesus Christ, since *Torah* for him points to something higher than itself (grace operating through faith). Paul might have sympathized with the sentiment expressed by a rabbi from two centuries before him, Simeon the Just, who said: "The world is sustained by three things: *Torah*, worship, and compassionate deeds."[4] Paul insists that those living under the cross gratefully worship and faithfully serve the God of all creation. *Torah* forms spiritual people for lives of sacrifice and compassion. Christians keep the essence of the Law in the concrete attitudes, commitments, and behaviors of their lives. Law works in conjunction with awe before God and solidarity with other human beings.

Unlike his later readers, who were undoubtedly influenced by Luther, Paul did not feel a need to denigrate the *Torah*, but rather to say that it operates in the context of the saving deeds of Jesus Christ. His problem was not with *Torah*, but with *Torah* separate from the saving deeds of God ("glory" as he puts it in 2 Corinthians 3:7–8). His reverence for *Torah* shines through whenever he tries to clinch a point, for he then invariably quotes the Old Testament.

The Jewish rabbis, meanwhile, counted 613 laws in the Pentateuch, covering subjects from avoidance of idolatry to injunctions against sexual, financial, and relational immorality, to rules against tattoos and strange haircuts. Some of the rules seem odd to us, but they may well have had great significance in their original setting. For example, we may wonder about rules for proper slaughter and what foods should be eaten. But many of the biblical rules about food do reveal a common theme: do not eat predatory animals, do not eat a parent animal and its offspring, do not eat blood. The concern does not seem to be with hygiene, by the way, since sheep and cows in ancient times were as prone to diseases dangerous to humans as pigs were. The rules want to protect Israel from barbarism, cruelty to animals, and callous disregard for the sanctity of life. True, all of the Laws are intended for Israel, not Gentiles, as Paul also notes. Still, when the church brought the Old Testament into its canon, it also undertook to make some spiritual sense of *Torah*, just as Israel has always done.

What sense, then, does *Torah* make for Christians? The easiest place to start is with the Ten Commandments, or Decalogue, in Exodus 20 and Deuteronomy 5. In both places, the rules follow a theological description of God's mighty deeds (Exod. 1-19; Deuteronomy 1-4). In ancient Near Eastern law codes, which Exodus and Deuteronomy resemble, the king who gives the laws often prefaces them with descriptions of his achievements. The Decalogue begins in the same way: God the king and lawgiver has graciously saved Israel from slavery and now calls them to be an ethical, compassionate, and worshipful people. Then the Commandments themselves follow.

By prefacing the rules with a theological justification, the text points out that God does not act arbitrarily. Rather, God's actions proceed from a desire to bless humans and be in relationship, covenant, with us. Morality for those who seek a biblical faith is rooted in the very nature and actions of Israel's Lord. Any moral rule (slavery, the ownership of women, female circumcision, and a long list of human customs) that does not reflect the nature of God cannot command our assent, no matter how time-tested and widely accepted the rule is. On account of human weakness, the *Torah* sometimes regulates problematic behaviors rather than abolishing them outright. However, by opening up vistas of the deeper meanings of God's care for all creation, the *Torah* also compels us to test the goodness of every economic, political, or family practice and discard those that are found wanting.

So, we do not come to the *Torah* with the attitude expressed in the unfortunate sentence that used to be popular among us, "God says it; I believe it; that settles it." The Bible does not cater to ignorance and prejudice in this way. Rather, the *Torah* in general, and the Ten Commandments in particular, set forth moral instructions that reflect the gracious character and behavior of God, in sharp contrast to the meaninglessness and brutality Israel experienced in Egyptian bondage.

In the Ten Commandments, the first commands focus upon this life by prohibiting idolatry. Humans liberated from slavery by God ought not to turn to entities that are not gods, that therefore cannot save. Even the very name of God should not be invoked in an oath when the oath-taker has no intention of executing it. To know of Israel's God is to be in awe of the astonishing deeds that have accompanied that people's deliverance.

The commandment that gets the most ink in these chapters is the fourth, regarding the Sabbath. Today, the Sabbath is a conspicuous way in which Jews live out their commitments to God. This is a day for study and worship, as well as rest and time spent with family, a day in which we too step out of our normal routine and live as we will live in eternity: "Remember the Sabbath to keep it holy."

The biblical text is especially keen on the Sabbath. Genesis 2 envisions it as the climax of God's creation, a theme that Exodus 20 also picks up. Deuteronomy 5, meanwhile, sees the day as a way of recognizing God's deliverance of Israel from Egyptian slavery. In Egypt, human beings were like beasts without rights. In Israel, however, even work animals, much less human beings, received gentle treatment on the Sabbath. Defining someone solely by his or her economic value violates Israel's basic character as God's elect. Just as God rescued defenseless slaves, so should Israel recognize that work and economic needs do not take precedence over the needs of human beings to rest, to be with loved ones, to reflect, and to worship.

The extraordinary treatment of the Sabbath reveals something about how the *Torah* worked. Far from being a burden imposed on Israel, it was designed to shape the community in such a way that all the nation not only remembered what God had done, but they actually lived in a way that reflected those saving actions every day in the relationships of work, law, and family. To be in covenant with the God of Israel defines one as compassionate toward others.

Christians reading the biblical law of Sabbath may easily be tempted to say, "Well, that applies to Israel, not to us. We're under a different regime now." But since the Old Testament is still part of the Bible—since we still encounter within it the Word of God—we need a more nuanced understanding of this problem. The concern for social justice, for the conviction that humans cannot be measured simply by their contributions to the economy, remains a central concern of all who would follow Jesus (who himself spoke of Sabbath as being made for humankind). The need to combine rest with reflection and worship also remains crucial to spiritual growth. The principle of Sabbath shapes our lives as pilgrims before a God who leads us to a promised land.

Of course, not all the laws of the Pentateuch are so readily understandable and applicable to us today. What about the material on the sacrificial system, for example? We are tempted to define these instructions as "empty ritual," and agree with the nineteenth-century satirist Ambrose Bierce in defining rite as, "A religious or semi-religious ceremony fixed by law, precept or custom, with the essential oil of sincerity carefully squeezed out of it."[5] Many of the rules on butchery and building the Tabernacle, for example, seem hopelessly obscure and irrelevant. Not so!

Take the Tabernacle first. Exodus 24–40 recounts its construction, giving a full description of the building and its furnishing not once, but twice. Sandwiched in the middle is the story of the Golden Calf, an image meant to represent the God of Israel. As a whole, these chapters draw a contrast between proper cult (the Tabernacle) and improper cult (the Calf). God cannot be represented in images, cannot be worshiped wherever Israel chooses, and cannot be honored in ways that simply fit human comfort levels. God does not belong to us; *we belong to God*. Worship is at its deepest an awareness of the *otherness* of God, a sense that God alone can command pure devotion.

But as we draw closer to the text, we discover other insights as well. Note that the interlude of the Golden Calf ends with a conversation between Moses and God (Exod. 33:12–23) in which Moses pleads for Israel: "See that this nation is your people!" (verse 13) God responds to Moses' intercession by showing mercy to those who so recently had rejected the center of the Ten Commandments, the prohibition of idolatry. Here we get a sense of the graciousness of Israel's Lord. Those who had "eaten, drunk, and risen to play" now experience the awesome presence of the creator of the universe, their deliverer.

This same graciousness also appears in the description of the sacrificial cult in Leviticus. The Bible explains in detail neither everything sacrifice accomplishes nor why the God of Israel insists upon it. But Leviticus does not merely command a ritual. It modifies practices that Israel shared with other cultures in order to point the Chosen People to their God, who surpasses the gods of other cultures, reminding us that God has deigned to let us approach him in ways that we can understand to some degree, in ways that are meaningful to us. Leviticus speaks of the "glory" of God, for sacrifice reminds us of the awe-inspiring nature of God.

Offering animals in sacrifices limits savagery by controlling the method of slaughter and the use of blood (Lev. 17:10-12), but this is hardly a full explanation. In part sacrifice removes sin; in part it serves to thank God for various blessings. There may be other reasons. What is clear is that the practice of sacrifice was a major concern in ancient Israel, as texts like Malachi

Incidentally, Jews cannot sacrifice animals today because there has been no temple in Jerusalem since the Romans destroyed it in A.D. 70. However, Samaritans still sacrifice on Mount Gerizim, which they believe to be the legitimate place of worship.

show. The practice, not surprisingly, later served Christians as an appropriate (though hardly complete) metaphor for understanding God's saving act in Jesus (see, for example, Hebrews 9:13-28).

For Christians, reading the *Torah* is always like reading someone else's mail. The moral laws seem bedrock to all Christian ethics—sexual, political, or economic. By contrast, the cultic laws seem alien, inexplicable. But here, perhaps more than elsewhere, we discover the holiness and graciousness of God who can deliver men and women, not only from slavery, but from social anarchy that comes from attributing what belongs to, and comes from, God something that is less than God.

Perhaps it is fitting to end this chapter as we began it, with a character facing danger. This time it is Moses, who has seen the destruction of the worshipers of the Golden Calf and now, having sacrificed to God, expects divine redemption. Just before giving the *Torah* to Israel again, just as before the idolatrous episode, God passes before Moses, announcing:

> The Lord, the Lord, a gracious and merciful God, slow to anger, abounding in steadfast love and loyalty, keeping steadfast love with thousands, forgiving iniquity and transgression and sin—but who will not acquit the guilty, repaying the parents' iniquity to children and grandchildren, to the third and fourth generation.
>
> —Exodus 34:6-7

After Moses asks God's grace, the Lord responds: "I make a covenant. Before all your people I will perform marvels greater than any done in all the earth or in any nation[...]" (Exod. 34:10).

The cult, for this story is set in the description of the sacrificial worship, reminds us that Israel may see—we may see—greater miracles than the liberation from Egypt. God can perpetually redeem a people. In the next chapter, we'll discuss what Scripture has to offer such a people as it worships, reflects, and, in short, lives a life with one foot in this world and one in the next. 🔥

6 Dancing to the Tune of Torah

In the fall of 1987, my wife-to-be and I were students in Israel. One day, we visited the Western Wall in the old city of Jerusalem. A large open courtyard fronts the wall, and since the Six Days' War of 1967, it has served as a synagogue. This particular day was the festival Simchat Torah—*"Joy of the* Torah"—*a day celebrating God's gift of* Torah *to Israel at Mount Sinai.*

Families had gathered, men and boys on one side of the courtyard, women and girls on the other. These Jews came from all over Israel and the world. Some were very old—perhaps survivors of the Nazi concentration camps? Gradually they began to form a circle and then to dance and sing. Fathers wearing blue and white prayer shawls carried sons on their shoulders. Some held high above their heads scrolls of the Torah. *Above them soared the wall that is all that remains of Herod's Temple, where Jesus himself had been circumcised. The songs, chanted, shouted, came from Genesis 1. Here people remembered God's creation, not as an event of long ago, but as an ongoing work, ever new.*

—Mark

I have often thought of this chance encounter and sometimes wonder why it has impressed me so much. On the one hand, nothing could be further from my previous experiences than dancing with *Torah* scrolls to the tune of Hebrew chants. Still, something about this event seems uncannily familiar, as if I too could understand how readers of Scripture could invest hopes, dreams, and commitments in it—or rather, in the God to whom it bears witness. The depth of the relationship between the text and its readers shines through in such an event. Perhaps we could do with more singing and dancing, Bibles in hand!

Jews can celebrate the words of Scripture because, generation after generation, it connects to the deepest aspirations and hopes of human beings. It does this through stories large and small, through calls to worship and laws for decent human behavior. It also does so in other ways, which we will now explore.

Reading the Prophets

Like the *Torah*, the prophets often confront their audience not just with their pride, destructive self-will, and abuse of power, but with the redeeming nature of God. Understanding these writings challenges even the most optimistic reader. Here let us consider *what* the prophets say and *how* they say it.

The challenge for us is to liberate the majestic prophetic voices from the tyranny of our own agendas, so often tainted by paranoia in the face of unwelcome change. Let us hear anew the bold challenges of those men and women who called Israel back to the covenant of Yahweh.

How shall we begin? Rather than discussing the prophets in general, a task that would cause the cutting of many trees, let us consider a text that illustrates their work. One may take some of the principles of interpretation that appear in the next few pages and apply them to other prophetic texts without too much difficulty. This way, the prophets' message of moral commitment and hope in the face of adversity will ring out to our age in vital, life-giving ways.

Isaiah 5 opens with the parable of God's vineyard, representing the southern kingdom of Judah. Despite the owner's attention to it, the vineyard bears only bad fruit. The owner will, therefore, uproot the vineyard and begin again. The chapter then continues with a series of oracles of woe against Judah. The poetry of the text is beautiful, but the message must have been painful indeed. Isaiah pulls out all the stops to say that God's terrible judgment is falling on those who claim to be most religious.

Step 1

After noticing the main point of the chapter, first ask how this chapter fits into the book of Isaiah. Notice that it concludes a long introduction (chapters 1-5) to the book. Chapter 6 describes the opening scene in Isaiah's ministry, his awe-inspiring vision of God in the Temple. Since the words of chapters 1-5 were spoken *after* Isaiah saw the vision recorded in chapter 6, it must be that the book of Isaiah is not arranged chronologically, but thematically. And, in fact, we find that many of the book's themes, especially those of the first 39 chapters, are stated first in chapters 1-5. Thus the first five chapters tell us that Isaiah will be a book about doom and hope, and chapter 5 in particular stresses that Israel has rejected God's grace in pursuing idolatry and injustice.

123

Step 2

After making a rough-and-ready estimate of the place of chapter 5 in the book as a whole, next move to consider how the chapter is organized. It consists of a parable (verses 1-7) and then a series of woe oracles (verses 8-10, 11-17, 18-19, 20, 21-24), concluding with a final description of God's anger and disappointment with the people. We do not know whether Isaiah spoke these verses all at once, or whether two or more speeches have been combined. Since the second woe oracle (verses 11-17) is much longer than the others,

it may be that the prophet or a disciple of his expanded the text at some later date. Whatever the prehistory of the text, these various pieces fit together in an integrated, intelligible whole, bearing a powerful message calling Judah to repentance.

Step 3

Now move from the structure of the text to its individual sentences. Isaiah opens with a parable and continues with woe oracles, both genres with which his ancient audience was familiar. Each sentence consists of a beautiful poetic couplet. For example, verse 7 offers the punch line of the parable:

> For the vineyard of the Lord of Hosts is the
> house of Israel!
> And each person of Judah is his treasured
> planting;
> Yet he hoped for justice, and there was
> bloodshed,
> for righteousness, and there was a wail!

The last sentence in Hebrew uses a pair of puns that help the prophet's audience remember what he says:

God finds bloodshed (*mispach*) instead of justice (*mishpat*), a wail from the oppressed (*tsa'aqah*) instead of equitable behavior (*tsedaqah*). The rest of Isaiah 5 abounds in such word plays, as well as with metaphors, similes, and direct quotations of God or the people. Presumably the use of such verbal artistry allowed hearers to remember the words and impressed them with the seriousness of the message.

The remainder of this chapter, again, consists of a series of woe oracles. The first one mentions rich persons who accumulate houses and vineyards. The reference to vineyards probably provided the hook that the book of Isaiah needed to connect the woe oracles to the parable just before it: "speaking of vineyards[...]." But the connections among the parts of the chapter are stronger than this simple metaphor of the vineyard. Throughout the chapter, God's attention falls on those in Judah who use their power purely for their own self-interest. Relentlessly, the prophet invites all his listeners, rich and poor alike, to consider their fate.

Step 4

Start the process over and repeat. In reading the Bible, one must reflect at length on its words. A quick one-time read-through will never suffice. Each reading will reveal new depths of meaning, new questions for us to ponder, and new moral and spiritual insights.

What do we learn from this short exercise? Prophets were poets who spoke for God, but how did they do so? To find out, ask in other chapters the kinds of questions we outlined for Isaiah 5. Start from the large and move to the small, and then move to the large again. By looking at the pieces of the book over and over again, we begin to see how they fit together, and thus we begin to understand their message more clearly.

Apparently, the prophets gave short speeches that they and their disciples later collected together into books. Isaiah 5 shows signs of just such a process of collection and reworking. First-time readers of the prophetic books often find them difficult to follow because they link together many short oracles, perhaps given at different times, and they sometimes even include later narrative in which the book's editor, either the prophet or some of his disciples, comments on the aftereffects of the prophet's work. The book of Jeremiah provides the clearest example of this phenomenon. It intersperses stories about the prophet, told in the third person, with oracles of his relating to various events of his time.

Another good example is the book of Micah, which divides into three large sections (chapters 1-2, 3-4, and 5-7), each of which consists of a series of doom oracles concluding with a single oracle of hope. The wild mood swing that one finds on first reading the text disappears once one realizes how the book has been put together. In general, the prophetic books are not *chronologically* arranged transcripts of speeches. Rather, they are *thematically* arranged in intricate ways that lay out a message step by step.

The Message(s) of the Prophets

Those who read the prophetic books in search of their significance for today often stumble upon their seemingly harsh oracles predicting the collapse of their society. Remember that the prophets do not lob verbal grenades at persons for whom they do not care, but rather plead with their own fellow-Israelites to live lives of equity and honor befitting their status as the Chosen People. Their grim words are not so much predictions of what inevitably *will* be, but exhortations to avoid what *may* be.

They insist that, unless Israel changes its ways, it will be annihilated. Consider Amos 3:12:

> Thus says the Lord: As the shepherd rescues
> from the mouth of the lion two legs, or a piece
> of an ear, so shall the people of Israel who
> live in Samaria be rescued, with the corner of
> a couch and part of a bed.

That is, Israel will only barely survive catastrophe. The prophetic books, especially those of the eighth century like Amos, Hosea, Micah, and Isaiah, and the late seventh and early sixth centuries—Jeremiah, Zephaniah, Ezekiel—abound with such statements.

These fearsome statements are not idle threats. They reflect the prophets' deep concern for the ethical behavior of the people of God, especially its leaders. To take a few examples, Nathan boldly accuses the adulterous David of oppressing a poor man (2 Sam. 12), Elijah attacks Ahab's theft of Naboth's vineyard (1 Kings 21), and Amos predicts the demise of a society that rewards the already powerful to the detriment of the poor (Amos 7). Our example in Isaiah 5 focuses on those who run the law courts (verse 22), the nobility. The prophets knew that power corrupts. Those who have much must give much in return.

Since God the sovereign Lord has created and redeemed Israel through the exodus, this new people must live in ways befitting the ethical and gracious nature of God. The prophets rarely state this obligation in terms reminiscent of the *Torah*, and they almost never refer to Moses. But they do insist on the same high moral standard that shapes the Laws of the Pentateuch. In addition to our example of Isaiah 5, which indicts those who amass wealth at the expense of others, using their power and influence to indulge their appetites for pleasure

(for example, see Isa. 5:22), consider a few further
illustrative texts:

> Swearing, lying, and murder, and stealing
> and adultery break out; bloodshed follows
> bloodshed. Therefore the land itself mourns,
> and all who live in it languish.
>
> —Hosea 4:2-3
>
> For three, yes four transgressions of Israel, I
> will not revoke the punishment, because they
> sell the righteous for silver, and the needy for
> a pair of sandals—they who trample the head
> of the poor into the dust of the earth, and
> push the afflicted out of the way[...].
>
> —Amos 2:6-7
>
> [Jerusalem's] prophets are reckless, faithless
> persons; its priests have profaned the sacred;
> they have done violence to the law.
>
> —Zephaniah 3:4
>
> As a well keeps its water fresh, so [Jerusalem]
> keeps fresh her wickedness; violence and
> destruction are heard within her.
>
> —Jeremiah 6:7

Chosen almost at random, these verses illustrate
how deeply the prophets feel the gap between God's
calling to Israel and the reality of their people's
behavior. Israel has not lived up to its calling to bless
the world by mirroring the behavior of its sovereign
Lord in all the relationships of life.

Three major concerns occupied the prophets:
idolatry, oppression of the poor, and abuse of power
by leaders (sexual sins occasionally show up, but
much less frequently). Since the problems they
address have never disappeared from any human
society, their calls to justice remain as fresh today
as they were centuries ago.

The prophets argue that polytheism causes injustice, and vice versa. Polytheistic ways of thinking often mirror the human world, with a king ruling arbitrarily at the top of a hierarchy, and humans falling victim to divine whimsy. In a polytheistic system, the god one serves enjoys a rank in the divine hierarchy equivalent to the worshiper's position in the human hierarchy. So, the king might worship one of the major deities, and a peasant would worship a minor deity.

Not so in Israel, as the prophets envisioned it. For them, all are to worship the one God, who creates and sustains all humanity. Everyone owes allegiance to this deity alone. The God of Israel demands ethical behavior: just as God has liberated slaves from Egypt, so must the slaves' descendants refrain from oppressing those weaker than themselves. This is the genius of the vision of a united people under the one God that the prophets outlined. Their message has lost nothing of its power as we also endure a world in which the powerful often focus more on their own pleasure than on the good of society as a whole.

> **Monotheism:**
> Today we take for granted the belief in one God, but in ancient times this view must have seemed wrongheaded to many people. All ancient societies, except Israel, were polytheistic—worshiping many gods (even if a few scholars may have imagined monotheism of some sort in Babylon). Many—often most—Israelites worshiped multiple gods. The prophets taught the oneness of God. God was not the deity of a class, a sect, a gender, or a location as the pagan gods were. God was the gracious sovereign of everyone and everything.

From Oral Word to Written Word

Israelites eventually wrote down the prophetic words in collections that we call prophetic books. Ordinarily, the writer was not the prophet himself, but one or more of his disciples (such as Baruch in the book of Jeremiah). The arrangement and explanation of the oracles (often by means of connecting paragraphs that functioned as commentary or fresh words of exhortation) fell to these disciples, who perhaps worked over fairly long periods of time.

In most cases, we can only infer this process from the texts we have. However, in one case, that of the book of Jeremiah, we can identify stages of literary development with some confidence. Jeremiah 36:32 offers a clue: after King Jehoiakim (Josiah's son) had burned a scroll of Jeremiah's writing, the prophet dictated another scroll containing his old oracles plus new, similar ones. This scroll, written by Baruch, was not identical to our book of Jeremiah, which contains speeches and stories later than the reign of Jehoiakim.

Another important clue comes from Jeremiah 51:64, "Thus far the words of Jeremiah." This implies that chapter 52 comes from a person other than the prophet who is looking back on his hero's life and the events thereafter. Still another clue comes from the textual history of the book. The ancient Greek translation (the Septuagint or "LXX") of Jeremiah, as well as some manuscripts from the Dead Sea Scrolls, exhibit a different order of chapters and slightly fewer verses than one finds in the standard Hebrew (Masoretic) text, indicating that at least two versions of the finished book existed in ancient times. The differences are minor, but they do exist.

So, we can see at least the following stages in the development of the book of Jeremiah: oral words of the prophet → the burned scroll → the second scroll → later additions.

Why did the prophet and his disciples bother with all this work of preserving and commenting upon the words to Israel? Because they recognized that the words of the prophets should not remain dead words locked in a forgotten past, they worked again and again in new situations to speak God's Word to a people with whom God wished to frame a new covenant. The prophetic books help us understand that the voice of the Lord of Israel speaks afresh to each generation through the life-giving words of Scripture. We always need to hear their call to justice, their criticism of too-easy religion, and their visions of a better tomorrow. When placed beside the narratives of Scripture, the words of the prophets remind us that the events of human history must correspond to a higher ethic than the inevitable compromises of those who judge everything in the light of their own self-interest. Far from a negative process that people of faith must fear, the ongoing use and interpretation of the words of the prophet signal the abiding work of the Spirit in the people of God who, together, gave us the words of Scripture.

Praying The Psalms

How do humans in God's community respond to these life-giving words? Within the canon of Scripture itself, one large group of texts offers us words for doing just that. The book of Psalms was the primary collection of hymns for the second temple in Jerusalem (ca. 500 B.C. to A.D. 70). Here we should consider 1) how the Psalms originated; 2) what they say and to whom; and 3) how they say it.

Songs were sung at the Sabbath sacrifice and during various holidays, and they were undoubtedly familiar to many religious people who found in them words that expressed their own longing for God's presence in their lives. The book of Psalms as a whole begins with a mixture of songs of laments and praise—tears and joy—and ends (Psalms 146 to 150) with a crescendo of hallelujahs in which all creation joins.

However, most of the psalms are older than the second temple, coming from the First Temple period (1000-586 B.C.). Written over many centuries, they were hymns for worship, mostly in the Jerusalem temple, but sometimes in private settings and perhaps even in sanctuaries in northern Israel. The people of Israel as a community sang the psalms as they faced various dilemmas that challenged their faith. The psalms' anonymous authors, mostly Temple singers, sought to express Israel's response to God's gracious actions among them.

There are various genres of psalms, each fit for a different occasion of worship:

- Laments of individual Israelites (examples: Psalms 6, 30, 38, 41, 88);
- Laments of the people of Israel (examples: Psalms 12, 14, 44, 58, 60, 74, Lam. 5);
- Wisdom psalms (examples: Psalms 1, 119);
- Historical recitations (examples: Psalms 78, 105);
- Hymns of praise (examples: Psalms 8, 19, 29, 33, 46, 47, 48, 76, 104, 135, 136, 145, 150);
- Psalms about kings (examples: Psalms 2, 18, 20, 21, 45, 72, 89, 101, 132, 144).

Each type of psalm plays a different role in the worship of God.

In reading a psalm of whatever type, recognize that it is poetry, not a set of propositions. Rich in metaphor, powerful in emotion, the psalms talk about the interior life of the believer, his or her life in the community of faith, and the ever-present search for God. They are deeply personal, but not individualistic. They bear witness to the involvement of each person praying them in the life of a community of shared histories and obligations. As James Kugel has recently put it, these texts (and the Bible in general) open up to us "another way of seeing" the cosmos as it really is, a level of perception that often escapes us in the modern world.[1] They are not chiefly objective theological propositions about "the way things are." Rather, they draw us into the world where truth exceeds logic and finds its fullest expression in the paradox of faith in the face of doubt, and hope in the face of fear.

Since the psalms have for so long and for so many opened windows into eternity, we must ask *how* they do so. Like the prophets, the psalms employ the basic features of poetry: metaphor, rhythm, alliteration, and so on. Normally, a sentence of poetry in Hebrew consists of two parts, conveniently labeled A and B,

> For a concise and lucid, though slightly idiosyncratic, introduction to Hebrew poetry, see James Kugel's *Great Poems of the Bible*.

which in some way balance out or complement each other (a feature usually called "parallelism"). Consider, among hundreds of possible examples, Psalm 80:6:

A. You have fed them tears for bread;
B. you have given them a full complement of tears to drink.

A. You have made us a laughingstock to our neighbors;
B. our enemies snicker among themselves.

The second part of each sentence repeats the basic sense of the first part, although with some supplementation. Again, this A/B pattern appears everywhere in the book of Psalms.

In addition, each psalm follows, in general, the structure and content of the genre of which it is a representative. Consider one example, which may stand for others. Psalm 80 expresses a lament of the people of Israel. It opens with an appeal to the

"Shepherd of Israel," whom it asks for relief from various enemies. Like other psalms of lament, this psalm opens with an address to God and proceeds to lamentation over disaster befalling the people. It ends with a final turning to God and a promise to praise him for deliverance. This basic pattern provides the structure for scores of laments in the book of Psalms.

Within the confines of this basic poetic structure, the psalmist soars to amazing spiritual heights, recognizing that God has previously saved Israel and can do so again. The appeal to the exodus in verse 8—"You brought a vine from Egypt"—simultaneously reminds the audience (and God!) of past deeds and expresses hope for similar actions in the future. Verses 14-16 continue the vine metaphor by tying it to present harsh realities. These verses probably refer to the destruction of the northern kingdom of Israel by the Assyrians in 721 B.C. (which one may infer from the mention of exclusively northern tribes in verse 2). Present reality and past reality thus blend into one arena of the activity of God, the shepherd of Israel.

Since the history of Israel is fundamentally God's history *with* Israel, the psalmist recognizes God's responsibility for the current situation. He asks *how long* God will allow the current calamities to continue, daring even to attribute them directly to God's decisions. Unlike the prophets, who agree that God has indeed caused disaster for his people, the psalmist does not think of the people as culpable, but as innocent victims of foreign enemies. This perspective, which finds its fullest biblical expression in the book of Lamentations, balances out the prophetic emphasis on human morality with a recognition that suffering sometimes exceeds the bounds of human tolerance. Sometimes arguing that suffering is the due reward for wrongdoing simply does not seem convincing.

If we had more space, we could say far more about this psalm and could examine it in detail. As with Isaiah 5, one should consider each layer of the text and try to connect it in its entirety with other texts that relate to it thematically, especially in the book of Psalms.

But what about the book of Psalms as a whole? How did all these individual hymns come together in a single book? Granted that it contains many powerful songs about suffering and longing and triumph, what is its purpose as a whole?

Take the first question first. Originally songs (for the most part) of the monarchic period of the history of Israel and Judah, the psalms at some point were collected together into a single work. (At first only a few psalms were associated with David, but his role grew in the minds of people over time until they eventually believed him to have written almost the entire Psalter.) The process of collection undoubtedly began before the Babylonian Exile, and it was not entirely finished until perhaps the second century B.C. This long process was necessary because the needs of Israel and its understanding of God grew over time in the light of greater revelation and profounder experience. The finished book of Psalms explores the many dimensions of a community at praise. It offers language for us when we need to cry passionately to God for help, to testify to God's repeated intervention on behalf of Israel and individuals, or to articulate our overwhelming attitude of awe before the sovereign creator of the universe who deigns to care about the welfare and behavior of ordinary human beings.

Now the second question. The book of Psalms opens with two introductory psalms that call upon the reader of the book to be wise (Psalm 1) and to trust, not in the power of arms and wealth, but in the strength of the one who sets his anointed one on Zion (Psalm 2). The book ends with a coda of five psalms of praise (Psalms 146-150) that invite the entire creation, not just Israel or even humankind in general, to join in praising the God who made everything and invites human beings to share in this magnificent handiwork. As Psalm 1 makes clear, the whole book of Psalms aims at the formation of a community of people who understand their place in a universe in which God has made humans "a little lower than the angels" (Psalm 8), has called us to a life of service and concern for the weak (Psalm 101), and has invited us to join the cosmos in bearing witness to the God who continually delivers Israel from bondage. The psalms form us as moral and spiritual beings in a community of shared values. No wonder so many Bible publishers put together the New Testament and Psalms!

Why does this matter today? Because we are still people who need to subject our experiences—positive and negative—to the wisdom, grace, and power of the Lord of the universe. And also because we do this most often as a community of people who can pray the psalms together as their prayers. We are, after all, the church of the one who quoted Psalm 22, "My God, my God, why have you forsaken me" and also heard, in the words of Psalm 16:8, "I saw the Lord always before me, for he is at my right hand that I may not be shaken[...]" (quoted in Acts 2:25). The Psalms speak to us of God and thus also of ourselves as the people of God.

The Words of the Wise

Like the prophets and psalmists, the wise men and women of Israel were concerned with the transmission of values from one generation to the next. These wise persons, or sages, often boiled down their observations of human life and ethics into short, pithy proverbs. Proverbs typically consist of two parts that complement, or contrast with, each other in some way. Consider a few examples:

"Better is a dinner of herbs where love is *than a fatted ox and hatred with it.*"

—Proverbs 15:17

"Many seek the favor of a generous man, *and everyone is a friend to a man who gives gifts.*"

—Proverbs 19:6

"He who keeps the law is a wise son, *but a companion of gluttons shames his father.*"

—Proverbs 28:7

This A/B pattern (like that in Psalms and the prophets) makes the proverb memorable and mentally stimulating. The list goes on, and the topics covered range from business to family to religious life to politics to social climbing.

The world of the wise appears primarily in the books of Proverbs, Job, and Ecclesiastes, though stories of wise men and women also exist in Genesis, 2 Samuel, and other places. Each of the three major wisdom works offers a complex treatment of key problems of life: How should a person live ethically? Why does suffering exist? How much can we say confidently about God?

Proverbs

The oldest of the three wisdom books is Proverbs. Chapters 1-9 form an elaborate set of speeches in which a sage, here a father, invites a young person to acquire wisdom. The father quotes a figure called Lady Wisdom, wisdom personified, who is contrasted to Lady Folly. Lady Wisdom offers life and happiness and integrity, whereas her counterpart Lady Folly offers first the illusions of life, but ultimately only disappointment and destruction.

The remainder of the book is a series of proverbs attributed to various authors, including the "men of Hezekiah" (probably scribes of that king who collected oral proverbs and composed new ones), Agur (Prov. 30), and Lemuel (Prov. 31). We do not know anything about these latter characters, who are not Israelites. In addition, Proverbs 22:17-23:11 freely quotes an Egyptian text called the "Sayings of Amenemope." Since many of the ideas of Proverbs 10-31 can be said by moral people of many faiths (or no faith), this is not too surprising.

However, the introduction to the book in chapters 1-9 provides a lens through which one can read the entire work. Far from being words of secular good advice that any thoughtful person can appreciate, the proverbs of the book, the opening chapters insist, relate directly to religious life: "Reverence for the Lord is the beginning of wisdom," says Proverbs 1:7 and 9:10 (verses forming bookends in chapters 1-9). The life of wisdom, balance, discernment, and discretion relates ultimately to awe before God, insists Proverbs.

While the middle chapters of the book can seem monotonous to one trying to read them straight through, collectively they convince the reader that wisdom in life ultimately derives from the pursuit of God. One cannot acquire true wisdom in the absence of faith, because to neglect faith is to deny a cornerstone of reality, a fundamental aspect of the human experience. Since God exists and is wise and ethical, those who seek to understand reality and the human role in it must also inquire into the ways of God. For Proverbs, religion *is* wisdom, by definition.

Additionally, to understand this book, one must know that the proverbs in it do not individually reflect absolute truth. Rather, they represent truth partially, from a point of view, and it is only in the combination of the proverbs and their jostling with each other that fuller truth emerges. A convenient illustration appears in Proverbs 26:4-5: "Answer not a fool according to his folly lest you be like him yourself. Answer a fool according to his folly, lest he be wise in his own eyes."

At first glance, these verses seem blatantly contradictory. Does one answer a fool or not? However, when one considers these two proverbs individually, one quickly realizes that each is *sometimes* true. Sometimes one must respond to a hurtful person in order to prevent further damage. Sometimes one shouldn't. Wisdom lies in knowing which condition prevails at the moment. In fact, a larger truth emerges from the combination of these seemingly contradictory smaller truths. This larger truth is one that could not as easily be perceived by listening to either one of the proverbs in isolation. One learns by comparing the proverbs that a wise person comes to understand the potential of others to learn better behavior in a given situation. The wise person acts on the basis of this discernment. To discern wisdom, one must *think* carefully about the complexities of a given situation and refuse to settle for simplistic black-and-white answers.

Job

This tension between complementary but not identical truths becomes much more pronounced in Job and Ecclesiastes. The book of Job, probably written after the Babylonian Exile, asks what would happen if a truly innocent, righteous person were to suffer horrendously. Would he or she repudiate religion and fall into despair or cynicism? Would friends and companions support the sufferer? From where would this suffering come, God or some other force?

The book opens with a wager between God and a character called *the* Satan. "Satan" means "adversary" or even "prosecutor." The definite article is important here because this figure is not described as a full-blown diabolical figure similar to what we see in, say, the book of Revelation. In Job, this adversary reports to God on his actions and is asked to consider the righteous figure Job. This figure does not act without divine permission—even provocation!—so we cannot ultimately understand him as the source of Job's troubles, much less as evil embodied, a force virtually equal to God. This is why the Satan does not appear in the closing chapter, where some sort of resolution is reached. The person whose actions are on trial here is God, and God alone.

Job the billionaire enjoys a huge family for whom he sacrifices routinely, just in case they might have sinned. His religion is transactional and legalistic: "if I do X for God, God will bless me in ways that my culture and I define as most relevant." When suffering comes—and it comes in torrents—this theology of blessing no longer makes sense, no matter how hard the book's various characters try to pretend it does.

The key to the book of Job lies not in the opening scene, important as that is, but in the dialogues that follow. After he has lost everything—wealth, family, health, and dignity—he is visited by three friends from the desert who at first sit in silent mourning with him, but then enter into a dialogue that spins horribly out of control. Job and his friends take turns speaking through most of the book (following the pattern Job → friend → Job → friend until each friend has spoken three times). The dialogue opens in Chapter 3 with Job's embittered cursing of his day of birth.

Job's radical questioning of the goodness of God distresses any religious reader of the book. Neither Job nor any of his friends question the existence or overwhelming power of God. They all admit at various times that they do not adequately understand the Creator's ways of working. What is at stake in their questioning is the benevolence and attentiveness of this deity. For example, in 9:15-19 Job describes what he fears will be his experience with God should an encounter take place:

> Though innocent, I could not answer him; I
> could only plead for mercy.
> If I cried and he answered me, I am not
> convinced that he would hear my voice.
> He would crush me in a whirlwind and
> unjustly multiply my wounds.
> He would not let me catch my breath, but
> would overwhelm me with suffering.
> If this is a contest of strength, look at him! If a
> court case, who will subpoena him?

The sufferer's cry to God—and against God—lays out many of the central themes of this book. Job does not feel that he will get a fair hearing from the deity. In fact, he struggles with how to understand his own suffering, which he is convinced that God has caused (and if we read chapters 1-2, we have to agree with him!). He attempts to sue God, absurd as that seems, so that he will at least get a hearing. He realizes, however, that in any legal proceeding, the divine defendant will also be judge, jury, and executioner. Job's chances of victory are thus almost nil!

After twists and turns, the book climaxes with the appearance of the Lord in Chapters 38-42. Yahweh, the covenant God of Israel rather than some anonymous deity, does speak from the whirlwind, does present unanswerable arguments to Job, and does intimidate him thoroughly, just as he had expected. But Job's worst fears do not come to pass, for not only does God allow him to speak, God also restores his fortunes. Job does not receive answers to his questions, which may be unanswerable, but he does receive something more precious, a relationship with the source of all wisdom, the answer to *all* questions, the God of Israel.

It is true, the book proclaims, that human existence is often unfair, unjust, and uncomfortable. It is also true that the universe is a much larger place than humans imagine. And, even more importantly, this somewhat chaotic world is orderly enough, just enough, good enough, for us to function as whole, creative beings ourselves. The book thus makes no effort to dismiss Job's extreme criticisms of the divine management of things, but neither does it fully accept his charges.

Moreover, the fact that Yahweh shows up at all completely changes the terms of the discussion that Job and his so-called friends have had. They have discussed the case at hand on the basis of incomplete information. They have spoken of the central character in the situation only on the basis of hearsay. Now that character has appeared and, without bothering to defend his actions, has completely altered everyone's understanding. No longer can Job be satisfied with the inadequate comfort of an intellectual explanation. He has received something more—the presence of God.

Ecclesiastes

The latest book of wisdom in the canon is Ecclesiastes, in which the author takes on the persona of King Solomon. Like the author of Job, he writes to question glib religious talk that claims all answers and silences all who disagree. Finding no ultimate meaning in this world, Ecclesiastes nevertheless invites us to enjoy the pleasures of family, friends, and comforts within the context of a balanced life lived in awe of God. In the canon of Scripture, Ecclesiastes functions to caution us against pushing religious claims so far that we assume we know more than we do or that our actions coincide exactly with the will of God for our lives. As such, the book serves as a bracing tonic to religious communities that so often become overconfident and complacent.

Wisdom as a Whole

The wisdom books raise questions about religious language that lacks content, that comes too easily. Such books may not state religious demands as straightforwardly as the laws or the epistles do, and they lack the moral straightforwardness of the prophets, but they advertise the fact that life can be complicated and that true religion encourages the use of the brains that God gave us. In a world in which wisdom is far less widespread than knowledge, these books offer a precious glimpse of God, the infinitely wise teacher from whom his prized pupils, human beings, may learn a thing or two.

Apocalypses

The attack on the complacency to which religious people often fall prey finds full expression in the closely related apocalypses Daniel and Revelation. The later book, from the end of the first century A.D., draws on Daniel, recycling its visions for a new age. Whereas Daniel was primarily concerned to show that God had acted in the past and would act again among Jews

Apocalypses may contain visions, descriptions of the beginning and end of time, and an emphasis on God's judgment of the wicked. In reading them, remember that the symbols refer to an ancient political or religious situation. Look for the text's words of encouragement about faithfulness and confidence in God. Apocalypses comfort the persecuted, reorient those distressed by political change, and give hope to those facing death. They do not lay out a detailed roadmap for events of the future.

groaning under the misrule of the Greek-speaking Seleucid kings of the second century B.C., Revelation expresses great confidence that the Lamb who was slain will yet triumph over the seemingly invincible Roman Empire. Apocalypses, a common literary type for several centuries, of which the two biblical books are the most powerful examples, reflect the experiences of groups who have fallen out of power (if they ever enjoyed it) and now experience great suffering and even persecution.

Many of us find reading these books difficult, in part because they have so often been the preoccupation of some of our odder fellow Christians. Paranoid readers have found everything from the papacy to grocery store bar codes and helicopter gunships in these books. So, the historical background of the texts remains an important safety net for interpreters, who need to recognize that both Daniel and Revelation were preoccupied with their own times. At the same time, their horizon was not limited to the historical moment. For example, Revelation expects Jesus' triumphant return soon. Timing matters far less than the overall message of hope.

Readers of these two books have long recognized their close relationship. Sometimes we have assumed that they were describing the same historical events, but this is unlikely. Instead, Revelation borrows the rich imagery of Daniel (and other Old Testament works, notably Ezekiel) to describe a situation as fraught with danger and as subject to divine redemption as that which the book of Daniel also describes.

An example: Revelation 13 speaks of a fearsome beast, identical to Rome, that arises from the sea. The beast's multiple heads and horns are reminiscent of *several* similar beasts described in Daniel 7, where the animals in question represent successive empires dominating the land of Israel. In Daniel, the final ruler is the eleventh horn, apparently the Syrian king Antiochus Epiphanes, whose power is checked by the Romans (see Dan. 11:30). Revelation's eleventh horn, meanwhile, is a Roman emperor not unlike the tyrannical Nero. In this case, as in many others, the two books describe similar (but not identical) historical situations with similar (but not identical) language to claim in ways that readers of the apocalypses understood that God would soon intervene in dramatic ways on their behalf.

We who read these texts millennia later can come to understand and appreciate the power of the books' message that God sometimes stands radically opposed to the political and economic powers of our world in order to bring in a new creation in which oppression ceases. We need not read Daniel and Revelation as histories of our own time written in advance. To ask of them precise information about history or the eschatological future is to ask the wrong questions. They focus not on *how* and *when* God will act, but on the powerful reality that God *will* and *does* act on behalf of Israel and those to whom Israel bears witness of a world beyond this one.

Epistles

Sharing this hope for the future are those Christian texts with which we end this description of the canon of Scripture, the epistles of Paul and others. In Paul's day, as in ours, letters were a common way of communication, and they followed set rules of composition. Ordinarily, they included an introduction, a body (with certain set introductory formulas), and a conclusion. Knowing how a letter worked helped an ancient person read it. To take a contemporary analogy, consider a letter often received in the mail:

> Dear Mr. Hamilton,
> You may already have won $10,000,000!
> Sincerely yours,
> Jane Doe

Someone who did not understand the rules of modern American letter-writing might find this confusing. "Dear"—does that imply affection? "Sincerely"—if an author says he or she is sincere, should we believe that claim? Or does making the claim prove insincerity? Someone who does not know that a letter like this is actually a sales pitch will be seriously disappointed not to win the vast fortune promised.

All of us know how to read modern letters. Ancient letters differ from them slightly, but the ancient forms can be learned with practice. Paul modified the normal form of his time a bit by beginning his letters with phrases like "grace and peace" and ending them with doxologies to God and Jesus Christ.[2] Long lists of persons to greet (as in Romans 16) are also unusual; but still, we can recognize his works as ancient letters, and because they take this form we know *not* to read them as narratives or theological treatises or handbooks covering every imaginable eventuality that the church might face for all time. They cover *specific* events in the life of the congregations in which Paul ministered.

This is not to say, however, that the letters lack theological content. Anyone who has read them with care has felt himself or herself drawn up into the tornado of the Christian encounter with the true and living God. Paul defies all our comfortable expectations of the Christian life. One New Testament scholar, Ernst Käsemann, once claimed that the apocalyptic mindset (apparent most obviously in Daniel, Revelation, Mark 13 and its parallels, and elsewhere) was the mother of the church. Certainly, the epistles of Paul especially give this impression. They address Christians "on whom the end of the ages has come" (1 Cor. 10:11). Paul, therefore, chooses to write a letter (not a philosophical treatise or some other literary genre) to respond to pressing ethical and theological issues of the churches he has founded in order to form them more fully as Christians awaiting the return of their Lord. Since they are closely rooted in a unique, unrepeatable situation, letters seem peculiarly suitable for churches living in the shadow of the end of the world, where little can be counted as permanent.

Of course, Paul was not the only writer of epistles in our canon. The New Testament includes Hebrews with its reflections on Jesus Christ as the ever-living embodiment of the *Torah* and Temple, James with its prophetic demands for justice, 1 & 2 Peter with their call for perseverance and virtuous living in the face of the delay of Christ's return, 1-3 John with their insistence on love for other Christians, and Jude with its (undeservedly obscure) charge to moral and spiritual purity. All these works let us hear the voices of many parts of the church as it struggled to survive in an environment hostile to her claim that the one God had saved the world and transformed men and women through the person of a crucified Jew, Jesus of Nazareth. But it is Paul who has captured the imagination of believers for two millennia. And his letters offer a fitting way to conclude this sprint through the biblical texts.

Paul was a first-generation Christian whose visions of the risen Lord drove him to mission work among churches around the Aegean Sea. He and his colleagues, such as Timothy, Silvanus, and others, wrote letters to address difficult problems that churches he had founded (and an individual, in the case of Philemon) faced in his absence. That is, his letters are occasional pieces, addressing *specific* situations in the life of a church. In reading them, we must be aware that Paul was not attempting to work out for all time every aspect of every issue he addressed. For example, 1 Corinthians addresses a series of questions that the letter's recipients had apparently asked Paul (1 Cor. 7:1, 11:34). Paul instructs them on ways to live that will reflect Christ's calling of them in *their* situation. His precise rules on head coverings or the display of miraculous gifts or the silence of women may not have been in force in other churches (then or now).

Paul focused on larger concerns than these external issues, important as they are in the everyday life of the church. He affirmed that God had decisively intervened in a sinful world through the person of Jesus Christ, the new Adam (Rom. 5), the one who had vanquished the old age of sin and death, and had ushered in the new world in which God's will triumphed.

Paul attempts various means of describing the life to which God has called Christians. Whenever the church's behavior does not befit its calling, he reminds his readers of their identity as a people under the cross. He can quote a hymn in Philippians 2:5-11 with its model of the humble Christ who "emptied himself" by assuming flesh and dying on the cross. As Christ lived, so must we live. Or he can caution against the use of miraculous gifts, which he can even imagine ending, as ways of dividing the church body and inflating the ego of the gifted. Instead, he notes the importance of love as the goal of Christian existence (1 Cor. 13). Or he can remind them of the words of institution of the Lord's Supper, which they probably quoted in their own worship services. Or he can end his epistles with lists of virtues.

Most of all, he quotes Old Testament Scripture and connects it to the suffering of Christ on the cross. For example, in 1 Corinthians 15:3-8, he cites this creed that the Corinthians must already have known:

> For I delivered to you as of first importance what I also received, that Christ died for our sins in accordance with the scriptures, that he was buried, that he was raised on the third day in accordance with the scriptures, and that he appeared to Cephas [Peter] and then to the Twelve. Then he appeared to more than five hundred brethren simultaneously, most of whom still live (though some are dead). Then he appeared to James, and then to all the apostles. Last of all, as to one born at the wrong time, he appeared to me.

This brief statement of the core of the gospel describes as well as anything else Paul wrote what animated him. The gospel has several key parts: Christ's death, burial, and resurrection; his connection to Scripture, the Old Testament, and hence to the grand story of Israel's redemption through exodus and return from exile; and appearances to the church, represented by apostles and others, Paul most of all. The events of Easter profoundly connect to what goes before and after it in the life of the community of people who serve God. Those who believe this gospel experience a radical transformation of values and behaviors that allows them to reflect more exactly the extraordinary nature of God's work in human existence.

This brings us to the final issue in Paul's letters that we shall consider, the vexing problem of his discussion of *Torah*. Paul, as a Jew who believed in the Jew Jesus Christ, had to ask repeatedly about the role of the Law in the life of faith. The problem is: if salvation comes through faith in Jesus Christ (Rom. 1:16-17 and Gal. 2:21; see also Eph. 2:4-10), what purpose does *Torah* serve?

Paul does not always say the same things about *Torah*. In Galatians, he faces radical Jewish Christians insisting on circumcision as a mark of salvation, and so he emphasizes the limits of the Law in order to argue against their position. In Romans, meanwhile, he addresses the question of the role of *Torah* in greater detail (and perhaps with a little less vehemence). He addresses the problem of its relationship to the gospel by arguing that: 1) *Torah* ultimately concerns the salvation of Israel (and thereby all the world, as Genesis 12 already notes) through faith (Rom. 4); 2) all of Scripture is about revealing God's splendor and grace to the world

(Rom. 2); and 3) Christ is a continuation of the story of Israel (Rom. 4-5).

To remove the possible objection that Israel's disbelief meant that we had moved beyond any need for *Torah*, he notes that Israel has disbelieved before—see the prophets!—yet still experienced eventual divine redemption. Moreover, this apparent disbelief will not last and merely serves as an opening for Gentiles to come to God (Rom. 9-11). He concludes his discussion of *Torah* by noting that "Whatever was written in the past was written to teach us, so that through endurance and the encouragement of the Scriptures, we might have hope" (Rom. 15:4). Paul felt no need to discard *Torah*, properly read. Rather, he experienced the wholeness and liveliness of the full canon as he read it in light of his encounter—the church's encounter—with God's work in Jesus Christ.

Conclusion

Along with Paul and the myriad readers of Scripture before and after him, we confront the urgent question of *what it all means*. The stories, poems, prayers, proverbs, letters, and apocalypses point us beyond themselves to the complex interactions between God and creation, most notably humankind. The words of Scripture, rich in metaphor and music, draw faithful readers into the unfolding story of God. The Bible forms us into persons and communities that consciously commit ourselves to lives of trust, openhanded and sacrificial generosity, forgiveness of those who fail us, and penitence toward those whom we fail. Attending to the multiple voices of Scripture helps us not to overemphasize one truth over another, but to balance the aspects of truth that point us to the one cardinal Truth: God in Jesus Christ is reconciling the world and will call us to be part of this salvation in the New Jerusalem. Scripture calls us to love God and our neighbor. All the rest is powerful, life-sustaining commentary.

Scripture draws us into a world in which men and women struggle to believe, and believe in order to struggle. We read the cry of despair and fury in Lamentations 2:5, "God has become an enemy!" And in the same book, one chapter later, we hear the songs of those whose houses have been burnt, whose children have been enslaved, whose wives have been raped: "The steadfast love of the Lord never ceases; his mercies never come to an end." We read the tale of Job, who suffers unjustly and uncomprehendingly, and struggle with the book's refusal to answer the question of "why." Here we hear the cries of a Jewish carpenter who promised a new tomorrow: "My God, my God, why have you forsaken me?" And we also hear the words spoken to Mary Magdalene, who first shared the gospel story, "He is not here; he is risen!" Scripture is not a pretty book for people who think they are good enough and merely want confirmation of that fact. It does not contain success tips for the privileged citizens of the First World. It speaks to humanity's deepest longings and sorrows and joys. It brings us into the world where men and women, flawed, selfish, yet sometimes surprisingly generous, saints and sinners—we ourselves—have met God.

Scripture brings us to a vision of the consummation of the ages. Augustine of Hippo (354-430) prayed at the beginning of his great autobiography, *Confessions*, "Our soul is restless until it rests in You."

And so it is. And yet, if we take Scripture as a whole, reading the Christian canon as a unit, we see a kind of resolution even in the anticipation of that rest. In Genesis we leave Paradise, and in Revelation we return to it. This pattern appears even on a smaller scale. The Pentateuch begins with Adam and Eve leaving Eden and ends with Israel standing on the verge of the promised land. The Christian Old Testament ends with Malachi's promise of a second Elijah who is a harbinger of a new era. And the Jewish Bible, which has a different arrangement of the same books as our Old Testament ending in 2 Chronicles, concludes with the story of Cyrus of Persia ordering the return to Zion. It is not entirely clear whether this pattern is deliberate, or whether we should read the whole Bible as a unit this way. But it *is* clear that Scripture points us to a state of being in which the lamb lies down with the wolf and gets away with it, when every eye is tearless, when there is no rich or poor, no hater or hated.

When we read with an attitude of faith, hope, and love, Scripture creates a world in which the walls separating us from each other crumble because it points us to our common destiny. As we share its words, in preaching, song, and Lord's Supper, as we live its words together, we hear in the distance the song of the crowds of readers: "Worthy is the Lamb that was slain, who was, and is, and is to come." Scripture points us to the time when dreams do not die and hopes do not fade, to the place where the accidents of skin color and gender will not determine worth or fitness for service. It points us to the time when our restless souls find rest in the God who brings the only real pleasure, Himself. And this is why reading Scripture well truly matters. 🌱

7
Reading Scripture with Ancient Eyes

The two preceding chapters oriented us to the literary diversity found in the Bible. They offered some key insights on how each genre of biblical literature should be read. But in addition to considering the demands of each genre, a careful reader must also recognize that the Bible was originally written for ancient audiences, and this fact places special demands on modern readers. With the foundation built in Chapters 5 and 6, we can begin to read Scripture as ancient readers would have read it—or, to change the image slightly, to hear Scripture as ancient hearers would have heard it. This kind of hearing is exciting, but it also requires us to cultivate a sense of hearing that can recognize the "songs" of old. We must develop a basic literary and historical literacy. To promote this literacy, this chapter describes a process for interpreting a passage of Scripture. We'll begin by exploring some of the challenges of interpreting Scripture in a diverse community and conclude by dealing with three special problems connected with the process of interpretation.

The consequences of bad interpretation can be serious. Though extreme, the following stories illustrate the cost of poor readings of Scripture:

In the early years of the third century, Origen read about those who "made themselves eunuchs on account of the kingdom of heaven" (Matt. 19:12). Origen castrated himself based on his reflection.

Daniel Wallace tells of a student at a Christian college who gouged his eye with a screwdriver based on his literal interpretation of Matthew 5:29, "If your right eye causes you to stumble, then take it out and cast it away from you."

The fiery demise of the David Koresh cult at Waco in 1993 illustrates the lack of understanding of apocalyptic literature by the FBI. One FBI agent thought that the Seven Seals were aquatic mammals.[1]

There are many other examples of misinterpretation, from the trial of Galileo in the seventeenth century, to the refusal of blood transfusions (based on Acts 15:29), to the many predictions of the end of the world, usually based on passages from Daniel and Revelation. Rather than dwelling on the many problems of misinterpretation, this chapter will focus on ways to equip the church to read Scripture *well*.

Simple & Complex

Before we can discuss how to interpret Scripture well, we need to address some of the resistance to intense study of Scripture. When it comes to studying Scripture, people often ask the following two questions: "So, do you have to be a Bible expert to be a Christian?" and "Why do scholars have to make everything so hard to understand?" These are legitimate questions that deserve honest answers. To the first question, we emphatically affirm that God's loving offer of grace through the sacrifice of his Son is understandable by all. In other words, the gift of salvation conveyed in the gospel does not require an expert to understand it.

The second question often expresses an understandable frustration with people who use education as a source of pride or power. We oppose both abuses of education. However, there are a number of good reasons why someone might think that Scripture contains some matters that are difficult to understand.

First, Scripture itself depicts the need for interpreters. In Nehemiah 8, we see interpreters present when Ezra reads the Law. In Acts 8, Philip asks the Ethiopian eunuch, "Do you understand what you are reading?" The eunuch responds, "How can I understand unless someone guides me?" Furthermore, Jesus' hearers did not always understand him; even his disciples were confused at times.

Scripture also describes itself as hard to understand. 2 Peter 3:16 indicates that at least one inspired writer found Paul "hard to understand." The same verse indicates that the "ignorant and unstable" can "distort" Scripture "to their own destruction."

In addition, studying God takes us beyond the powers of human reason. As finite beings, humans will find complete understanding of an infinite God impossible. Why is it that physics is considered a complex topic, but God—the creator of the universe—is not?

Finally, modern readers are separated from the Bible by time, culture, and languages. If we were assigned to study a book written in China over two thousand years ago, we would certainly welcome help. But when it comes to the Bible, some seem to shun, and even celebrate the absence of, help. So, is there a place for the person in the pew? Is there a place for the expert? To both questions, we answer, "Yes."

Why Doesn't Everyone Agree with Me?

Can't everyone pick up the Bible, read it, and agree? Apparently not; many groups claim to follow

> "Both read the Bible
> day and night,
> But thou read'st black
> where I read white."
> —*William Blake*
> *"The Everlasting Gospel"*

the Bible, yet Christianity remains fractured into many groups. Why is that? This section tries to describe why good people sometimes find it difficult to talk about,

much less agree on, the Bible. Although the reasons are many, we will examine three.

Different Backgrounds

Anders Stephanson, a professor of the freshman Contemporary Civilization course at Columbia University, began his course with these words: "John F. Kennedy was killed on November twenty-second, 1963. Is that an objective statement?" Students returned blank stares. When forced to vote by raising their hands, most of the students raised their hands in agreement. Stephanson continued, asking what the year was in the Jewish or the Chinese calendar. The students then realized that how we record time in the West is a convention not shared by all cultures.

This story, from David Denby's *Great Books*, illustrates the point that we are shaped by the society in which we are raised.[2] Our culture gives us "default modes;" we're not even aware of some of them. More importantly, we do not even realize that our ways of thinking are culturally conditioned. For those who have grown up in the American culture of individualism, a culture that values the group is hard to understand. As an example, consider my experience while a professor at Lubbock Christian University:

Alumni from Japan returned to LCU for Homecoming. A young girl of 18, about the same age as the roughly one thousand students in the college auditorium, gave a description of herself to the translator. Part of her self-description surprised me. The translator read, "I would like you to know that I obey my parents and that I am very polite." I was startled. No college *student in the West would stress those qualities in describing him or herself. They would tell how unique or different they were, or how they did something few other people had done. I realized the depth of individualism in our culture and the hollow ring "family values" must have for those in the East, especially when that message comes from the West.*

—Ken

This story illustrates only one of the hurdles that culture brings to mutual understanding. When we add other differences born of ethnicity, region, race, gender, education, family, political party, income, and age, then *any* agreement among people seems remarkable! When we factor in diverse views about religion, God, the nature of the Bible, the interpretation of texts, and ideologies, then matters can get really complex. In other words, we do not all share the same presuppositions about a number of topics, many of which affect our interpretations of the Bible. For example, the Japanese woman mentioned above probably does not wonder why Paul includes murderers, God-haters, fools, and those disobedient to parents in the same list of vices (Rom. 1). On the other hand, my Western students are almost always surprised by Paul's inclusion of the phrase "disobedient to parents."

Different Types of Appeals to Scripture

The type of appeal to Scripture provides another stumbling block to interpreters. What does "type of appeal to Scripture" mean? For me, one of the more illuminating discussions on interpretation occurred in a New Testament ethics class at Yale taught by Richard Hays. Building on the ideas of ethicist James Gustafson, Hays described four types of appeals to Scripture: rule, principle, paradigm, and understanding of God or humanity.[3] Readers who interpret a text on the rule level in effect say, "If the Bible says it, do it" (literally). For them, the Bible provides a *list* of do's and don'ts. Those who read a passage on the principle level look for the *intent*, recognizing that sometimes commands are dressed in the culture of the time. Others who read a passage on the level of paradigm look for *examples* depicted by the text; here Hays means accounts describing exemplary or corrupt behavior. Finally, many read a text assuming that it reveals *insights* into the nature of God or humanity. So, where's the rub?

The rub comes when different people read the same passage with different assumptions about the text. For example, a group of people who read, "Greet one another with a holy kiss" (2 Cor. 13:12) on the rule level will demand that everyone greet each other with a kiss (that is, "it says it; we do it"). Another group, reading the same text on the principle level, sees the *principle* of greeting one another as authoritative, but the *method* ("with a holy kiss") as optional, depending on the culture. In other words, for the second group the passage means, "Greet one another in a culturally appropriate way."

This example is not too threatening for most people, but when the passage treats a disputed issue like women's roles in the assembly or baptism, then the stakes change for many in our churches. The great benefit of recognizing one another's assumptions is not that we will now suddenly agree. Rather, the benefit is that if we can recognize *why* we disagree, then we can begin to have a substantive conversation about our differences. Too often disputes arise and persist because we are not operating with the same assumptions. Change the assumption, and understanding, even agreement, becomes possible.

Different Sources of Authority

Another challenge to finding agreement on an interpretation is the fact that different religious groups often operate with different sources of authority. In addition, they rank those sources of authority in different ways. For most groups, some combination of Scripture, tradition, reason, and experience functions as the source of authority. Almost all Christian groups value Scripture. However, for some groups Scripture does not rank at the top, or it has equal status with other sources of authority. For Churches of Christ, Scripture has ranked at the top with the power to trump any of the other three. In other words, if tradition conflicts with Scripture, we follow Scripture; if reason or experience conflicts with Scripture, we still follow Scripture.

How does this analysis help? Perhaps the greatest area of help is in conversation with other Christian traditions. For example, Catholics generally view

Scripture and tradition as twin pillars, providing the voice of authority for faith and practice. So, a Catholic, when reflecting on infant baptism, may arrive at a different conclusion than someone who values Scripture above all else. Again, the benefit of recognizing this source of disagreement is not instant agreement; rather, now equipped with this information, the conversation partners can recognize the problem and have a substantive discussion. The disagreement may still persist after the conversation. But at least they now understand *why* they disagree, and they can continue in dialogue over the actual differences. That is, the disagreement is not always about the disputed practice itself, but sometimes about the *rationale* for the practice. Agree on the rationale, and agreement on the practice becomes possible—not guaranteed; disagreements may still exist, but now dialogue does as well.

The Process of Interpretation

Leaving some general problems of interpretation, we turn to a specific description of *how* to interpret a text. Unfortunately, a "magic formula" for the interpretation of a text does not exist. We can, however, take advantage of the scholarship and wisdom of many who have preceded us. We can learn to ask appropriate and helpful questions, and to avoid bad questions. For example, after reading "For all have sinned and fall short of the glory of God" (Rom. 3:23), one could say either that Paul thought Jesus sinned, since he says "all have sinned," or that Paul did not think Jesus was human, since Paul thinks that all humans have sinned. In fact, *neither* is true, and pursuing these questions will only create problems for the reader. In this instance, Paul is not answering a question about Christ—how Jesus could be both divine and human at the same time. Rather, Paul is answering a question about humans, that is, "What is the condition of humankind?" Clearly, this example illustrates that much is at stake in beginning with an appropriate question. Helpful questions point us in the right direction and eliminate some wrong options. Learning to ask the right questions is a tool that will help us hear the text with ancient ears.

What Did the Author Write?

Since none of the original copies of any of the books of the Bible exist, a necessary first question is, "Are we reading what the author wrote?" Even though none of the autographs of any of the biblical books still exist, we are blessed with over five thousand texts, from small papyrus fragments to entire manuscripts in book form, for the New Testament alone. How does a reader of an English translation know if there is a problem? Better translations usually provide a note at the bottom of the page indicating that other readings exist. For instance, most translations rightly skip from Acts 8:36 to Acts 8:38, omitting Acts 8:37. How does a teacher find out if Acts 8:37 should be included as part of a lesson on Acts 8? The most convenient book for a brief discussion about a disputed passage of the New Testament is Bruce Metzger's *A Textual Commentary on the Greek New Testament.* Unfortunately, the explanations can be technical, and no comparable book exists for the Old Testament. If

Metzger's book leaves one dissatisfied, then the next, most accessible resource is likely a commentary on the particular book.

Which Translation Should I Use?

Although reading an English translation creates specific challenges for interpreting the Bible, these problems are not insurmountable. If we had to select the three most helpful pieces of advice on the topic of translation, we would say 1) be aware of the reading level, 2) know the type of translation, and 3) have more than one translation.

Reading Level

The most accurate answer to the question, "Which translation should I use?" is not the most satisfying one. The most accurate answer is, "That depends on what you want to use it for." Reading level is sometimes a key variable to consider. For example, a class taught to fourth graders should take into account reading ability, and the NIV (New International Version), written on a seventh grade level, would take preference to the NASB (New American Standard Bible), written on the eleventh grade level. Recently, some students in my classes mentioned how helpful the NIrV (New International Reader's Version) was in working with homeless people, who sometimes have limited reading skills. Although reading levels differ slightly from paragraph to paragraph and from book to book, it still helps to know the average reading level of a translation. For further information, consider the following table showing the reading level of some of the major translations:[4]

Translation	Abbrev.	Reading Level by Grade
New International Reader's Version	NIrV	2.86
Easy-to-Read Version	ERV	3.87
Contemporary English Version	CEV	4.70
The Message	Message	5.36
New Living Translation	NLT	5.61
Today's English Version	TEV	7.29
New International Version	NIV	7.80
Living Bible	LB	8.33
New Revised Standard Version	NRSV	8.39
Phillips	Phillips	9.55
Jerusalem Bible	JB	10.10
Revised Standard Version	RSV	10.40
New American Standard Bible	NASB	11.32
King James Version	KJV	12.00

Type of Translation

An understanding of the type of translation is equally important in equipping oneself to read the Bible well. Generally speaking, there are three types of translations. Some translations strive for more of a word-for-word translation. These *literal* translations have advantages and disadvantages. One advantage is that, in a particular New Testament text, a literal translation can often tell a reader of the English text whether the same Greek word is used at different places in the text. So, if an actual word were at issue, then the NASB would probably be more helpful than the NIV, since the NASB is more likely to preserve a word-for-word translation than the NIV.

On the negative side, a literal translation can be extremely wooden, straining English syntax

165

and hurting readability, such as one sometimes encounters in the NASB. Furthermore, a literal translation may not convey the actual meaning in any foreign language. For example, the French words in the phrase "pomme de terre" literally mean "apple of the earth," but an accurate translation is "potato." An example from the New Testament occurs in Philippians 1:8, which literally states, "For God is my witness how I long for all of you *with the intestines* of Christ Jesus." Recognizing that Hellenistic thinkers located the emotions in the region of the stomach, less literal translators correctly render the italicized phrase *"with the affection* of Christ Jesus."

Another type of translation is *dynamic equivalent* translation, which attempts to translate idea for idea. Though usually a sound way to translate, dynamic equivalent translation can become too interpretive, such as when the NIV translates "flesh" as "sinful nature" in Romans 8:3 (and elsewhere), implying the Calvinist idea of total human depravity. This type of translation attempts to keep the historical and cultural features of the text, although some terms like weights or measures are often put in footnotes. However, dynamic equivalent translations update the language, grammar, and style of the original language.

Idiomatic translation attempts to modernize both the language and the ideas of the original, making the translation as accessible as possible for current readers. Also called paraphrases or free translations, idiomatic translations include the *New Testament in Modern English* by J. B. Phillips, the *Cotton Patch Version* by Clarence Jordan, the *Living Bible* by Kenneth Taylor, and *The Message* by Eugene Peterson. An oft-cited example of an idiomatic translation from the

Living Bible is the translation of "lamp" as "flashlights" in Psalm 119:105. It is worth noting that idiomatic translations are not necessarily "translations." For instance, the "translator" of the *Living Bible* did not translate from the original languages, but paraphrased from an existing English translation.

In summary, each of the three types of translations makes decisions for the reader, so that *all translation is interpretation of some type.* Translators decide other matters as well—whether quotation marks should be present (for example, 1 Cor. 6:23a; 7:1b) and whether a sentence should be a question or a statement (for example, Rom. 8:33b, 34b). Each translation has pluses and minuses. For instance, the gain in readability that readers receive in the NIV's translation of the Gospel of Mark becomes a loss in the sense of immediacy that Mark's rough Greek conveyed to its original hearers. To take another example, the accessibility of an idiomatic translation may also make the language sound dated in a few years. Knowing the types of decisions made by the translators helps create more informed readers.

Multiple Translations

Because no single translation can meet all the demands of English readers, owning several translations is highly advisable. We recommend carrying and studying one translation to aid memorization and study. Many readers will identify with the following experience: "I don't know where the passage is in Matthew, but I know it's on the right side in the top right corner." However, it's also wise to own one translation from each of the three types, so that readers can be alerted to problems in translation. Furthermore, new insights almost always come from reading and comparing other translations. The following chart, adapted from Fee and Stuart, will help in selecting from the range of translations.[5]

Literal			Dynamic Equivalent		Idiomatic
NASB	RSV	NIV	ERV		Phillips	Message
KJV		NRSV	NIrV CEV			LB
			TEV	NLT		

What Did the Author Want to Say?

The type of translation is not the only factor to consider in becoming an astute reader of the Bible. Discerning contextual clues is also a key skill to develop. Consider the following illustration: What does the word "seals" mean in the sentence "Seals are not permitted"? It could refer to an aquatic mammal, a military group in the U.S. Navy, a sticker associated with Christmas or Easter, a symbol of an office or state (for example, the Presidential Seal), or something that secures—from wax on a letter to foil on a bottle of medicine. Context usually makes the meaning clear. As modern readers, we have become more aware of the "indeterminacy of texts"—the fact that texts in and of themselves can be interpreted in a number of ways.

Most people think it is important to search for the *intention* of the author. However, the search for authorial intent creates some difficulties that must be addressed. First, discerning the author's intent is complicated by the fact that we all bring presuppositions and prejudices to a text; no one can read a text without presuppositions. Indeed, all readers should attempt to recognize their presuppositions as a necessary step toward a faithful interpretation.

Additionally, modern readers of Scripture face the difficulty that no one has direct access to the intent of an author. Thus, it makes sense to avoid claims of absolute certainty. Although it is impossible to know with certainty what an ancient author intended, the spectrum from impossible to certain contains a number of other options: possible, probable, likely. Thus, we can often speak with confidence about *understanding* an author. In other words, while we do not possess all the information to be able to claim that we *know* what the author meant, we still can *understand* what the author meant.

E. D. Hirsch, literary and cultural critic, offers a helpful distinction between meaning and significance. In *Validity in Interpretation,* Hirsch defines "meaning" as what an author literally intended, and "significance" as what the text means for readers today, what we might call "application." For "meaning," Hirsch recognizes the restrictions placed by time, place, and literary genre. For "significance," Hirsch rightly allows a range of possibilities. In some ways, it is like interpreting a piece of music. Although conductors and musicians are constrained by the notes on the score, the ways they interpret the music will still vary.

What does all this discussion have to do with reading a text? How *do* we know what an author wanted to say? Despite the problems discussed above, discerning the author's general intent is not impossible. Like many other literary texts, the Bible has a number of factors that limit the possible number of meanings: language (Greek, Hebrew, Aramaic), grammar, historical context, literary genre, literary context, and the author's own body of writings. Thinking of these factors as ways to zero in on the author's meaning, like concentric circles of a bull's-eye, helps us to recognize that many times we can proceed with confidence; other times, however, the absence of evidence may leave several interpretive options open. As an example of the latter, Paul mentions "those who are baptized for the dead" in 1 Corinthians 15:29; occurring just once, this phrase has elicited numerous interpretations, and its precise meaning will likely remain a mystery, unless further evidence is found. However, such interpretive quandaries are the exception, not the rule, in studying the biblical texts. Most of the time, the author's meaning *can* be determined by the careful consideration of the factors listed above.

What Is the Historical Context?

Along with genre (discussed in Chapters 5 and 6) and translation, historical context is another factor to consider in hearing the Bible with "ancient ears." The events of the Bible occurred in history—a particular person in a specific place wrote at an actual point in time. Unfortunately, we are separated by more than 1900 years from the most recent events of the Bible. Knowing about the author, time, place, and culture helps us to understand a writing. For instance, understanding the role of a proconsul in Roman government explains how the proconsul Gallio can ignore the beating of Sosthenes (Acts 18). A proconsul is the supreme ruler in a province; he can recognize or dismiss any case he chooses. Knowing the value of a *lepton* gives special power to the story of the "widow's mite" found in Mark 12:41-44. Given the first-century price of sparrows (Matt. 10:29), her two *lepta*—"all she had"—could have purchased only half a sparrow! Other examples abound, ready to reward curious readers.

As with any historical project, modern readers of Scripture do not always possess all the information they would like to have. A good study Bible will help by giving equivalents for technical terms like weights and measures. A more thorough grounding in the historical background of a text often requires reading an article in a Bible dictionary. A minimum level of historical literacy includes the ability to place key individuals and empires on a time line, and key places on a map. Gradually, one adds other areas of study, such as the religious, philosophical, political, economic, social, and cultural aspects of biblical civilizations. For instance, many Christians picture the early Christians meeting in buildings like those of today, rather than the house churches that existed in the towns and cities of the Roman Empire.

The benefits of doing historical research easily outweigh the work involved. Most significantly, the meaning and "bite" of some passages cannot be understood without the historical and cultural background. Without a sense of women's roles in the first century, the significance of Jesus' female supporters may go unnoticed in Luke 8:1-3. Without an understanding of the hostility between Jews and Samaritans, the parable of the good Samaritan loses much of its impact.

Interpretations based on historical investigation have greater integrity, since some of the reader's previous viewpoints may have been reshaped or refuted by the realities of history. Good historical work also allows us to enter the story, giving a greater sense of "being there;" we move from merely reading the passage to *experiencing* the passage. In addition, we teach and preach with greater depth and confidence, since we know more than we actually tell. Finally, with a newfound sense of the historical background, we can more easily imagine and recognize analogies to the present situation, allowing us to apply the text in meaningful and faithful ways.

What Is the Literary Context?

Another factor that must be considered in the interpretation of Scripture is the literary context. The literary context includes two aspects, the literary genre and the immediate context of a passage—how a passage connects to what precedes and follows. Since we already discussed the need to pay attention to the literary genre in Chapters 5 and 6, we know that the Bible conveys truth in different ways and requires specific approaches for reading particular genres. With those ideas in mind, we now focus on the value of paying attention to the immediate literary context. Perhaps the best way to argue for that value is to show some examples, one from a gospel and another from the narrative of Acts.

One of the characteristic features of Mark's Gospel is what is sometimes called "Markan sandwiches," meaning those passages in Mark where he begins a story, stops this first story before its end, tells a second story, and then finishes the first story—an A/B/A structure. The second story does not merely *interrupt* the action; it *interprets* the action. For example, Mark tells about a synagogue ruler named Jairus who begs Jesus to save the life of his young daughter. On the way to Jairus' house, Jesus is touched by a nameless woman with a flow of blood. Although this woman does not have any social status, she does possess a remarkable faith that heals her. When Mark then returns to the account of Jairus' daughter, we discover that the daughter is now dead. What is the relationship between these two women, these two "daughters" (Mark 5:34, 35)—one who suffered for twelve years, the other whose life ended after twelve years (Mark 5:25, 42)? Mark both repeats these terms ("daughter" and "twelve"), connecting the two women, and provides the structural feature of the "sandwich" to show that the healed woman demonstrates the kind of faith that Jairus needs to exhibit now that he has heard the words, "Your daughter is dead" (Mark 5:35). Attentive readers will notice a number of other "sandwiches" in Mark's Gospel.[6]

In the book of Acts, Luke periodically uses "contrasting panels." By placing contrasting narratives side by side, Luke emphasizes both the good of the positive portrayal and the bad of the negative portrayal. For instance, Acts 5 begins with the account of Ananias and Sapphira. What is the point of this passage? By looking at the end of Acts 4, we find a clue. Luke describes the unity and generosity of the Jerusalem community, presenting Barnabas as an example of generosity. Barnabas thus functions as the positive example, made even more striking by Luke's placement of the account of Ananias and Sapphira next to it. In fact, both passages are seen in greater relief *because* they are placed side by side. The unfortunate chapter division between Acts 4 and 5 does not help the modern reader; it actually hinders most readers from noticing this connection. Recognizing Luke's use of contrasting panels, readers will be more likely to notice other panels, such as those in Acts 17, 18, and 19.

Although Mark and Acts serve as positive examples of the clear gains made by close attention to the context, this recommendation applies to *any* biblical passage. Looking at passages in terms of the relationships among their surrounding verses and chapters will function as a valuable tool for discovering the meaning of texts.

Special Problems of Interpretation

As this chapter has illustrated, the process of interpretation is more complex than often portrayed. The old saying "It says it; we do it" is not an adequate prescription for Bible study. For instance, we do not pluck out our right eyes (Matt. 5:29) or wash one another's feet (John 13:15), despite the fact that these are direct commands of Jesus. Some Christians debate over the appropriateness of worship activities like clapping or raising hands. These examples point to a problem—our often simplistic process of interpretation has not been equal to the complexity of Scripture. Most people have an intuitive sense that, for example, Christians should not pluck out their right eyes. We need, however, to go beyond intuition; we need to be able to articulate *why* we do not follow this command of Jesus literally. We will pass over the recognition of figurative language (Matt. 5:29), since most people readily understand that concept. However, the problems of the role of culture, the silence of Scripture, and the diversity of Scripture need further exploration and discussion.

The Role of Culture

Since the Bible describes various types of governments, styles of dress, and postures of worship, we assume that God did not ordain only one culture. What parts of Scripture, then, are *merely* cultural and what parts are not? We say *merely* cultural because every activity is cultural; it is vital to discern what is specific to the culture of a particular time and place, and what is not. Although fixed rules for this kind of discernment are difficult to state, there are some "rules of thumb" that can guide us in many circumstances.

With an acknowledged debt to Fee and Stuart's work, we proceed with some claims and some examples. To begin, items occurring in lists of vices are universal, not merely cultural. The burden of proof should be on those who claim that a vice is *merely* cultural. To be sure, vices have cultural *aspects*. For example, every society's legal definition of murder does not match exactly. Nevertheless, even though definitions of murder differ slightly from culture to culture, murder's status as a vice does not; all cultures still forbid murder.

Second, in determining the role of culture on the interpretation of a passage, it is often helpful to ask, "Would this be an issue if the Bible did not mention it?" For example, would we even wonder about headcoverings for women if they were not mentioned in 1 Corinthians 11? The answer is almost assuredly, "No." While it's true that some individuals can be so far from God's will that they do not ask important, moral questions, for honest seekers of God's will, this question still remains a useful one to ask.

It is also often helpful to ask whether the intent of a command could be accomplished by another method. For example, going back to the command "Greet one another with a holy kiss," we contend that the *principle* of "greeting" is normative, but the *method* ("with a holy kiss") is not. What then do we do with an action like baptism? Is it acceptable to select another culturally appropriate way to express our commitment to God other than immersion? No, because the method—immersion—is directly linked to the core of the gospel, namely the death, burial, and resurrection of Jesus (1 Cor. 15:3-5). In Romans 6, Paul explicitly connects his description of baptism to Jesus'

> **1 Corinthians 15:3–5**
>
> "For I delivered to you *as of first importance* what I also received, that Christ died for our sins in accordance with the scriptures, that he was buried, that he was raised on the third day in accordance with the scriptures, and that he appeared to Cephas, then to the twelve."
>
> —*RSV*

death, burial, and resurrection. Thus, we believe that the burden of proof lies with those who would substitute another practice for one that is *directly connected to the cross*, such as baptism and the Lord's Supper.

Finally, to determine the universality of a given command or teaching, it is worth considering what other options were known, available, or possible at the time of the writing of the passage. For example, what do we do with the presence of slavery in the Old and New Testament? Should we support slavery today? By no means! Given the pervasive presence of and economic dependence on slavery in ancient times, what is surprising is the presence of anything in Scripture against or undermining slavery. And yet, we *do* find such passages, most notably, in Deuteronomy 23:15-16, in Galatians 3:28, in Philemon 15-17 and 21, in the theological warrants of Colossians 3:22-24 and 4:1, and in Revelation 18:13.

> **Deuteronomy 23:15**
> "You shall not give up to his master a slave who has escaped from his master to you."
> —*RSV*

The Silence of Scripture

Many people in the Churches of Christ have heard the statement, "Where the Scriptures speak, we speak, and where the Scriptures are silent, we are silent." It was used early in the nineteenth century by Thomas Campbell and many others in the Restoration Movement and became a part of our speech and eventually our culture in the Churches of Christ. However, as a philosophy of biblical interpretation, this statement has problems. It is probably helpful to begin by noting that this phrase is not a quotation from the Bible. Indeed, some reflection will reveal that Churches of Christ have a number of practices about which the Bible is silent. For instance, we utilize many things not mentioned in Scripture: microphones, air conditioning, songbooks, pews, overhead screens, church buildings, bulletins, translations, and baptistries. We also have in our congregations a number of practices that are not specifically mentioned in Scripture: using communion trays, making announcements, having "Sunday School" classes, commenting before the Lord's Supper, and singing during the Lord's Supper, to name but a few examples.

Our slogan has often kept us from substantive discussions about whether the silence of the Bible permits or prohibits something. In practice, we have applied the slogan inconsistently, satisfying our preferences. Furthermore, Churches of Christ have tended to show more acceptance toward those who interpret silence as prohibition rather than as permission.

It is also important to recognize that neither permission nor prohibition is part of the nature of Scripture itself. However, when we reflect theologically, some implications favoring permission emerge. Reflection on the nature of law and the gospel, as well as on examples from Scripture, illustrates this point. As we reflect on law, we should ask, "How appropriate is it for Christians to create new 'laws'?" James states, "there is one lawgiver" (James 4:12), and that lawgiver is God. Thus, if we make laws where God has not, then we may do what is reserved for God; at the very least, we must proceed with extreme caution, lest we create laws where God has not. We see an example of that caution in the decision of the council at Jerusalem to lay upon the Gentiles "no greater burden than what is necessary" (Acts 15:28).

What does the gospel have to do with this question of silence? Turning to Galatians, we notice that Paul uses freedom as an image describing salvation. Paul says in Galatians 5:1, "For freedom, Christ has set us free. Therefore, do not again be subject to a yoke of slavery." Paul writes these words in a context where some want to compel Christians to be circumcised (Gal. 6:12). The stakes are huge, since, as Paul says, "if justification were through the law, then Christ died for no reason" (Gal. 2:21). Elsewhere, Paul describes the freedom that Christians have in Christ; we are people who are "not under law, but under grace" (Rom. 6:15). In summary, if Christ's sacrifice brings freedom, then we should be wary of acting contrary to the implications of the cross by creating laws or rules not named in Scripture.

Perhaps the most instructive example in Scripture occurs in Romans 14:1–15:13, which records Paul's reflection and instruction on some matters of silence. Romans 14:1–6 describes two issues. In 14:2 the "weak eat only vegetables," while the strong "believes he can eat anything." Further, in 14:5, the weak judge some days more important than other days, while the strong judge all days alike. The ensuing descriptions of the strong and weak sound strikingly contemporary. The strong are tempted to "despise" the weak, looking down on them as simple and unenlightened, while the weak are tempted to "judge" the strong, condemning them to hell (Rom. 14:3).

Without going through a verse-by-verse analysis of the text, what can we learn? What are Paul's major points? To start, in disputes over matters of silence, all parties need to hear and presume that the others are striving to honor God; notice the three-fold repetition of the

Romans 14:6

"He who observes the day, observes it *in honor of the Lord*. He also who eats, eats *in honor of the Lord*, since he gives thanks to God; while he who abstains, abstains *in honor of the Lord* and gives thanks to God."

—*RSV*

phrase "in honor of the Lord" in Romans 14:6. This presumption of good intentions is often one of the first things lost in discussions of this type.

Paul attempts to keep the Christians in Rome focused on core issues, such as "righteousness, peace, and joy in the Holy Spirit" (14:17). Some issues are more important than others, as Jesus himself taught when he stated that loving God was the greatest commandment (Matt. 22:34-40). The realization that there are "weightier matters" is an important step before the identification of these "weightier matters" can take place.

> **Matthew 23:23**
>
> "Woe to you, scribes and Pharisees, hypocrites, because you tithe mint, dill, and cumin, but you neglect the weightier matters of the law—justice, mercy, and faithfulness."

Part of Christian maturity is thus the ability to distinguish things that do not matter (*adiaphora*) from things that do matter. Paul explicitly helps Christians identify matters of indifference in his letters (1 Cor. 7:19; Gal. 5:6, 6:15). Today, most Christians easily recognize some nonessential matters. For instance, few—hopefully none—would argue that a kitchen in a church is a matter of faith.

Paul's point here is that it is *never* permissible to use one's freedom in matters of silence to destroy the faith of another (14:20). Paul does *not* call on Christians to violate their convictions; actions should proceed from faith (14:23). The call for the weak is therefore to grow, to be built up (15:2), and the call for the strong is to bear the weaknesses of the weak and to welcome the weak because "Christ did not please himself" and because Christ welcomed us (15:3, 7). In other words, Paul calls the strong to behave in a Christlike way, connecting the appropriate response to the cross. In fact, the cross is the means by which

Paul determines what a Christian response should be. A number of similar passages showing the centrality of the cross could be cited; perhaps the most famous is Paul's use of Christ's example in Philippians 2:6–11 to shape a congregation facing differences and conflicts (Phil. 2:2–4, 14; 4:2–3).

Before we close this discussion, it is important to emphasize what we are *not* saying. Obviously, these guidelines for dealing with the silence of Scripture can be and often are abused. For instance, someone could say, "Since the Bible is silent about computer fraud and since it does not specifically say '*Larry* can't steal,' then I guess you'd say that Scripture permits those things." Granted, computer fraud is not mentioned, but we can legitimately extrapolate from theft, which *is* condemned in Scripture, to computer fraud. Also, such an over-literalism, as in the argument based on the fact that the words "*Larry* can't steal" are absent from the text, is clearly absurd. In fact, both of these types of arguments are so obviously false that it seems unnecessary even to mention them. However, the capacity of humans to rationalize or misconstrue is always an issue.

At the same time, even honest seekers of truth can have a real, sincere concern about where such reasoning about silence could lead. For that honest questioner, we included the brief exposition above of Romans 14:1–15:13. The answer to "Where does it end?" is in part, "Faithful responses to the ever-changing realities of life begin with Christians who are able to think theologically, who look to relevant passages like Romans 14:1–15:13 for instruction, and who keep what is central, such as the cross, as their guiding principles."

More substantially, we are *not* saying "can do" always means "should do." In other words, we do not claim that we should do everything that the freedom of the gospel allows. As already noted, we should not destroy the faith of a brother or sister by insisting on using our freedom (Rom. 14:20; 1 Cor. 8:11). Rather, we strive for what brings peace, what is good, and what builds up (Rom. 14:17; 15:2). Of course, what builds up a brother or sister may not always be what is comfortable for him or her! Churches should not always defer to the weaker brother or sister, because then the faith and practice of the church would be determined by the least mature. Obviously, these situations of disagreement require strong and wise leaders who recognize that change is difficult, slow, and emotionally charged.

Finally, we are *not* saying that silence on a given subject automatically implies permission. Nevertheless, given the opposite tendency in our fellowship's past, it seems important to state the *theological* and *scriptural* reasons for seeing the silence of Scripture as permissive. Perhaps some may now consider permissive conclusions about silence. Yet, some astute readers will already have thought of examples where biblical silence does *not* mean permission. Indeed, we acknowledge the prohibitive side of silence for many activities—from atrocities like female circumcision to absurdities like Frisbees in the assembly.

How does one interpret biblical silence in the real world? When do we act and when do we defer? Philippians 3 may provide some help. Notice that Paul can speak quite strongly: "Watch out for the dogs; watch out for the evil workers; watch out for the mutilation!" (3:2). However, later in the same chapter, Paul gently says, "Therefore, as many of us who are *mature*, let us think this. But if you think anything differently, God will also reveal it to you" (3:15). What happened between 3:2 and 3:15? In 3:2, Paul addresses a matter of the gospel. Apparently, circumcision was being bound on the Philippian Christians in a way that nullified the cross (see Galatians 2:21). In contrast, Paul deals with a matter of *maturity* in 3:15. Regarding an issue of maturity, Paul allows the kind of room for growth that we all want granted to us and should grant to others. In summary, we should proceed with what is right when the issue is a matter of the gospel. In matters of maturity, which are often matters of biblical silence, we can exercise patience and allow time for growth. In other words, with issues of silence there is a *hermeneutical* task, recognizing what is an issue of silence; there is a *theological* task, separating the core from the periphery;

Hermeneutics:
The study of the principles of interpretation.

and there is a *pastoral* task, calling on leaders to find ways for people to mature in a community where people are at different levels of maturity.

A modern example may help explain how churches might reflect on such an issue. To this point, we have primarily been concerned with church practice. Therefore, let's consider the use of drama in worship. Scripture is silent on this issue. So what should churches do? We submit that this issue is a matter of indifference; there is nothing inherently sinful about dramatic skits. In fact, churches often use skits with puppets in children's classes. This realization does not, however, conclude our reflection.

Where might one begin? One should reflect on the nature of worship. Doing so, we notice that worship constitutes praise to a holy God and that our actions should edify the church (1 Cor. 14). Certainly, we would also want to notice the motives for introducing drama; because other congregations are doing it, or because it could "liven up" our services do not qualify as solid reasons. Rather, those reasons reflect a pandering to our culture unworthy of the gospel.

Instead, we might ask the question, "Is drama a legitimate teaching method?" The biblical witness suggests the answer "Yes." One can find Old Testament prophets performing symbolic acts to teach the people of Israel (Jer. 19:1-13; Ezek. 5:1-12), some of which we might even find disturbing (Isa. 20:2-5; Hos. 1:2). We see Jesus telling parables, as well as engaging in logical arguments. We also see Jesus couple symbolic acts with his teaching (John 13), much like the symbolic acts of the prophets.

Other questions remain—some practical, others pastoral. Do we have people with talent for acting? Do we have people who can recognize or write good drama? How often would we use drama? How much time would we allot? What would we omit? How would the congregation react? Could some teaching help people with the change? Would the change upset more people than it would edify? I suspect that in most congregations, this last question would prove most decisive. Nevertheless, it seems that drama *could* be done well and be quite edifying; it also *could* be done poorly and for the wrong reasons. When tradition becomes the issue, many people will balk because of their comfort level, a matter that leaders will weigh carefully.

What about other questions of silence, like stem cell research or abortion? These questions can be extremely difficult, and the eager reader will have to wait until Chapter 8, where we propose a model for searching for theological significance, and Chapter 9, where we reflect on how to foster theological literacy in our congregations.

The Diversity of Scripture

Silence is not the only difficulty in biblical interpretation, however. What do we do when the record of Scripture itself is diverse? For example, Scripture records a number of images to describe salvation: redemption, justification, reconciliation, peace, forgiveness of sin, and new birth. Any of them is appropriate to use, but religious groups tend to use one image and disapprove when others are employed, or even mentioned. Or, when we consider prayer, we notice that a number of different physical postures are mentioned in the Bible. We see raised hands (1 Tim. 2:8), standing (Mark 11:25), and kneeling (Luke 22:41). Is only one posture authoritative? Which one? The diversity of Scripture itself suggests latitude in practice. In other words, diversity in Scripture invites diversity in practice.

Perhaps a helpful distinction to keep in mind in dealing with diversity in Scripture is the difference between a prototype and an archetype. To take a cue from the automobile industry, a *prototype* is the first car produced so that problems can get worked out. After the engineers go back to the drawing board, then an *archetype* is produced that will be the template for the next hundred thousand or so cars produced on the assembly line. In a similar way, as we read Scripture, some of what we read is merely the *first* way that the early church lived out its life as a body of God's people. Other times Scripture provides an archetype, an *example* that future Christians should believe or do. Diversity in Scripture provides part of the information we use to decide whether a belief or practice should be considered an archetype or a prototype.

Conclusion: Paddling Lamb, Swimming Elephant

As an undergraduate student, I took an art appreciation course. Ever since that time, I have loved going to art museums. Whenever I go, I try to take advantage of the tours that museums normally offer. Although I can appreciate the art without a tour, I find that I learn and enjoy the experience so much more with a guide; inevitably, I see much that I would never have noticed on my own. In a similar way, this chapter is intended to help Bible readers find *even more* rewards in their study of the Bible.

We must all realize that *interpretation is not optional; every reader interprets.* Readers have to decide whether they will interpret poorly or well—whether they will be uninformed interpreters or informed interpreters. It is also vital that all readers give themselves time for growth. Recognizing that the careful study of Scripture is difficult, readers must think of the struggles as "growing pains," not unlike the pain that comes with improvements in physical fitness. Since Christians are called to grow, these struggles are good, equipping us all for the challenges that will come our way. Finally, readers should be confident that they *can* interpret Scripture! Granted, challenges will arise, but difficulties will remain for even the most intelligent or spiritual Christians. Scripture is like that; as Bernard of Clairvaux said, "In the ocean of this sacred reading the lamb can paddle and the elephant swims."[7] ❧

185

8

Searching for Theological Significance

As Arthur opened his Bible to prepare his Wednesday night Bible lesson, Exodus 36 stared back at him; he wondered, "How am I supposed to get a lesson from the description of the dimensions of the temple?" He decided to work on his Sunday morning Bible class instead. The New Testament was no kinder. The assignment of 1 Corinthians 8 prompted him to ask himself, "What am I supposed to teach? What does eating meat sacrificed to idols have to do with the Adult 1 class? No one is struggling with eating meat offered to pagan gods."

Unfortunately, Arthur's experience is not uncommon. Typically, Churches of Christ have done well with facts. We can recite the books of the Old Testament and New Testament in order; we go to Bible Bowls; we have memory verses for children. However, when it comes time to apply the text to real life, the teacher often offers a proof text or some cursory comments in the last five minutes of the lesson, usually on some moral point. In fact, if the passage does not mention some sin (or virtue), then the teacher struggles even more to find something to say. Of course, at the other end of the spectrum, another teacher may excite the class with dazzling applications, but the class is left wondering, "Great ideas, but where did he get that from the text?"

How does a teacher take the data of Bible study and craft it into a lesson that allows God's Word to address the church today? How can names, dates, outlines, and word studies challenge the church to live faithfully? If the teacher cannot *think theologically*, then the lesson is often a mind-numbing, soul-deadening experience. If the Bible lesson is *only* a history lesson, then the church will not be fed. Facts are good; they form the foundation upon which theological reflection is built. But churches cannot live by facts alone.

Recovering Faith & Practice

With its focus on the recovery of the practices of the early church, especially baptism and the Lord's Supper, the Restoration Movement has served Christianity well. We have, however, tended to ignore the restoration of the *theology* of the early church. The presence of theological meaning is important because in its absence church practices tend to devolve into mere ritual and legalism. However, when practice and theological meaning are connected, then our actions are not primarily an expression of our own willpower. Rather, Christians should act because of what God has done and because of who they now are as his people. In addition, it is important to recognize that having a theological foundation provides some protection against being overly influenced by bad, but popular, theology.

> Practices that are done in response to God's action tend to flow from thankful hearts and promote desire to worship God and serve others.

An example is probably the best way to illustrate the way that practice can become separated from theology. Allow me to give an example from the church in which I grew up, a church that blessed me immensely. If someone asked the question "Why should I get baptized?" he would have heard something like, "Because Acts 2:38 says so." Now, on the one hand, this response deserves praise; Scripture *should* inform our practice. But, in terms of being informed by the theology of the early church, the response misses the mark in at least two crucial ways.

First, this response ignores the historical realities of the earliest Christians. For example, a Christian in Corinth in A.D. 56, for instance, would not have said, "Because Acts 2:38 says so," since Acts 2:38 had not been written yet! What then would a Christian have said in the first century? Probably something similar to the idea that baptism is a participation in the death, burial, and resurrection of Christ, an idea echoed in Romans 6. As Christ died, we Christians die to sin. As Christ was buried, we Christians are buried in the waters of baptism. As Christ rose to newness of life, so shall we too find new life in Christ. This answer connects baptism to God's redemption of his people through the cross.

The initial response also neglects the theological *meaning* of baptism. The questioner should hear *both* practice *and* theology, both the demand and the reason. In essence, we have too often answered inquiries about baptism with "Just because," when Scripture articulates a rich, meaningful reason, founded on the death, burial, and resurrection of Christ. So, it is not that the first answer is wrong, but that it is theologically impoverished.

The same dynamic could be illustrated in a number of ways. One more example will suffice. If the same questioner were now to ask, "Why does the church give on the first day of the week?" the response would (likely) have been, "Because 1 Corinthians 16 says so." Here the respondent stands on shakier ground, since 1 Corinthians 16 describes a special contribution for the Christians in Jerusalem, not for the weekly, local needs in Corinth. However, the same lack of theological foundation is present. Notice that 1 Corinthians tells *that* the Corinthians gave, *when* they gave ("first day of every week"), and *how* they gave ("as one prospers"), but not *why* they gave. For the theological warrant for giving, 2 Corinthians 8:9 stands out in a discussion spanning two chapters: "For you know the grace of our Lord Jesus Christ, that although he was rich, he became poor for your sake, in order that you might become rich by his poverty."

In other words, when Paul answers the question, "Why give?" he responds, "Because it is a Christlike thing to do. When you give and become poor for others, you imitate the example of Christ." Consider the warrants for giving that you have heard in the past: duty, guilt, the right thing to do, humanitarian reasons. None of these have anything *necessarily* Christian about them; the same appeals could be made for a new computer at a PTA meeting! We should strive for a response founded on the cross, which enriches the understanding and motivation of the giver.

The Necessity of Theological Reflection

Theological reflection is necessary not only in the study, teaching, and preaching of Scripture, but also in the daily life of individual Christians and the church. Each day Christians are faced with questions and challenges that require reflection on God's will.

For instance, Clarice, a young woman in her twenties, considers a job change in Oregon. Does Scripture have anything to say? Not specifically, since the Bible does not mention job changes in Oregon for young women named Clarice. But prayer coupled with reflection on passages that address gifts and calling will provide Clarice some insight. Larry, a man in his sixties attending to his mother with Alzheimer's, faces the financial and emotional challenges of caring for a sickly parent. Does Scripture mention Alzheimer's? No. No study Bible or concordance will explain or direct him to a passage, but if he can think theologically, other passages will inform and strengthen him. He could grow in his understanding about suffering and dying, as well as about honoring his parent.

Churches face other, equally difficult questions. First Avenue Church finds itself in a downtown area that has become poverty-stricken and drug-infested. What should the church do? Sell the property and relocate to the suburbs, where most of the members live? Stay and reach out? What is the best way for the congregation to reach out to the community? Start a soup kitchen? Become involved in drug rehabilitation?

Second Avenue Church faces growth problems. Should the congregation build a new building? How large should it be? Should it have a gymnasium? Should the church rent a facility? Would multiple services best solve the problem? In both of these instances, the most devout Bible scholar will not find a passage that directly addresses the situation of either the First Avenue or Second Avenue Church. The Christian equipped with data is only partially prepared to address the challenges of real life. However, Christians who can think theologically can find insight in Scripture. This chapter first describes how a Christian might move from

Scripture to a message for today, and then concludes with reflection on moving from the challenges of real life to a response shaped by Scripture.

From Scripture to Significance

Scripture truly functions as Scripture only when it shapes the life of a person or community. Yet, sometimes the challenge can appear great. For instance, how does one translate Haggai's admonition to complete the construction of the temple into a compelling lesson for a group of teenagers in the 21st century? Learning how to *think theologically* equips one to answer these kinds of questions.

Before any attempt to describe this endeavor, a few preliminaries are in order. These items are "rules of thumb"—*not* a formula into which one can plug data and automatically be presented with the theological substance of a passage. The process is somewhat individual; that is, what works for me may or may not work for others to the same degree. Yet, it is *not* true that the search for God's will is *totally* individual.

In the words of one of our authors, the search for theological substance is "like teaching art. You can teach technique, but knowledge of technique—even mastery of technique—does not make a great artist." In other words, the search for the theological substance of a passage is both an art and a science. Every interpreter is aided by the study of theology and Scripture. However, the scholar may not have the deepest insight on a particular text. Someone else's gifts and experiences—both triumphs and tragedies—may have prepared him or her to understand the depths of a particular text more fully than anyone else in the whole congregation.

It is wise, therefore, to learn from others. By paying attention to those writers, speakers, and teachers who read Scripture insightfully, one can gain understanding from their example. One of the most helpful practices is noticing the kinds of questions they ask.

Of course, all of this (as well as the following discussion) assumes that the interpretive work of Chapter 7 will be done—the essential attention to historical context, literary genre, and literary context. That research provides an indispensable foundation for reflection. Readers who have "lived" with the text will notice details that the casual reader does not.

So, what does a process for discerning the theological substance of Scripture involve? It encompasses a number of items. Intense prayer fills the whole process. A close reading of Scripture and sustained theological reflection normally precede an attempt to translate the message for a specific context. The following reflection describes each element in greater detail.

Pray

Bathe your whole effort—your study and reflection—in prayer. What does praying over a text mean? Numerous examples could be given. Asking God for insight, confessing a lack of understanding, and requesting help for weaknesses exposed by the text are three ways prayer flows from the study of Scripture. Perhaps most foundationally, one can pray focusing on the themes of the text. Somehow wrestling with Scripture in prayer provides clarity and insight that other disciplines do not.

Read the Text

Now read the text again. Read the text at least a dozen times more than you think you should! Read the text in different translations, spanning the spectrum from extremely literal (NASB) to completely idiomatic (*Message*, Phillips, *Living Bible*) to those in between (NRSV, NIV). You will be surprised what you notice.

Outline the Text

Constructing an outline demands a close reading of the text, exposes the structure of the passage, and reveals the main themes of the passage. Forced to identify the main points, we will also notice the subordinate ideas—and then struggle to describe the relationship among all the parts. Immersed in the text, we will be addressed by the demands of the text. In other words, this call to immerse ourselves in the text is not only *practical*—the more we read, the more we notice—but also *theological*; that is, the more time we spend immersed in God's Word, the more opportunity God has to mold our hearts and minds.

This sentiment finds expression in Scripture. The writer of Hebrews describes the Word of God as "living and active," penetrating the innermost parts of the self (Heb. 4:12). Luke commends the Christians in Berea who "received the word with all eagerness" and "examined the scriptures daily" (Acts 17:11). Finally, Luke notes that when the Word is sown in a "good and noble heart" (Luke 8:15), it bears fruit.

Reflect on the Text

Here is a call to work in two opposite directions at the same time. On the one hand, we pay attention to connections with our own experience. As we study and reflect on the text, we will be surprised how often a news item, TV program, movie, or personal experience relates to and illuminates the passage. Write down these ideas; they often prompt deeper insights. In addition, they often help an audience connect to the message.

Perhaps even more significant, notice what is *different*, what does *not* seem to make sense. What bothers, dumbfounds, surprises, embarrasses, or scares should also be pursued. These bothersome questions are likely many of the same questions that will arise in the minds of others. By listening to these questions, we often tap into sentiments and reflections common to the human condition.

In fact, the most difficult texts often yield the greatest insights. As an example, after reading the account of the woman who anointed Jesus with ointment worth almost a year's wages (John 12:1-8), I had the following questions:

> Why would Mary use her hair to wipe Jesus' feet? Why do I find myself feeling sympathetic toward Judas' sentiment about selling the ointment and using the proceeds to help the poor? Am I *bad* for thinking so practically? Why? Why does Jesus defend her action? What does the sentence "The poor you always have with you" mean? Is Jesus *against* helping the poor? Should I rethink benevolence? What would this action look like today if someone in my congregation did something analogous to her action? Why can't I think of anything analogous today? Are there *no* Christians today who act in a similar way?

On the basis of these ponderings, I began to reflect on the nature of grace, how it is both lavish and offensive, lavish because it overflows beyond any expectation, offensive because it falls on impure hearts (John 12:6). The film *Babette's Feast* came to mind, a film where a young woman spends all her lottery winnings on a single meal for her friends. Passages of Scripture also sprang to mind, such as the parable of the workers in the vineyard (Matt. 20:1-16) and the parable of the prodigal son, especially the older brother (Luke 15:11-32), where grace both defies description and disturbs.

This first round of questions produced yet another round of questions for me:

> What would happen if Christians behaved in grace-filled ways toward non-Christians? Should we expect both positive and negative responses? Is it the case that only an act of grace will be arresting enough to break bitterness, cynicism, or moral callousness? Does the act have to involve something worth so much money? Can something like forgiveness or a small act of sacrifice accomplish the same transformation? What would I, or my congregation, look like if the message of this passage were living in me? What was impure in my heart that made me sympathize with Judas?

Hard questions should not be avoided, but embraced! However, further reflection and study do not guarantee "great ideas." Sometimes they yield only small insights—or even nothing at all. Nevertheless, Christians are called to struggle with God's Word. And even when the struggle does not bear the expected fruit, God still uses that struggle to shape his people.

Remove the Text

What does "remove the text" mean? Simply, it is often helpful to ask, "What if this verse—or passage, or even a whole chapter—were lost?" For some reason, answering the question, "What is this passage about?" becomes easier when it is expressed in negative terms—"What does this book now lose with this passage omitted?" For instance, what if 1 Corinthians did not have 1 Corinthians 10:1-13? What is lost? After all, how does this Old Testament example relate to the discussion of meat sacrificed to idols? Why does Paul mention baptism at this point? What does Paul mean by "the Rock was Christ" (10:4)?

Additional study and reflection on 1 Corinthians 10:1-13 might lead a reader to ask, "What if other actions beyond eating meat sacrificed to idols were also at issue, such as engaging in immorality, testing God, and grumbling?" Furthermore, perhaps not only the Corinthians' *actions*, but also their *attitudes* are at issue. Perhaps their attitudes arise from a misconception about baptism. If this hypothesis is true, then Paul's illustration from the Old Testament allows him to address a number of issues with one example and moves the conflict from Christian against Christian to Christian against God. We might end up with the same conclusion through direct, analytical research, but the "long way home" often exposes new vistas, breaks through impasses, and paradoxically becomes a "shortcut."

Ask Theological Questions of the Text

Behind this suggestion is the conviction that the substance of a biblical text is most likely to be found in theological expressions. That is, the writers of Scripture were primarily concerned with shaping a community faithful to God. In so doing, they taught about the God whom the community worshipped.

"But as the one who called you is holy, be holy in your conduct."
—*1 Peter 1:15*

What we believe about God matters. Scripture shows that we become like what we worship, which can either be for good (Lev. 19:2; 1 Pet. 1:15) or for ill (Psalm 115:8; Jer. 2:5). Also, the biblical writers describe the nature and identity of God's people (Israel, the church) because they hope for a people who will behave consistently with God's call.

Unfortunately for purposes of interpretation, readers are naturally drawn to the people in Scripture, especially in narrative material. Not surprisingly, the lessons that emerge from those readings often go awry in a number of ways, ranging from psychologizing to moralizing. Let me illustrate.

Once I was sitting in on the conversation of some Bible teachers. They were preparing to teach a lesson from Genesis 13 (Abraham's separation from Lot) to a group of children. Because Abraham gave Lot first choice of the land, the teachers concluded that a lesson about generosity should be taught. Although generosity is a good lesson for children to learn, I suspect that Genesis 13 is not about generosity. This is a category of misinterpretation I call "true, but wrong." That is, a lesson about generosity is a good and true lesson, but Genesis 13 is not about generosity. In making this point, I neither question the integrity nor the intentions of those teachers; they were doing the best they could, and I include them among the best Christians I know. They do, however, join a number of other teachers who immediately draw a moral lesson from the text without reflecting whether the text teaches that lesson or not.

What is wrong with moralizing? Not much in terms of content, since Scripture teaches moral lessons. Nevertheless, the stakes are significant. First, we miss out on the actual message of that passage when we replace the message of the text with our own biases. Second, we separate the *norm* from the *warrant*. When the norm is separated from the warrant, then the result is moralizing. However, when the norm and warrant are connected,

Norm:

The rule or behavior; *what* we should do.

Warrant:

The rationale; *why* we should do something.

moral instruction and formation result, because our actions are based on our convictions. Practically speaking, as we examine a text, we need to ask both "What?" and "Why?" Curiously, the full message often emerges only when the ratio is two or three consecutive whys for every what.

What does it mean to ask theological questions of a text? Two basic questions to ask are: "What does the passage say about God?" and "What does the passage say about God's people?" When teachers search for and express the message in those theological categories, they are most likely to capture the message of the text. Beyond these two, simple questions, it is often helpful to read the text with seven standard theological categories (i.e., God, Christ, Holy Spirit, sin, salvation, church, eschatology) in mind. By reflecting on what

Eschatology:

The study of end times.

the text says about each theological idea, one emerges with a more comprehensive understanding of the theological contours of a passage.

To return to the example of Genesis 13 above, I would say that Genesis 13 teaches about a God who is faithful—even when his people have failed in the past, about a God who is faithful—even when the future appears dim, and about his people who are called to be faithful—even when faithfulness does not seem prudent or personally beneficial.

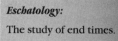

199

Translate the Message for Your Context

At this point, we seem to have reached the goal;
we have identified the theological message of a given
text. But identifying the theological message does not
end the process. Rather, it begins another, because
now each interpreter must translate that message for
his or her specific context and culture. It is vital for
interpreters to ask how the message can have the
same "bite" that it originally had.

Although one cannot bottle those "A-hah!" moments,
it is possible to offer some modest suggestions. To begin,
in our experience those moments occur most often
during periods of preparation such as those already
described. Some questions and reflections tend to
prompt that moment of insight: What are the stakes for
this congregation? What is the issue in this passage?[1] If
the church faithfully applied this text, what would the
congregation change or do? Selecting up to a half dozen
individuals, consider a conversation about this text with
each particular member. How would I explain the text
in language that each member would understand? What
questions would each ask? How does this text challenge
or comfort each of these individuals?

There is also no substitute for regular practice.
We grow as we study God's Word, and we improve as
we exercise our theological muscles. The more we
engage Scripture, the more we develop our "court
sense," and the more sensitive our "instincts" become.
Nevertheless, despite our best efforts, God's word for
our time remains in some sense elusive, a gift given,
free from any efforts to confine or constrain it.

Our translation of the message of the text can take a
number of forms. For instance, if we were to translate
the theological message of the parable of the good
Samaritan into action, we might show compassion

and love for our neighbor by bringing a meal to a sick neighbor, mowing a lawn, watching children for an afternoon, buying a homeless person a meal, befriending the outcast at school, ministering to AIDS victims, and so forth. The theological message is not exhausted by any one context. Rather, our contemporary context shapes and gives life to the message.

In summary, to hear God's message to his people, we must go beyond data, beyond moralizing, and beyond mere summaries. We must invest *ourselves* in our search. Yet, if we are willing to struggle with the complexities that Scripture presents, God will bless us richly.

From Real Life to Theological Discernment

The popularity of the book *Experiencing God: Knowing and Doing God's Will* (over two million copies sold)—as well as the number of conversations that begin "God told me…"—attests to the pervasive desire and apparent attainment of knowing God's will. The search for God's will raises some interesting questions, as the following anecdote illustrates.

I know a couple—we'll call them Alice and Bob—who illustrate the spectrum well. In a hurried trip to the supermarket, Alice snags a prime parking spot and whispers a prayer "God, thank you for the parking spot," convinced that God is active in the world and that it was God's will for her to have that particular parking spot. Almost a deist (that is, someone who believes that God wound up the universe like a clock, and now the universe is running by itself), Bob, her husband, would never utter such a prayer. He would also prefer that his wife not mention hers, although he truly believes God is active in the world and faithfully prays for God to answer prayer. He just has a hard time "knowing" that something is God's will, since, as he might say, "God doesn't leave notes under my pillow."

Like the Alices of this world, we too should desire to thank God for the many graces of each day. But like the Bobs of this world, we may sometimes wonder what God's will for our life is. Although we may not have the certitude for which Bob yearns, most Christians can see the hand of God in retrospect. That is, at the moment of decision, doubt may still linger, but in retrospect even the most "Bob" of Bobs will acknowledge seeing the hand of God at work in his life, even though he may not have admitted or known so at that moment.

Individual Discernment

We began this chapter moving from the study of Scripture to the application of God's Word to real life. What happens when real life forces Christians to respond? How then does Scripture inform our response? Are Christians left without guidance when life's realities force them to respond?

We answer with an emphatic "No," even though we may not know with full assurance the right course of action in every circumstance. For instance, Becky wonders whether she should marry Colby or not. Would a time of reflection and discernment help? Provide an answer? We think so, despite the many ways that such a process can and does go astray. As humans, we have an incredible capacity for self-deception. Pride and selfishness, to name but two vices, always remain poised to pounce on our good intentions. The basic commitment to God's will, however, stands at the foundation of our conviction, going back to the words of Jesus himself—"not my will, but yours, be done" (Luke 22:42). We also see individual reflection in the person of

Mary whom Luke describes as "pondering" the meaning of God's action in her life (Luke 1:29; 2:19, 51), echoing the Old

> "Mary treasured all these things, pondering them in her heart."
> —*Luke 2:19*

Testament description of Jacob (Gen. 37:11). What might a process for discernment look like?

Pray

Students enjoy asking professors questions like, "If God already knows everything, then why do we need to pray?" Although there are several possible answers, I usually point out how prayer transforms the one who prays. Allen Verhey offers some insightful and prophetic comments on the role of prayer in ethical reflection. He points out how prayer to God reminds us that we are creature, and God is Creator, keeping us humble; how prayers of confession remind us of our weaknesses, keeping us from being judgmental; how prayers of intercession remind us of others, keeping us from hatred.[2] As we address God in prayer, seeking his will, we are shaped by those petitions. What was shiny becomes gaudy; what was alluring becomes repellent; and what seemed a real possibility becomes shallow. Prayer reveals what is not of God, such as impure motives. Ideally, prayer leaves us with a godly perspective and (perhaps several) options. By emptying ourselves, we become vessels capable of being used by God.

Prayer, however, does not work merely by negation, that is, by removing the dross of our sin. Rather, it also provides strength and insight. The Gospel of Luke shows the value of prayer in a number of ways. We see Jesus praying at significant times in his ministry: at his baptism (Luke 3:21), before the selection of the twelve

> "At this time, he went out to the mountain to pray, and he spent the night in prayer to God."
> —*Luke 6:12*

203

(Luke 6:12), and before his death (Luke 22:39-46). In addition, Jesus consistently seeks time for prayer. In Luke's gospel, we see Jesus praying in the wilderness (5:16), in private (9:18), and on mountains (6:12; 9:28; 22:39-41). Elsewhere in the New Testament, James counsels the one who lacks wisdom to "ask God" (James 1:5). Later James describes this "wisdom from above" as "first pure, then peaceable, gentle, open to reason, full of mercy and good fruits, without uncertainty or insincerity" (James 3:17 RSV). To enter into a time of discernment without prayer is not only foolish, but also faithless.

Study & Reflect on Scripture

Scripture provides insight into the nature of God and his will; we see who God is by what he says and does and by how God is described. At this point in the process of discernment, we benefit from reading Scripture and collecting passages pertaining to our question. Concordances, Bible dictionaries, and even some commentaries will be helpful, usually in that order. After those passages have been collected, intense research and reflection will further shape the heart and mind of the interpreter.

Scripture does not answer every issue directly. But even in its silence, Scripture can accomplish several important things. It can exclude some options. Some options will clearly not be godly and should not be considered. In addition, especially with ethical issues, Scripture can help us focus our reflection by forcing us to consider an issue in light of our identity, purpose, and central convictions. For instance, we should be asking questions like, "What kind of community is created when we do this behavior?" "How does the cross relate to this issue?" "How does our identity as God's people inform our understanding on this issue?"[3] Furthermore, Scripture can give us language for framing our discussion. As an example, Paul's reflection in 1 Corinthians 6:12-20 and 9:1-27 excludes the language of "my rights," however American, from discussions of abortion.

Listen for the Guidance of the Holy Spirit

The Spirit not only helps us in our prayers (Rom. 8:26-27), but also in our understanding. 1 Corinthians 1-4 discusses the Spirit as revealer. As Christians, "we have received the Spirit which is from God, in order that we might understand the gifts given to us by God" (2:12). Paul teaches that God reveals himself to us "through the Spirit" (2:10). Since we can easily be tripped up by the "wisdom of this age" (2:6), Christians are blessed to have the Spirit as, in Carl Holladay's words, a "guide to the interior of God's mind."[4] The Spirit teaches Christians to "have the mind of Christ" (2:16)—to discern how to apply the cross to diverse situations. It is not accidental that Paul begins 1 Corinthians by sketching out the implications of the cross before he addresses specific problems like immorality and lawsuits in chapters 5 and 6, since only the Spirit-informed, cross-shaped mind can fully discern godly responses to life's complexities.

Since Scripture describes growth (1 Cor. 3:6) and understanding (Phil. 3:15; 2 Tim. 2:7) as results of God's activity, it seems reasonable to look to God for insight. Practically speaking, how does God reveal that insight? On the one hand, it would be presumptuous to claim to know how God reveals his will in every circumstance, since God moves in mysterious ways beyond the understanding of humans (Rom. 11:33-34). Furthermore, a degree of caution is in order, since some have committed atrocities in the name of God. On the other hand, we can make some claims. It is clear that God speaks through Scripture and the life of Jesus (John 1:18). In addition, since God communicated in "various ways" (Heb. 1:1) in the past, it seems likely that God might also use various means

> "I planted, Apollos watered, but God caused the growth."
> —*1 Corinthians 3:6*

today, such as fellow believers, times of prayer, and the events of our lives to provide insight. Although it may be difficult to discern God's Word for today, Christians must still listen patiently.

Find & Use Every Pertinent Resource

A necessary prerequisite, the ability to listen allows Christians to take advantage of the abundant resources available. Unfortunately, we often neglect all of the resources at our disposal. Do we seek to hear the strongest arguments for *all* sides of an issue? Can we describe the strongest arguments *against* our position? Too often we seek only what we *want* to hear. James lists "openness" as one of the characteristics of wisdom (3:17). We would do well to remember how often God has acted in ways that have *surprised* his people. Are we a people open both to confirming past convictions and to perceiving new insights? Listening does not require agreement, but it does require openness.

With a plea for openness in place, it is appropriate to address one of the greatest resources Christians have—the community of believers. It makes sense to emphasize community. Christians are more likely to find a faithful answer among the community of faith. Dialogue with people of faith is an invaluable resource for a number of reasons. For one, it provides us accountability. Fellow Christians will challenge our rationalizations, keeping us honest. As others inquire about our ideas, our assumptions are questioned, and our ideas are clarified. With the aid of the community's critique, some of our bad ideas are even jettisoned, saving us from our shallow or sinful thinking.

Looking through the eyes of others also enables us to see different questions. Many times new ideas emerge as we are forced to look at a question from a different perspective.

In addition, communities of believers provide access to other Christians who have gone through a similar experience or have considered the same question. Where else but the church can we find other people with the same convictions, but who offer rich perspectives because of differences in age, gender, education, ethnicity, race, income, or career? For example, while pondering a move to a different city, I asked over twenty people their opinions. Their responses ranged from "If you do, you're throwing away your career" to "If you don't, you are a *bad* husband." Although not always pleasant, this diverse input forced me to ask hard questions and gave me wisdom that I would not otherwise have discovered.

Christianity has often identified four major resources for theological reflection: Scripture, tradition, reason, and experience. Since we have already mentioned Scripture and experience, a word about tradition and reason is in order. Tradition can be used in a negative way (Matt. 15:8-9), or it can preserve the very foundation of the Christian faith (1 Cor. 15:3-8). Mature Christians are able to see both the strengths and weaknesses of tradition, affirm as much as they criticize, and profit from the experience and reflection

207

of those who have attempted to live faithfully. Readers will want to reflect on the more extensive discussions of tradition and community in the first volume of this series, *The Crux of the Matter.*

Reason, like tradition, is a tool to be used wisely. Some matters are beyond reason (for example, "What happens after death?"). Other matters elude reason. For instance, is it reasonable to give up vacation time to build homes for the poor in Mexico, apart from the Christian faith? Nevertheless, we will profit by considering the presuppositions, coherence, and implications of the reasoning behind our decisions. Reason will also help us evaluate the warrants and goals of our actions.

Prayerfully Decide & Act

Everything that has been described to this point—from prayer to resources for theological reflection—has been preparation for making a decision, since at some point, everyone must act; deliberation cannot go on forever. Rarely do we have all the information we would like. In fact, a response of faith requires some risk. At the point of decision, certain questions are often helpful. First, it is often helpful to reflect on the *nature* of the decision, asking, "What is Christian about this decision?" Second, reflecting on the *basis* for the decision, we should ask, "What is the rationale for this decision?" Third, considering the *goal* of the decision, we can ask, "What is the purpose of this decision?" Often these questions can save us from self-deception or confirm a decision as a faithful response.

But how do we *know* what the right decision is? That is a difficult, if not impossible, question!

Sometimes no single, right decision exists; a number of godly responses may exist. Nevertheless, many Christians report noticing a number of events that seem to "come together," pointing in a definite direction. Others may experience a sense of peace. At other times, it is only in retrospect that confirmation comes (Luke 24:32). Any remaining uncertainty should not be surprising, since what we have attempted to articulate is a faithful response to the discovery of God's will and not a "magic formula."

Communal Discernment

How does a process for communal discernment differ from one for individual discernment? In many respects, it remains the same. From Acts 15, we see how Christians gathered to consider how Scripture (15:16-17), tradition (15:5), reason (15:2, 6-7), and experience (7-11, 12) informed the church about the activity (15:4, 7-9, 12, 14) and will of God. From the Old Testament (Jer. 28) to the New Testament (1 Thess. 5:19-21), communities of faith have been forced to exercise discernment. The Christian tradition also contains many examples of those who have attempted to reflect on the discernment of God's will. One can tap into, for example, the model of Ignatius of Loyola, who wrote six rules for communal discernment.[5]

No matter what model is followed, difficulties and opportunities abound for communities engaging in a process of discernment. One of the challenges for

The Ignatian model:

1. Become aware of as many dimensions of the decision as possible, gathering information, considering all the possible consequences, soliciting insight, weighing the pros and cons.

2. Devote a period of time to considering the alterna-
(continued on next page)

tive the community is least inclined to choose, using the imagination to settle into that alternative, praying about it, noticing the emotions, sensations, and thoughts that either attract the group to or repel the group from the choice, reflecting on whether the sources of those various stirrings are divine, demonic, or neurotic.

3. Repeat the process for the same period of time with the other option to which the group was originally more attracted.

4. Reflect with both heart and head on the two reflective time periods, weighing information and comparing various feelings to determine which choice gave rise to a deeper sense of consolation—an experience of life, love, freedom, peace, joy, creativity, and communion.

5. Make a tentative decision, living with it for a period of time in order to see if the decision is confirmed by a sense of peace through prayer.

6. If the decision seems to be confirmed, take action.

this process in the context of American culture is the high view of individualism; not everyone will want to work together or work for the common good. Another challenge includes deciding about the pace of change. Other Christians simply will not think that a process of discernment is necessary or helpful. Unfortunately, some churches may find it tempting to disguise "what we want to do" as "a time of discernment." Other times "a time of discernment" can degenerate into doing what the majority will permit—discernment as polling, so to speak. In another case, the decision may be clear, but difficult to do. It is hard to do what is right when unity is threatened. Our history, however, tells us that leaders must sometimes make hard, not simply popular, decisions. For instance, for too long churches waited to enact and support racial integration. In summary, we recognize that communal discernment is not without its hurdles.

Given the diversity of challenges and contexts, it would be difficult to be too specific. However, it may be helpful to point out some of the items that congregations will need to consider: timetable, process, precise phrasing of the question, sources of information (for example, panels, speakers, books), representation (whole church or a representative committee), activities (for example, prayer, fasting), the means of communication to the congregation, and the process for coming to a decision. Each congregation will work out details consonant with the culture and convictions of the members.

Conclusion

Why do we include a chapter on discerning the theological significance of Scripture? What does theology have to do with either the church or Scripture? We believe that Christians have something significant to say about the issues facing modern society. To say something significant, the church must be able to *think theologically* because so many current issues are not directly addressed in Scripture. Nicholas Lash rightly claims, "To think as a Christian is to try to understand the stellar spaces, the arrangements of micro-organisms and DNA molecules, the history of Tibet, the operation of economic markets, toothache, King Lear, the CIA and grandma's cooking—or as Aquinas put it 'all things.'"[6] If the church wants to be taken seriously, it needs to *think seriously*. But before tackling national or international quandaries, we must be able to cope with personal and congregational issues. The next chapter will propose ways to foster theological literacy in our churches, as well as address the many ways that Scripture can enrich our personal and congregational lives. ❧

Training in Godliness

A tradition of my boyhood was Mom reading a passage from the Bible at breakfast. We would discuss a passage or often a proverb before I left for school. Wednesday nights and Sunday mornings meant memory verses, races to see who could find a Bible passage first, and Who Am I cards, stressing knowledge of biblical characters. Summer brought Vacation Bible School and the books of the New Testament song. We always brought our Bibles to church. Virtually every year my grandmother read through the Bible, giving her formidable questions to ask me, the "Bible major." In short, Scripture permeated my life, and I grew to love it.

—Ken

As we state in the preface of this book, one of the goals of this volume is to encourage a love for Scripture. In Psalm 119:16, the psalmist writes of the delight that God's Word provides him. That delight should characterize God's people. Scripture will be loved if it is read, understood, and lived. However, Scripture seems to be used less and less in more and more of our congregations, resulting in lowered biblical literacy. For instance, which of the following statements are true (answers in sidebar on p. 216):

213

1. The image of the lion lying down with the lamb comes from the Old Testament.
2. The New Testament describes wise men who visit baby Jesus in a stable.
3. The innkeeper tells Joseph and Mary, "There is no room at the inn."
4. The book of Revelation mentions the "Anti-Christ."
5. The book of Revelation mentions four "riders," popularly known as "the four horsemen."

We the authors want more than biblical literacy; we want to foster theological literacy and renewal as well. Thus, we propose ways that Scripture can be used in worship, in Bible classes, and in the home. Why is Scripture so important for the worship of the church? Scripture nourishes, challenges, and transforms the church. Furthermore, Scripture shapes and sustains the identity of the church, as we saw in Chapter 4.

The Use of Scripture in Worship

A View from the Trenches—And a Parable

Differences in worship preferences make people uncomfortable at best and cause division at worst. One of the sanest diagnoses of the problem came as an email in April 2001 from Chris Seidman, a minister in Texas:

> I wonder if we put too much pressure on our assemblies to generate a spirit or experience of "worship renewal." What if "worship renewal" on Sunday mornings has a lot more to do with what's happening in the believers' lives Monday through Saturday? I'm currently with a church that for the last few years has been exploring and appropriating a freedom and innovation

in the assembly that many folks dream about happening in their church.... But when I asked the leadership about the evolution of the body's worship experience and the renewal that's taken place here, they never pointed to these forms. They talked about how the core of the church several years ago, meaning elders/deacons and their wives along with others, began to be heavily involved in Bible Study Fellowship.... The bottom line is, this church leadership's answer was that what led to a sense of renewal in their collective worship experience on Sunday was the fact that they as individuals were more immersed in disciplined interaction with God in the Word and prayer Monday through Saturday.

Or let me put it in the form of a modern day parable... When I was in Florida a few years ago, FSU was preparing to play Tennessee in the Fiesta Bowl for the national championship. Merchants in Tallahassee were so sure that FSU would win and were wanting so much to be the first to produce national champ T-shirts that they printed hundreds of thousands in advance of the game so that as soon as the game was over, the shirts could be sold in the streets. Well, the Vols won, and guess what? The merchants still tried to sell the shirts at a tremendous discount. No takers. So then they tried to give the shirts away on the streets. They had to clear out their warehouses. No takers. Why? Why not take free, gorgeous, national championship T-shirts? Because nobody is in the mood to celebrate something that hasn't really happened. I would suggest that sometimes that is what we are trying to do in our assemblies. Celebrating some things that haven't been happening recently for a lot of us as individuals. We sing songs about surrender, when we have no intention of surrendering and haven't surrendered in a while. We sing songs about freedom when the truth is we've been in bondage.

The hard, dry, empty heart is unlikely to be stirred by any combination of worship forms—traditional or contemporary. Rather, as we draw near to God, God draws near to us (James 4:8). Scripture breaks hearts and shapes minds, turning the church to God.

The Public Reading of Scripture

Although there are a number of passages illustrating the public reading of Scripture, a personal favorite is Ezra's reading of the book of the law in Nehemiah 8—a text previously discussed in Chapter 1. As Ezra opens the book to read, the people stand because they respect God's Word (8:5). Ezra reads from morning to noon, and interpreters help the crowd to understand what is read (8:3, 8). And because they understand, the people weep (8:9). The respect, eagerness, and understanding of the people, as well as the impact the text has on them, are striking—something churches should strive to recover. But how do we recover that level of respect for God's Word?

Respect is learned. When our children see us attending to the public reading of Scripture with interest, then we model behavior worthy of imitation. However, have we ever caught ourselves using that time to write out the check for the collection, to read the bulletin, or to look up the next song? Interestingly, we tend to value good speaking more than good listening. For example, we tend

Answers to the quiz...

Only statement 5 is true (Revelation 6:1-8). For the other statements, see
1. Isaiah 11:6-9; 65:25.
2. Matthew 2:11.
3. Luke 2:7.
4. 1 John 2:18, 22; 4:3; 2 John 7.

to judge ministers on the basis of their ability to preach well, but we usually spend much less time reflecting about *our* responsibility to listen well! Scripture, however, emphasizes the responsibility to listen well. Notice the conclusion to the parable of the sower in Luke 8:18: "Therefore, pay attention to *how* you hear. For whoever has, more will be given to him. And whoever has not, even what he thinks he has will be taken from him." Giving God's Word less attention than our favorite television program hardly conveys respect.

Part of the respect for Scripture comes in the commitment to plan for good public readings of it. It is necessary to highlight two key aspects of planning. First, congregations need to *value and teach* good public reading of Scripture; it does not happen by accident. Readers need to receive the passage *in advance* so that they can prepare. Churches can train readers by giving a handout with advice for preparation. We know of one congregation that gives a worship manual to all who serve publicly. Though a laudable beginning, a hand-

> *Preparation for public reading:*
> - Pray;
> - Study the passage;
> - Practice the reading in advance;
> - Prepare the audience;
> - Provide a conclusion.

out or manual is not sufficient without some mentoring and practice. The positive results of this training will be a context in which everyone who reads publicly is aware of the high expectations for readers of Scripture.

In addition, the readings must be *selected* on some basis. Some congregations read through whole books, one chapter per week; others have an Old Testament reading and a New Testament reading that coordinate with the theme of the sermon; most often, the reading presents the sermon text for the day. Other possibilities exist as well, such as coordinating readings with a prayer, a song, or the Lord's Supper. Congregations may also choose multiple readers for passages with multiple characters; they may read Scripture in unison, or responsively, as Psalm 136 likely was.

Churches who plan in these ways will foster respect for God's Word and encourage well-executed readings. How do good readings happen? We claim no control over the way the Spirit addresses our hearts through God's Word. We can, however, be responsible public readers and practice a few specific activities to improve our public reading.

Pray

Prayer should permeate the whole process from start to finish. Nevertheless, the public aspect of reading Scripture presents challenges to the one who prays and those who hear alike. For the one who prays, it is important to remember that reading Scripture publicly is not about the reader; it is all about communicating the message of God's Word. The attention of the congregation should not be directed toward the reader. The reader's energies should focus on conveying the message of the passage. To maintain this focus, it is appropriate to express a silent prayer for a pure heart. Also, a prayer to prepare the hearts of the congregation is entirely appropriate.

Study the Passage

Since Chapter 7 focused on strategies for interpretation and Chapter 8 dealt with searching for theological significance, only a few reminders are in order. Determine the message of the passage, asking key questions. The following questions constitute a bare minimum for the purpose of the public reading of Scripture: Who wrote the passage? What is the book about as a whole? How does this passage fit into the whole book? How does this passage connect with what immediately precedes and follows it? What is the gist of the passage?

Practice the Reading in Advance

How many times have we heard someone stumble over the name of a person or a place in a public reading? We grant that the Bible contains some fairly challenging names and places—Maher-shalal-hash-baz and Ptolemais come to mind! However, if we were scheduled to read a proposal at a town meeting or deliver a speech televised on the national news, we would likely prepare. Poor preparation for the public reading of Scripture conveys a lack of respect; it says, "The Bible was not important enough for me to take the time to prepare." I suspect we have all experienced a sense of awkwardness and loss in those situations.

With the message of the reading understood and with the motivation to prepare, it is now possible to discuss several tools at our disposal to aid in the oral presentation of the reading. The easiest to use are pause, rate, and volume. We need to use those tools to stress what the passage stresses. For instance, we can read parallel items with equal rate and volume, helping the hearers to grasp the structure of a passage. We can emphasize

Vocal "tools"

- Pause
- Rate
- Volume
- Tone
- Pitch
- Enunciation

a repeated theme in the passage, aiding the hearers in recognizing what is significant. I often put pencil marks in the text to remind me; I use a vertical line to indicate a pause and underlining or italics to indicate a stress. For example, 1 Corinthians 8:6 might look like this:

> But for us there is <u>one</u> <u>God</u>, | the father, | from <u>whom</u> are all things and <u>for</u> <u>whom</u> we exist, | and there is <u>one</u> <u>Lord</u>, | Jesus Christ,

| through whom are all things, | and through
whom we exist.

More difficult is the use of tone and pitch. Consider
how a reader might use tone to convey different
emotions, such as sadness or excitement. How might
one read to express a sense of awe or anger? How
should one express the stubbornness of Pharaoh or the
sarcasm of Amos? Questions like these are appropriate
to consider. Experiment with reading the passage
in different ways until you are able to capture the
message in your presentation. The key to any of these
oral techniques is *practice*. Readers should practice the
passage aloud a number of times, so that the focus is
not on execution, but remains on the message.

Practice reading loudly and clearly, and enunciate.
Readers often drop final consonants—"and" becomes
"an." And sometimes vowels are pronounced sloppily.
It is easy for "to" and "for" to become "tuh" and "fer."
After preparing the passage, ask someone to listen
as you read the passage aloud. This input can be
extremely helpful. And yes, the critique can also be
painful, but it's for the benefit of the congregation!

Prepare the Audience to Hear the Passage

A call to hear, such as "Hear the Word of the Lord,"
will direct the attention of
the congregation to hear the
reading. The passage ought to
be mentioned at least twice,
so that those who want to
follow along can do so. Allow
time for the audience to look
up the passage. Also, *briefly* describe the context
and content of the passage, equipping the listeners to
hear and understand the message. In summary, a basic

A basic introduction for a public reading:

1. A call to hear;
2. A mention of the scriptural citation;
3. A brief description of the context and content.

introduction includes the call to hear, mention of the Scripture citation, and a brief description of the context and theme, as the example below illustrates:

> Hear the Word of God from 1 Corinthians 5:1-13. Previously in 1 Corinthians 1-4, Paul criticized the Corinthians for their factions, immaturity, and exclusion. Turning to church discipline and restoration, Paul describes yet another example of their immaturity, but now he commands them to exclude one of their number. 1 Corinthians 5:1 begins....

Provide a Conclusion

A comment, usually a blessing, at the end of the reading provides closure to the reading of the Word. For example, after the completion of the reading, the reader could say, "May God bless the reading of the Word." Obviously, this comment is but one possibility. The reader could also prompt an "Amen" from the congregation with some statement like "And the congregation said...." Congregations may also become accustomed to the practice and not require a prompt.

Enriching Worship with Scripture

Thus far, the discussion of the use of Scripture in worship has been limited to reading Scripture well in the church. The possibilities, however, are virtually endless. It is the goal of this section to present a few suggestions regarding preaching, singing, praying, presiding at the Lord's Supper, and closing a service.

Preaching

As previously mentioned, readings from Scripture can accompany and illuminate the sermon text. Some churches use a lectionary, a listing of Bible texts for each Sunday of the year. Each Sunday contains four readings—one reading each from the Old Testament, Psalms, Gospels, and Epistles. The lectionary has strengths and weaknesses. On the positive side, the lectionary covers much of the Bible and collects passages on a similar theme. This wide coverage of the canon forces preachers to go beyond their favorite texts and to address hard texts they might prefer to avoid. The collection of parallel passages aids those planning worship by providing other scriptures on the same theme. The lectionary informs the congregation in advance what scriptures will be addressed, allowing members to prepare for worship with study and prayer. Using a three-year cycle based on Matthew, Mark and Luke, the lectionary focuses on one gospel each year, resulting in a Christ-centered menu of preaching. Finally, the broad focus on both the Old and New Testament brings balance to the congregation's diet.[1]

Lectionary:
A book listing Scripture readings for each Sunday of the year.

Nevertheless, the lectionary is not without weaknesses. It does not treat some books. It does not encourage preaching through the Old Testament as much as it does the New Testament. It divides some readings in odd places and makes some questionable choices for parallel passages. Despite these problems, the lectionary still remains a wonderful resource for coordinating services around a theme and for introducing multiple readings into worship services.

The lectionary is not the only way to integrate sermons and Scripture. Some congregations coordinate the sermon texts and the Bible classes so that the Bible classes study the same passage as the preaching topic. This planning allows churches to explore Scripture more deeply, since classes bring opportunities for additional teaching, questions, and reflection.

Singing

Songs also present opportunities for Scripture to play a more formative role in the life of the congregation. Since many of the songs in our hymnals repeat the words of Scripture, or at least were inspired by passages of Scripture, congregations can easily coordinate songs and readings. Readings can either precede or follow the song. The practice can enrich both the singing and hearing of God's Word. Another option is for song leaders to comment occasionally about the biblical background of a song, providing insights and connections that some in the congregation might otherwise overlook.

Prayer

Scripture can also enrich the prayers of a congregation. It is necessary, however, for congregations to plan in advance. Those who lead a prayer must know, for instance, the theme of the service so that they can prepare their thoughts. With that information, they can reflect on that theme or text, as well as other related passages, and then incorporate the language, images, and thoughts of Scripture into the prayer of the congregation. Prayer and Scripture can coordinate in other ways as well. Congregations can pray some of the prayers in the Bible in unison. A notable example is the Lord's Prayer. Clearly, these ideas are only suggestions, representing examples of some ways that Scripture can enrich public prayers.

Lord's Supper

The Lord's Supper offers incredible opportunities for enriching worship. Although the words of institution from the Gospels or 1 Corinthians are absolutely appropriate, the richness of the themes present in the Lord's Supper opens the doors to a number of possibilities.[2] Appropriate themes include thanksgiving, covenant, remembrance, future expectation, participation, and the redeeming death of Christ. A reading of Scripture, coupled with some reflection on one of these themes, can expand and deepen the experience of the Lord's Supper. Such reflection directly connects to the meaning of the Lord's Supper. In 1 Corinthians 11:26, Paul says that as often as the church eats and drinks the Lord's Supper, it "proclaims the Lord's death." The church's reflection on the Lord's Supper should link the church's partaking of the Lord's Supper with the grand story of God's redemption, as has been mentioned in Chapter 4.

Closing the Service

To close this discussion of Scripture's use in worship, a brief mention of the practice in the congregation I now attend might provide a useful example. At the conclusion of each service, one of the elders reads a passage of Scripture. Sometimes the passage emphasizes or complements the message of the sermon or one of the songs; other times, it provides an opportunity to share a passage that addresses a concern in the congregation or that has been the topic of reflection by the elder. In any case, it conveys the importance of God's Word to the congregation, since Scripture is the last thing that the congregation hears as it leaves to begin each new week.

Biblical & Theological Literacy

Scripture should permeate the minds and lives of Christians. In the first part of this chapter, we noted various ways that Scripture could be used to enrich worship. In this next section, we explore the vital role that Scripture plays in both biblical and theological literacy and suggest ways to promote both of these types of literacy.

A Call for Biblical Literacy

I'm reminded of my experience at the Broadway Church of Christ in Lubbock, Texas. Every five year old had to know the books of the Old Testament, the books of the New Testament, the names of the twelve apostles, and the entire Twenty-third Psalm before graduating to first grade Sunday School. I remember one parent saying, "No five year old can memorize all that!" The longtime teacher responded, "Every five year old here has for the last thirty years."

—Ken

The key role that Scripture plays in the formation and spiritual life of each Christian is powerfully demonstrated in Jesus' responses to the devil in Luke 4:1-13. Each time Jesus answers, his response contains a quotation from Scripture. Jesus used Scripture as his defense in a time of temptation. It is worth noticing, however, that the devil also quotes Scripture, which points out the need for more than a superficial knowledge of God's Word.

Scripture was important in the life of Jesus (Luke 4:16-30), and it plays an integral role in the life of our congregations as well. What can we do to equip our children to love Scripture and benefit from its message? This plea is not merely a call to learn a mass of facts. As the personal reflection about my experience at the Broadway congregation in Lubbock suggests, however, memorization, or at least basic literacy, forms the foundation that permits study at a greater depth. For children, memory verses, immersion in the overarching story of God's dealing with his people, and a knowledge of some basic stories provide a necessary foundation.

225

Previous chapters in this book have shown the formational power of knowing the story of God's gracious redemption of his people. That story can be taught in a number of ways. Active learning with songs or puppets, as well as reinforcement and affirmation at home, make the tasks of learning and connecting facts fun for the entire family; Mom and Dad may even profit from a review of the order of the minor prophets! As children grow older, other opportunities like Bible Bowls arise.

What does biblical literacy look like? In broad strokes, the following represents typical objectives for different age groups. The content for younger children usually includes basic stories like Adam and Eve, Noah, and David and Goliath, as well as facts like the books of the Old and New Testament. As children progress, teachers add longer narratives like those of Joseph, David, and Jesus. In addition, students can study longer blocks of historical material like those found in Genesis, Exodus, and Acts. Eventually, students will begin to study concepts like covenant and faith. During their junior and senior high years, teens should begin to put together the flow of biblical history. Along with the capacity to think abstractly comes the study of biblical themes like grace and the church. Teachers must strive to connect these and other themes to real-life situations, modeling for the teens how to think theologically. Furthermore, as teachers connect these themes to God's story of reconciliation, a coherent theological vision emerges in the minds of the students. It is vital to discuss how to present all of these ideas in convincing and compelling ways. Before discussing the craft of teaching, however, it is necessary to explain ways to foster theological literacy.

A Call for Theological Literacy

Chapter 8 explained the need for theological literacy and issued a call to reclaim our theological heritage. It is now time to answer that call with some greater depth. How can churches teach theological literacy? To be sure, neither biblical nor theological literacy occurs by accident. Traditionally, Churches of Christ have taught biblical literacy well. Unfortunately, they have not done as well teaching *theological literacy.* Any number of examples could be explored. The following discussion uses film as a point of entry into this question.

It is likely that the average Christian can say something theological if the film retells a biblical story (for example, *The Ten Commandments*), or has an explicit reference to religion (such as *Chariots of Fire*). Likewise, if a film has a biblical idea or symbol—like angels—or treats a moral issue (like adultery in *Fatal Attraction*), then Christians can comment productively. But what about books, films, music, television shows, current events, cultural trends, or crises in our lives that neither retell a biblical story nor refer directly to religion and morality? Are they devoid of theological content? No! *Everyone* has values, presuppositions, and convictions about theological matters. It is the task of the church to help our congregations become theologically literate enough to respond substantively.

How to teach theological literacy is a huge topic; I offer a modest proposal for teaching theological literacy in our congregations. To begin with, churches need theological categories to organize their reflection. Basic theological categories such as God, Christ, Holy Spirit, sin, salvation, church, and eschatology provide the skeleton. Then, it is necessary to add "flesh" to each of these categories by discussing the typical questions associated with each topic, along with representative answers to those questions.

227

For example, previous reflection on the existence of God and the relationship between faith and reason prepares someone for a substantive discussion after viewing the movie *Contact* with a non-Christian. We could illustrate this point with a number of other topics: free will and the *Truman Show*, Christ-figures and the *Green Mile*, and theodicy and *Amadeus*.

Theodicy:

Consideration of the question, "Why does evil exist if God is all-good and all-powerful?"

Second, it is necessary to model theological reflection. Budding theologians need many examples. Those who are theologically trained can help others see the theological significance in the ordinary. For instance, a conversation at a potluck luncheon can become a reflection on "calling," and "Mrs. Smith" can see her time in the kitchen making blackberry cobbler as an expression of her God-given gifts. In Connecticut, my wife, the youth group, and I did a free car wash for the community. Because we talked beforehand about Christlike service, the youth responded with incredible insight to those in the community who were puzzled and *asked* (a nice dynamic!) *why* we would wash cars for free.

One effective way to model theological reflection is with the use of story or autobiography. Some sample anecdotes can show that even reflection on our own lives provides grist for theological reflection. The author Frederick Buechner practices this type of theological reflection well. Buechner views the ordinary events of his, or anybody's, life as potential moments of insight. He claims, "It is precisely through these stories in all their particularity, as I have long believed and often said, that God makes himself known to each of us most powerfully and personally."[3] In the same vein, Peter Hawkins claims that our lives are "a sacred text capable of revealing nothing less than divine truth."[4] By training individual members to think theologically about their own lives, we equip them to see the theological significance of their jobs and daily trials, to give but two examples.

The church will also need practice thinking theologically. Mere information cannot prepare the church for the complexities of real life. One way to access the experience and wisdom of others is through case studies. A case study recreates the events of a dilemma, usually in a page or two, and describes the parties and the conflict. One major benefit is the opportunity to consider a "sticky" problem without the cost of personally going through the dilemma. In addition, the process of discussing the problem allows the congregation to profit from the insights and experiences of others. These times of reflection are opportune moments. It is wise to introduce other theological categories (for example, creation, covenant, freedom, forgiveness), while they are immediately relevant. This practice is extremely demanding; working on an issue requires continual movement back and forth through Scripture, theology, and actual events. However, the effort is worthwhile; each journey through new passages, ideas, and events produces improved skills and insights.

Finally, the church needs a theological compass that will orient it while it journeys among an array of possible choices. When faced with excruciatingly complex situations, the church needs a sense of "true north" to guide it. What are those foundational theological commitments? We can name several. We already described the grand story of God's gracious pursuit of sinful humanity in Chapter 4. Reflection on that story brings images, themes, and examples to mind that inform and ground the church. It is necessary to add other resources previously, but briefly, mentioned in

Chapter 7, such as the greatest commandments—love of God and love of neighbor (Matt. 22:34–40). Chapter 7 also described how Scripture says that some things are more important, such as "justice, mercy, and faithfulness" (Matt. 23:23) and "righteousness, peace, and joy" (Rom. 14:17) and showed how the cross provided the lens through which Paul sought insight when facing both theological and pastoral challenges (1 Cor. 15:3–5). As the church becomes more accomplished at applying the cross to diverse situations, it will develop "the mind of Christ" (1 Cor. 2:16; Phil. 2:5).

Teaching Scripture Well

Discussing teaching brings a curious mix of sobriety and excitement, sobriety because I know that those who teach will receive a "greater judgment" (James 3:1), excitement because there is little I enjoy more than teaching. Bad teaching usually falls in one of two ditches. In one ditch, the teacher finds amazing insights and tells great stories, but hardly ever refers to Scripture. In fact, Scripture is only mentioned because the teacher feels obliged to connect the lesson to *some* passage from the Bible. In the other ditch, the teacher is incredibly well-prepared, expounding on the historical background of a passage with an impressive command of names and dates. However, the teacher is clueless when trying to answer the questions, "So what? What difference does this passage make in the way I believe or live?" Actually, the class could have stayed home and read a history book or a commentary and not lost anything. The outstanding teacher, however, is able to weave *both* research *and* application into a seamless whole.

How do churches train teachers who can perform both tasks well? Since the recipe for great teachers is one part gift and another part training, we can only focus on the training part. Because most people incline either toward the research or toward the application side, the remedy, in most cases, is to force them to have balance and ask various types of questions. One of the simplest and clearest models is that of Roberta Hestenes.[5]

Hestenes calls for teachers to ask three types of questions: observation, interpretation, and application. Observation questions help orient and inform the class. The setting, characters, structure, context, order of events, and themes are all elicited through questions to the class. The test for an observation question is, "Can the question be answered from information in the text?"

Asking good questions...

In general, teachers should avoid questions that can be answered with a simple "yes" or "no;" these kinds of questions typically do little to encourage thought or discussion. The one exception may be the "yes-or-no" question that allows the class to notice a key point, and then is immediately followed up with a "how" or "why" question.

Interpretation questions explain key terms, interpret actions, and illuminate the purpose of the author. The test for an interpretation question is, "Does the question illuminate the *meaning* of the passage?" Finally, application questions address the relevance of the passage *for today.* Application questions answer the question, "So what?"

With these basic building blocks in place, teachers should consider the flow from question to question, striving for clear transitions. Consistent attention to a theme will focus the efforts of the teacher into a coherent and compelling lesson. Finally, the teacher has to contend with the fact that some class members may come to class tired or distracted by the events of the day; in short, they may not be as attentive as they should be. Good teachers ask, "How can I make the class *want to know* about this topic?" Often a puzzling question or an activity can help focus the class on the lesson. What does such a lesson look like? As an example, consider the outline of a class on Luke 4:1-13:

The First Temptation of Jesus: Luke 4:1–13

I. Introduction

- According to a 1995 *Newsweek* poll, what percentage of adult Americans believe the devil exists? What percentage of adult Americans say they have been tempted by the devil?

II. Observation

- What is the verbal connection between Luke 4:1-13 and what precedes it (hint: look at 3:38)?
- What do we learn about Jesus and/or his situation from verses 1-2?
- What is the common feature in the first and third temptations?
- What is the connection between Luke 4:1-13 and what follows in 4:14-30?

III. Interpretation

- In 4:3, 9, does the devil question whether Jesus is the Son of God or not (note the "ifs")?
- Does the devil tell the truth in 4:6? Support your viewpoint.
- How would you characterize the three types of temptations? What is the appeal of each? What is the cost of each?
- How is the third temptation different from the first two?
- Why was the time the devil chose to tempt Jesus "opportune" (4:13)?

IV. Application

- When are you most vulnerable to temptation?
- What do you learn about resisting temptation from Jesus' responses? What helps you overcome temptation?

The Personal Use of Scripture

We conclude this chapter by describing various ways that individuals incorporate Scripture into their lives. Scripture has played a vital role in the life of God's people for centuries. Consider the words of Deuteronomy 6:4-9:

> Hear, O Israel: The Lord our God, the Lord is one. Love the Lord with all your heart and with all your soul and with all your strength. These commandments that I give you today are to be upon your hearts. Impress them on your children. Talk about them when you sit at home and when you walk along the road, when you lie down and when you get up. Tie them as symbols on your hands and bind them on your foreheads. Write them on the doorframes of your houses and on your gates. (NIV)

Christians can surround themselves with Scripture in many ways. Some attempt to read through the Bible each year using a daily schedule.

> "Train yourself in godliness."
> —*1 Timothy 4:7*

Others may read one Psalm or book each day for a week or longer, searching for greater depth and insight. For those desiring some resources to aid in intensive Bible study, a listing of recommended reference works is provided in Appendix 2. Still other Christians spend time writing down passages or committing passages to memory. A more devotional use of Scripture is the practice of *lectio divina* ("meditative reading"), in which Christians focus on contemplating and praying a passage of Scripture.[6] Some Christians find it more helpful to read with a partner or a group.

Christians can also purchase a daily calendar with a passage from the Bible. Tapes and CDs now allow those who commute to work to listen to their favorite version of the Bible, with further choices of traditional or dramatic readings. Christians can even *watch* Scripture with the *Visual Bible*—the recent videos depicting Matthew and Acts. The possibilities are about as limitless as the human imagination. Whatever option is chosen, Christians should strive to become "religious readers" not "consumerist readers."[7]

For many Christians, sustaining Bible reading proves difficult at some point. A few suggestions may be helpful from one whose commitment has waxed and waned. A planned time, place, and duration can go a long way toward helping you remain faithful. Variety can also keep things fresh. For instance, change the genre. After reading the Gospels, try Job; after a long dose of Paul's letters, Psalms may be just the right choice. Or, change the way you read Scripture, trying one of the various examples mentioned above. You should also be willing to take a planned break. Try reading a devotional writer. Music, literature, and film can also enrich your study of a book or topic.

Not every personal use of Scripture involves study or devotional reflection. Scripture also calls God's people to act. Doing must accompany hearing. Obedience not only honors God, it also transforms the doer. Christians can experience the transforming power of *doing* God's Word in innumerable ways. Serving a meal to the homeless, teaching a class of fourth graders,

Two types of readers...

Consumerist readers are interested primarily in moving quickly from one text to the next in search of things that will excite, titillate, entertain, empower, and give them some advantage over others.

Religious readers, on the other hand, assume they have come into the presence of a text with inexhaustible depth. They read with reverence, humility, obedience, and the presumption that difficulty in understanding reveals more about their limitations than the excellence or effectiveness of the text. Religious readers incorporate, internalize, and memorize texts. They read slowly, hoping not to miss anything adopting an unwanted child, building a house in Haiti or in inner-city Houston—all these activities, and more,

"Be doers of the word, and not hearers only, deceiving yourselves."

—*James 1:22*

provide opportunities for God to shape his people. These opportunities are often times of struggle and growth, providing insight into the nature of God and illuminating one's own strengths and weaknesses.

Conclusion

What the church does with Scripture will have an enormous impact on the church. Our worship services and our Bible classes will shape our children and our churches. Our choices can foster a love of Scripture and sound training in God's Word. Equally important, our decisions will determine whether our churches are shaped by the story of God's grace and equipped for the challenges of our culture. In other words, our decisions will affect our identity and our ability to respond to significant issues. Without the ability to engage our culture, the church will only seem more and more irrelevant to those outside the church.

Fortunately, the opportunities are great. Strong biblical preaching and Bible study still abide in our congregations, as much as in any Christian fellowship. A hunger for God's Word still exists in our culture. But the study of the Bible must address the issues of real life that only careful examination and theological reflection bring out. To those hungering and thirsting for meaning, the church tells the story of the cross and embodies cross-shaped lives. Shaped by the cross and equipped with the Word, the church can again "turn the world upside down." 🍃

235

10
An Ending—And a Beginning

In writing this book, we have attempted to communicate our love for both Scripture and the churches
that can experience transformation through its pages.
We believe that playing off the Spirit against the text as
many of us have done poses the problem in the wrong
way. Just as rigidity and sectarianism do not mark a
person as a faithful Christian, neither does a refusal to
submit to the voice of Scripture mark one as a spiritual
person. God's Spirit can work through all the manifold
experiences, emotions (negative as well as positive),
and thoughts that faithful people have. At the same time,
God is not bound to our conceptions or experiences, but
is free to act in surprising and redemptive ways.

The Bible tells the story of this redemption—past,
present, and future. It also records the paradox of
human response to the story: we long to hear its words
and make them our own; yet we fear them as well,
because they demand nothing less than our hearts,
souls, minds, and strength.

The Bible's words do not lie sleeping on sheets of
paper, but, like holy fire, burn their way into the hearts
and minds of those readers who hear them in humble
faith, with an inquiring mind. We have written this
book because we believe that what our congregations
need now are not fancier church growth formulas, more

clever pastoral gimmicks, or more ornate and inviting sanctuaries. Rather, we need to hear once again those words that speak to our deepest needs, that challenge our comfortable illusions about ourselves, and that force us to ask questions about life and death, heaven and hell.

The unleashing of Scripture will draw Christians into worship that depends less on ourselves and more on God. Shaped by our stories, songs, proverbs, letters, and apocalypses, churches will become stronger witnesses to what God does among them. We will offer a clearer voice against injustice and hate, even when they cloak themselves in the language of faith. God's Spirit will use Scripture to equip the church, not merely a few members of a class of professional clergy, to serve the God who has called us all to be a kingdom of priests.

Our Plea

In this book, we have attempted several things, all in extremely abbreviated form. Much more deserves to be said. But we trust that this book, despite its inadequacies, will stimulate much more thinking across the church, in America and beyond.

We have argued that all of Scripture should become a source of moral guidance and theological insight in the life of the church, the Old Testament as well as the New. Reclaiming the *entire* Bible will enrich our understanding of the nature and activities of God. It will deepen our comprehension of our obligations to other human beings, giving us the resources for overcoming the extreme individualism and materialism that corrupts our culture. It will supply us with the language and concepts for making sense of life and death, suffering and pleasure, the presence and apparent absence of God. In short, God in Scripture will lead Christians far deeper into the real world than we can go through any other avenue. While so much contemporary religious literature seems calculated to encourage prosperous Christians to escape any concern with the painful reality that many of our fellow human beings face, Scripture itself brings us back to earth, showing us God's hand in redeeming a world fit to house the incarnate Son of God amid the poorest of Israel.

We have also tried to indicate some practical ways in which churches can enhance the reading and study of the Bible, and thereby can enrich the spiritual lives of people. We know from experience that these suggestions, some basic and others more difficult, will gradually work to draw all the church into the enriching process of Bible study in ways that are spiritually and psychologically healthy for all the body of Christ.

Finally, we have tried to reorient our study of the Bible. We do not study Scripture in church solely in order to arrive at the right answers to our preconceived questions. We do not pose the question, for example, "What organization must we have in our congregation?" and then go hunting down verses that seem to give us an answer, even if the texts from which they come show little interest in our question. Rather, we listen to the voices in Scripture, making its questions our own. Thus we learn in Deuteronomy about loyalty to God's calling, in Amos about compassion for the poor and restraint in our acquisition of wealth, in Matthew about keeping the heart of *Torah* as well as its letter, in Romans about living in response to abounding grace, in Revelation about serving faithfully in the shadow of the Second Coming, and so on.

We can discover the power that comes when, though we do not know the answer to every imaginable question, we trust that the God who created our beautifully complex world knows more than we. Someday our faith will become sight. But not here, not now. Until it does,

239

we learn what we can together and commit ourselves to be the people God is calling us to be.

These are some of the goals that this book aims to accomplish. We have written it for a worldwide communion that we cherish, from all of whose members we hope to learn, with all of whom we pray to grow in ever-deeper fellowship.

Speaking Always Anew

Ours is a time of momentous opportunity and breathtaking change. In such a time most of all, Christians must concentrate on the resource that most fully reveals God's work in the world, Scripture. This time of change offers us virtually unprecedented opportunities for growth in our comprehension of the Word of God, and thus for our growth as the people God calls us to be.

Over the past century, Churches of Christ have grown from a small group, mostly in the southern United States, to a worldwide movement. Indeed, a slight majority of this fellowship now lives outside the United States. Its centers of growth and vitality lie in Africa and other parts of the Third World. The implications of this change for the spiritual lives of American Christians, and even for our interpretation of Scripture, have just begun to make themselves felt. Those of us who have taught, and learned from, students from the so-called developing world can attest to the profound limits that the American experience imposes on us in reading the Bible. African brothers and sisters deepen our understanding of the family dynamics in the Old and New Testaments. Koreans remind us of the depth of the image of God as father. Those from the former Soviet bloc help us appreciate more the struggles with the powers that be that lie behind Daniel and Revelation. And on the list goes. God is blessing us with a broader circle of the sanctified who can teach us more than we have experienced before.

The era when the Christian story dominated Western culture has ended. Today, our story must stand on its own merits. Habit and custom no longer serve to prop it up. This new reality, however difficult to accept, should excite Christians because it means that the pure story itself can live free from the additions we have laid upon it. At our best in the American Restoration Movement, we have pled for just such a return to Scripture, not as a blueprint for church organization, but as a model for a theologically informed, morally robust, sacrificial life of the entire people of God. At this moment, our plea seems more vital than ever.

Ours is an era seeking spiritual meaning. We in the church can return to our roots in Scripture to seek there the true spiritual depth that one finds, not by looking in the mirror of our own souls, but into the very face of God. For too long, churches have exhausted their spiritual and physical resources merely by meeting felt needs, neglecting the innermost need that all human beings share, the lifesaving encounter with the God whom Scripture reveals. Now we are free to seek not merely a better marriage or better friendships, indispensable as those are, but God—and thereby ourselves.

Now we stand at the threshold of a new era, full of challenges and opportunities. Now we hold in our hands the guide by which Christians of every age, every place, and every culture have negotiated change before. We hear in Scripture the words of the One who does not change, whose Word remains forever. A holy fire lights the way from this world to the next. Equipped for the journey, let us join the company of saints, apostles, prophets, and martyrs who tread the path. With them, let us hear the ancient words that speak always anew. ✺

Notes

Chapter 1

1. Stanley Hauerwas, *A Community of Character* (Notre Dame: University of Notre Dame Press, 1981), 14–22.
2. N. T. Wright, *The New Testament and the People of God* (Minneapolis: Fortress, 1992), 123.

Chapter 2

1. Bruce Metzger, *The Canon of the New Testament: Its Origin, Development, and Significance* (Oxford: Clarendon, 1987), 107.
2. Raymond F. Collins, "Inspiration," *The New Jerome Bible Commentary*. Ed. Raymond E. Brown, Joseph A. Fitzmeyer, and Roland F. Murphy (Upper Saddle River, NJ: Prentice Hall, 1990), 1027.

Chapter 3

1. In rabbinic literature, see *t. Sanhedrin* 12.10; *b. Sanhedrin* 101a.
2. St. Justin Martyr, "The First and Second Apologies." Trans. Leslie William Barnard. *Ancient Christian Writers* 56 (New York: Paulist, 1997), ¶67.
3. N. B. Hardeman, *Hardeman's Tabernacle Sermons* (reprint ed.; Henderson, TN: Freed-Hardeman University, 1990), 38–9.

4. For more on this verse, see E. K. Simpson and F. F. Bruce, *Commentary on the Epistles to the Ephesians and the Colossians* (Grand Rapids: Eerdmans, 1957), 237-9. See also Markus Barth and Helmut Blanke, *Colossians*, Anchor Bible 34b (New York: Doubleday, 1994), 369-72.
5. Krister Stendahl, *Meanings: The Bible as Document and as Guide* (Philadelphia: Fortress, 1984), 68.

Chapter 4
1. James Sanders, *From Sacred Story to Sacred Text* (Philadelphia: Fortress, 1987), 67.
2. Robert Jenson, "How the World Lost its Story," *First Things* (October 1993), 22. See also Jenson's "Can We Have a Story?" *First Things* (March 2000), 17.

Chapter 5
1. David Weiss Halivni, *The Book and the Sword: A Life of Learning in the Shadow of Destruction* (New York: Farrar, Straus, Giroux, 1996), 69.
2. For a classic scholarly treatment of the shape of the Pentateuch as a whole, see Martin Noth, *A History of the Pentateuchal Traditions* (Atlanta: Scholars, 1981). More recently, see Joseph Blankinsopp, *The Pentateuch* (New York: Doubleday, 1992).
3. David Noel Freedman, *Psalm 119: The Exaltation of Torah* (Winona Lake, IN: Eisenbrauns, 1999), 89.
4. "Chapters of the Fathers." ("Pirqe Avot"), 2.
5. Ambrose Bierce, *The Collected Works of Ambrose Bierce*. Vol. 7: *The Devil's Dictionary* (New York: Gordian, 1967), 297.

Chapter 6
1. James Kugel. *The Great Poems of the Bible* (New York: Free Press, 1999), 36.

2. On Paul as a letter writer, see William G. Doty, *Letters in Primitive Christianity* (Philadelphia: Fortress, 1973). See also Jerome Murphy-O'Connor, *Paul the Letter-Writer: His World, His Opinions, His Skills* (Collegeville, MN: Liturgical, 1995).

Chapter 7

1. See Eusebius. *Ecclesiastical History* 6.8. See also Daniel B. Wallace, *Greek Grammar Beyond the Basics* (Grand Rapids: Zondervan, 1996), 681; and *Newsweek* (October 11, 1993), 27.

2. Story told by David Denby, *Great Books: My Adventures with Homer, Rousseau, Woolf, and Other Indestructible Writers of the Western World* (New York: Simon & Schuster, 1996), 40-2.

3. For further discussion, see Richard B. Hays, *The Moral Vision of the New Testament: A Contemporary Introduction to New Testament Ethics* (New York: HarperCollins, 1996), 208-9.

4. John R. Kohlenberger III, *Words about the Word: A Guide to Choosing and Using Your Bible* (Grand Rapids: Zondervan, 1987), 60-1. Kohlenberger cites a 1978 study by Drs. Linda Parrish and Donna Norton. Gratitude goes to Ken Berry of the World Bible Translation Center for calculating the reading levels of the NIrV, CEV, *Message*, NLT, and NRSV.

5. Gordon D. Fee and Douglas Stuart, *How to Read the Bible for All Its Worth*. 2nd ed. (Grand Rapids: Zondervan, 1993), 37.

6. See Mark 3:19b-35; 6:7-30; 11:12-21; 14:1-11; 14:53-72; 15:40-16:8, and perhaps also 4:1-20 and 14:17-31. For a helpful article on this topic, see James R. Edwards, "Markan Sandwiches: The Significance of Interpolations in Markan Narratives" *Novum Testamentum* 31 (1989), 193-216.

7. Quoted in *The Act of Bible Reading*. Ed. Elmer Dyck (Downers Grove, IL: InterVarsity, 1996), 30.

245

Chapter 8

1. For a great discussion on this point, see Eugene Lowery, "Surviving the Sermon Preparation Process" *Journal for Preachers* 24.3 (2001), 30.

2. Allen Verhey, "Praying with Dirty Hands" *From Christ to the World: Introductory Readings in Christian Ethics.* Ed. W. Boulton, T. Kenney, and A. Verhey (Grand Rapids: Eerdmans, 1994), 400–3.

3. Some of these questions are modified from, but inspired by, Richard B. Hays, *The Moral Vision of the New Testament: A Contemporary Introduction to New Testament Ethics* (New York: HarperCollins, 1996), 193–200.

4. Quote from Carl Holladay, "Shaped by the Cross," Pepperdine Lectures, 2001.

5. Note the discussions of several religious traditions of communal discernment in Ruth Fletcher, *Take, Break, Receive: The Practice of Discernment in the Christian Church (Disciples of Christ)* (Indianapolis: Homeland Ministries, 1999), 6–8. The quotation of the Ignatian Model is from page 7.

6. Nicholas Lash; quoted in Stephen E. Fowl, *Engaging Scripture: A Model for Theological Interpretation* (Malden, MA: Blackwell, 1998), 163.

Chapter 9

1. *The Revised Common Lectionary: Consultation on Common Texts* (Nashville: Abingdon, 1992), 9–10.

2. I draw here on a lecture on the Lord's Supper by Abraham Malherbe.

3. Frederick Buechner, *Telling Secrets* (New York: HarperCollins, 1991), 30.

4. Peter Hawkins and Paula Carlson, eds., *Listening to God: Contemporary Literature and the Life of Faith.* Minneapolis (Augsburg Fortress, 1994), 37.

5. Roberta Hestenes, *Using the Bible in Groups* (Philadelphia: Westminster, 1983). See especially

pages 57–75. For more on Hestenes' model, see the example later in this chapter and the template in Appendix 3.

6. For a more extensive description of *lectio divina* with an example, see Marjorie J. Thompson, *Soul Feast: An Invitation to the Christian Spiritual Life* (Louisville: Westminster John Knox, 1995), 17–30.

7. Frederick Niedner, "Forming Students through the Bible: Ground Zero" *Christian Century* (April 18–25, 2001), 19. Niedner draws on the insights of Paul J. Griffiths for this quotation.

Appendix 1:
How to Build a Library

Brevard Childs, one of my Old Testament professors, offered some helpful advice on building a library. With thanks to him and with my own modifications, I pass on his advice.

—Ken

Plan Your Library

Many poor purchases result from impulse buying. Buyers should be able to name their next three purchases.

Purchase Reference Works First

Almost everyone is tempted to buy the book that looks interesting or will help in teaching a lesson or series; those kinds of purchases have their place. However, their usefulness usually ends after one reading. Reference works have continued value and promote further growth. The first tier of reference works should include: a good study Bible, several translations, a concordance, a Bible dictionary, and a synopsis of the Gospels. A synopsis shows the particular emphases of each gospel writer; it differs from a "harmony of the Gospels," which mixes the gospel accounts together.

After this first tier of reference works, buy commentaries on the most-studied books of the Bible. Thus, the first two commentaries should probably be ones covering Genesis and one of the Gospels, with special preference to Matthew, Mark, or Luke, since they overlap so much. Purchase both detailed and quick reference books, since sometimes depth is necessary, and other times a quick answer suffices.

Avoid Buying a Complete Commentary Series

Resist temptation again. Many people are tempted to buy a whole set of commentaries. Unfortunately, from any one series, you will usually get from three to six quality volumes for each testament. Instead, plunder the best ones from each commentary series. The dust jackets may not match, but you will definitely be more satisfied in the long run.

Consider Buying from the Internet & Second-hand Bookstores

The most cost-effective purchases come from used bookstores. For instance, such stores often sell many different translations at minimal cost. Real "finds" come to those who frequent these stores regularly, such as weekly. Other "finds" make it to the Internet—see <www.abebooks.com> and <www.ebay.com>. To browse a wide selection of books and Bibles, see <www.christianbooks.com>. Try <www.bestwebbuys.com>, which searches the web for the lowest price and which is usually 30–50% less than the local bookstore. You may, however, wish to support the local economy, not wish to pay shipping, or need the book immediately; if that is the case, local bookstores often have the desired volume.

Strive for Balance

Despite the previous emphasis on reference books, a good library needs a variety of works. Seek out quality devotional books, as well as those that focus on theology, history, and literature. Introductions to devotional books and recommended devotional books are found in the Recommended Reading at the end of this volume.

Examine the Book or Ask Someone Knowledgeable Before Buying It

You will save dollars and heartache if you use a book before you purchase it. You can borrow it, check it out from the library, or read a section while standing in the bookstore. In the absence of such direct access, seek out someone knowledgeable or read a review; *Leaven*, for example, consistently reviews books on particular biblical books or topics. By taking these precautions, you can save yourself from a book that is either too technical or too shallow.

Have a Loan Policy

Be generous and allow others to use your books. However, you may avoid buying the same book again if you write down the borrower's name and loan the book for a specific time period. With all this discussion about building a library, some individuals and churches may want to begin immediately! In Appendix 2, we provide a list of recommended reference works.

Appendix 2:
Recommended Reference Works

Though we do not agree with everything in each book listed below, we think that the following recommendations will help those searching for a book from one of these subject areas.

Study Bibles

HarperCollins Study Bible (NRSV). Revised ed. San Francisco: HarperCollins, 1993.

NIV Study Bible. Ed. Kenneth Barker. Grand Rapids: Zondervan, 1995.

Translations

The Complete Parallel Bible (NRSV, REB, NAB, NJB). New York: Oxford UP, 1993.

The Contemporary Parallel New Testament (KJV, NASB, NIV, NLT, NCV, CEV, NKJV, Message). Ed. John R. Kohlenberger III. New York: Oxford UP, 1997.

Eight Translation New Testament (KJV, LB, Phillips, RSV, TEV, NIV, JB, NEB). Wheaton, IL: Tyndale House, 1974.

Today's Parallel Bible (KJV, NIV, NLT, NASB). Grand Rapids: Zondervan, 2000.

Concordances

Goodrick, E. W. and John R. Kohlenberger, III, eds. *NIV Exhaustive Concordance.* Grand Rapids: Zondervan, 1990.

Strong, J., ed. *Exhaustive Concordance of the Bible* (KJV). Iowa Falls, IA: World Bible Publishers, 1986.

Whitaker, R. E. and J. E. Goehring, eds. *Eerdmans Analytical Concordance to the Revised Standard Version of the Bible.* Grand Rapids: Eerdmans, 1988.

Whitaker, R. E. and John R. Kohlenberger, III, eds. *Analytical Concordance to the New Testament: New Revised Standard Version.* Grand Rapids: Eerdmans, 2000.

Young, R., ed. *Analytical Concordance to the Bible* (KJV). Nashville: Thomas Nelson, 1982.

Dictionaries

Anchor Bible Dictionary. Ed. D. L. Freedman. New York: Doubleday, 1992.

Civilizations of the Ancient Near East. Ed. Jack Sasson. Peabody, MA: Hendrickson, 2000.

Dictionary of Paul and His Letters. Ed. G. Hawthorne and R. Martin. Downers Grove, IL: InterVarsity, 1993.

Dictionary of Jesus and the Gospels. Ed. J. Green and S. McKnight. Downers Grove, IL: InterVarsity, 1992.

Eerdmans Dictionary of the Bible. Ed. D. N. Freedman. Grand Rapids: Eerdmans, 2000.

HarperCollins Bible Dictionary. Revised ed. Ed. P. J. Achtemeier. New York: Harper-Collins, 1996.

Mercer Dictionary of the Bible. Ed. W. E. Mills. Macon, GA: Mercer UP, 1990.

Synopses

Endres, John, et al. *Chronicles and Its Synoptic Parallels in Samuel, Kings, and Related Texts.* Collegeville, MN: Liturgical Press, 1998.

Synopsis of the Four Gospels. Ed. K. Aland. Stuttgart: United Bible Societies, 1995.

Bible Study

Fee, Gordon and Douglas Stuart. *How to Read the Bible for All Its Worth.* 2nd ed. Grand Rapids: Zondervan, 1993.

Atlases

Pritchard, J. B., ed. *Harper Concise Atlas of the Bible.* San Francisco: HarperSanFrancisco, 1997.

Backgrounds

Dictionary of New Testament Backgrounds. Ed. C. Evans and S. Porter. Downers Grove, IL: InterVarsity, 2000.

Ferguson, Everett. *Backgrounds of Early Christianity.* 2nd ed. Grand Rapids: Eerdmans, 1993.

Harrington, D. *Invitation to the Apocrypha.* Grand Rapids: Eerdmans, 1999.

Mazar, Amihai. *Archaeology of the Land of the Bible, 10,000–586 B.C.E.* New York: Doubleday, 1990.

Stern, Ephraim. *Archaeology of the Land of the Bible: The Assyrian, Babylonian, and Persian Periods, 732-332 B.C.E.* New York: Doubleday, 2001.

History of Interpretation

Kugel, James. *The Bible As It Was.* Cambridge, MA: Harvard UP, 1997.

Kugel, James and Rowen Greer. *Early Biblical Interpretation.* Philadelphia: Westminster, 1986.

Textual Criticism

A Textual Commentary on the Greek New Testament. Ed. B. Metzger. Stuttgart: United Bible Societies, 1998.

Introductions to the New Testament

Johnson, L. T. *The Writings of the New Testament: An Introduction.* Revised ed. Minneapolis: Fortress, 1999.

Commentary Series

Berit Olam (Old Testament). Ed. Jerome T. Walsh, et al. Collegeville, MN: Liturgical Press.

Interpretation: A Bible Commentary for Preaching and Teaching. Ed. James L. Mayes, et al. Louisville: Westminster/John Knox.

Sacra Pagina (New Testament). Ed. Daniel J. Harrington. Collegeville, MN: Liturgical Press.

Word Biblical Commentary. Ed. David A. Hubbard, et al. Dallas: Word.

Appendix 3:
Template for Bible Study

In preparing to lead a discussion about a passage of Scripture, you might find the following template helpful. As a general rule, avoid questions that can be answered with a simple "yes" or "no." Assuming that you've read the description of Hestenes' model in Chapter 9, now create a flow from question to question (and section to section), asking penetrating questions from each of the three types of questions (observation, interpretation, and application). Strive for faithfulness to a theme in the text. Ask at least three observation questions, three interpretation questions, and one application question.

Text
1 Corinthians 11:2-16 (for example).

Hook
How you are going to introduce the class to the text? How are you going to make someone want to know what you are about to teach? You can begin with an arresting question or an activity. State the question or describe the activity.

257

Observation

Ask questions that introduce the class to the basic facts needed for an understanding of the text.

1.
2.
3.
4.

Interpretation

Interpretation questions explain key terms, interpret actions, and illuminate the purpose of the author.

1.
2.
3.
4.

Application

Tell how this passage is relevant for today. Answer the question, "So what?"

1.
2.

Study Guide

Introduction

This guide has three sections. Discussion questions for each chapter are designed to assist readers in processing the material in the book as well as to challenge them to deeper reflection and prayer. These questions can be used by individuals to enhance personal insight or by groups in various settings to improve sharing and discussion.

The congregational scenarios offer readers an opportunity to explore the implications of *God's Holy Fire* in true-to-life situations. Discussion questions are included for each scenario to assist people in probing the issues presented in them. The scenarios also provide models for individuals or churches to use in framing some of their own unique situations and to see how the material from the book might be used to address them.

Finally, the case study and teaching notes provide readers a chance to enter the biblical world through fictional characters to discuss issues of biblical interpretation vital to the community of faith then and now. This particular case, "The Strong Ought to Bear With the Weak," is based on Paul's teachings in Romans 14 and 15. For further information about case teaching, the Association for Case Teaching offers a useful website at <www.caseteaching.org>.

—Jeanene Reese & Tim Sensing

Chapter Discussion Questions

Chapter 1

For Study & Analysis:

1. In your experience, have members of Churches of Christ in recent years been more inclined to study popular Christian literature in Bible classes, workshops, and retreats than to study just the text of the Bible itself? If so, what do you think are the reasons behind these inclinations? What are the results? What, if any, changes would you like to see made in these areas? Share specific examples that support your response.

2. Describe what you think biblical literacy would look like in today's world. Do you agree with the assertion in *God's Holy Fire* that the Bible is still prominent in many parts of our culture, yet Christians today are less biblically literate than in the past? Why or why not? Share specific examples that support your case.

3. The authors assert that the loss of knowledge of biblical stories reflects the loss of "vitally important memories of who we are." How do you think the "Back to the Bible" emphasis in the Restoration Movement made Scripture central to our identity? How does your understanding of the current identity crisis in Churches of Christ confirm or challenge that idea? Do you think our present self-understandings in Churches of Christ still emphasize Scripture as key to who we are? Explain your response.

4. What are the ways that Scripture is described as "useful for teaching"? In your opinion, are some of these more important than others? If so, which ones and why?

5. How is Scripture useful for "rebuking and correcting"? Why is this function of the Bible so difficult for some modern Christians to face? How can Christians reclaim this important use of Scripture without the abuses that have often gone along with it?

6. Describe how studying promotes "training in righteousness." Where do you see this function of Scripture most needed among Christians today?

7. The authors state: "Throughout the history of Christianity, moments of renewal have been preceded by the rediscovery of the Word of God. Few people doubt that the current period of secularization has confronted the church with a special challenge. The church will be tempted to respond to a general resistance to the Bible by placing Scripture at the margins of our lives" (p. 22). Do you agree or disagree with these statements? Explain your response. What place do you think Scripture is likely to take in your congregation? Why do you think the church will make this choice?

For Reflection & Prayer:

1. Reflect on the current ways the Bible is used in your local congregation in each of the following contexts: Children's classes; Adult classes; Worship; Congregational decision-making; Personal decisions.

2. What does this reflection say about your church's strengths in use of Scripture or its need to rediscover the Bible?

3. Read Deut. 4:9-10, Exod. 12:26, and Josh. 4:16. What questions do your children ask about your faith and practice? How do the authors suggest we respond to them?

4. How do you think reclaiming God's Word could renew your congregation?

Chapter 2

For Study & Analysis:

1. In what ways do people in Churches of Christ hold a high view of Scripture? How have we lived as a people under the Word of God? How is this similar or different from the experiences of believers in past centuries?

2. List six factors from the chapter that show the human element in the transmission of the Bible. Which of these elements has the most potential to challenge your faith in Scripture and why? Which most strengthens your confidence in Scripture and why?

3. How do you understand the term "inerrant"? Why do you think this term is useful or misleading in the current discussions? What do you think is generally believed in our churches concerning inspiration? Read Luke 1:1-4 and describe the view of inspiration that emerges from Luke's self-description in this passage.

4. Christians at various times in history have tried to harmonize the Gospels by giving the church a simple chronological document that smooths away apparent discrepancies

in the accounts. Why are we drawn to these harmonies or parallels? What do you think might be lost in such an endeavor? What possible fallacies undergird such an attempt?

5. What do the authors mean when they say "the Bible [is] more in danger from its friends than its enemies" (p. 43)? Do you agree or disagree with this statement and why?

6. The authors assert that the Bible is "occasional" in nature. That is, each book addresses particular situations and times. With this in mind, are there contemporary issues that are not addressed directly by Scripture? Give some examples. How does the church discern God's intention on these matters?

For Reflection & Prayer:

1. How has the discussion presented in this chapter enhanced your appreciation of Scripture as the Word of God?

2. Why do you think it is important for the church to participate in discussions about inspiration? What are the potential gains? What are the risks?

3. Spend time in prayer for your congregation.

Chapter 3

For Study & Analysis:

1. What do the authors mean by the statement, "a hole exists in the Bible"? How do they suggest it be filled? Why do you think it is important for *all* of Scripture to play a role in the canon?

2. If many in Churches of Christ have previously dismissed the Old Testament in inappropriate

ways, what would be a more appropriate way to understand the differences between the covenants? Why do you think the Old Testament is vital to the Christian faith? Identify specific ways that you think the Old Testament could enrich church life today.

3. In his writings from the second century, Justin Martyr affirms the place of the Old Testament in Christian worship. On a scale of 1 to 5 (1 = low, 5 = high), how effective do you think Justin's strategy might be for churches trying to reclaim the effectiveness of the Old Testament today? Explain your response.

4. Identify the "bedrock tenets of the Christian message" outlined by N. B. Hardeman in his second sermon in 1922. What effect did his view and use of Scripture have on the understanding of the Bible in Churches of Christ? Why do the authors of *God's Holy Fire* think these views need to be re-examined? Do you agree or disagree with them, and why?

5. What sermons have you heard or known about in recent years that have had a similar impact on how we understand and use Scripture in Churches of Christ? Describe why you think these recent sermons were so significant.

6. Why do the authors think the Old Testament needs to have a more important place in the canon? What do they mean when they claim the biblical canon does not provide "a single fixed perspective?" How do multiple perspectives from the canon especially benefit Christians today?

7. The concept of humans made in "the image of God" found in Genesis 1:26–27 is central to our understanding of who we are and how he made us. Evaluate what you think would happen to our perception of God and of ourselves if we did not have the Old Testament as a backdrop against which to examine the concept of the "image of God."

8. Read Colossians 1:15–23 and 3:1–10. If our understanding of the "image of God" came only from a synthesis of these New Testament passages, what would that image look like?

9. From this exercise, discuss why you think both testaments are vital for a fuller sense of what it means for human beings to be created in the "image of God."

For Reflection & Prayer:

1. What do you think would happen at your church if the Old Testament were given a more prominent place? What adjustments would have to be made?

2. How do you think greater respect for and involvement with the Old Testament might enhance your church's understanding and appreciation for the New Testament?

3. Reflect on the authors' assertion that on key issues the Bible speaks with one voice, while on other issues it has more than one perspective. How does this statement challenge or aid the church seeking to determine what issues are most central to the Christian faith?

4. Share the prayer concerns that grow out of what you have read in this chapter.

Chapter 4

For Study & Analysis:

1. What effect do stories have on our lives? How do they shape community? What happens when we no longer have stories to live by? How has the biblical story affected the way your congregational history is told? Give examples of the importance of story in your community of faith.

2. What do you think the authors mean when they say Israel had a portable faith? How was this phenomenon influenced by the nation's story? Why do you think churches often relegate the telling of the biblical stories to children and not adults? What are the common results of this practice?

3. How did the recitation of Israel's story affect its worship? How are these practices similar to or different from the way early Christians participated in baptism? in the Lord's Supper? What is significant about grounding our religious practices in their biblical roots? How does this grounding tie us to the larger story of faith?

4. Why is it important to understand the larger narrative of Scripture? What difference does this perspective have on the way we view the smaller stories in the Bible? According to the authors, how are believers potentially affected by the biblical story? Think of other ways we might be personally affected by the stories of Scripture. Describe a time when a story of Scripture affected your faith.

5. What rules about biblical narrative can help readers better enter the story? Why is each

of these rules critical to avoiding either over-
or under-interpretation of the texts? What
do you think happens when Christians find
themselves located in the biblical story?

6. The authors remind us that the biblical story
gives us a new way of looking at the world. How
did ancient believers live in a way that reflected
this understanding? How should this perspective
affect the way we live our lives today?

7. Examine the sermons and speeches in
Acts (2:14-40; 3:11-26; 4:8-12; 7:1-53;
13:13-42; 17:22-34; 22:1-22; 24:10-21;
26:1-29; 28:17-29). How do these sermons
retell the biblical story?

8. Look more closely at the "word of exhortation" in Acts 13:15. In 13:16-37, Paul retells
the stories, citing various examples from the
Old Testament. He draws a conclusion in
13:38-39. Finally, Paul exhorts his audience
to respond in 13:40-41. Can you find this
pattern elsewhere in Scripture? Would this
pattern serve as an appropriate model to
imitate for classes and sermons in the 21st
century? Why or why not?

For Reflection & Prayer:

1. What does it mean for you personally that we
as readers of Scripture are "the next chapter
of the story"? How are the heroes of faith
counting on us?

2. How prepared are you and your congregation
to live out the end of the biblical story? What
can we do to prepare ourselves better for
waiting until the Lord delivers all that he
has promised?

3. Reflect on how your own life has or has not been a faithful continuation of the biblical story. In what areas do you need to trust God more?

4. Spend time in prayer about meaningful ways your community of faith can continue to live out God's story and tell it to others.

Chapter 5

For Study & Analysis:

1. Why is it important to understand "what the Bible does and how it does it" in order to reach the depths of Scripture? What does it mean for the text to form a society of readers who can live by faith?

2. The authors differentiate between the terms history and story. Evaluate the distinction.

3. Why do you think they spend so much time retelling the story? As you read through their review of the biblical story, what discoveries did you make?

4. Summarize in 2-3 sentences what you understand to be the primary purpose of each of the following: The Pentateuch; The Deuteronomistic History; Chronicles, Ezra, Nehemiah; Ruth and Esther; The Gospels; Acts of the Apostles.

5. How does knowing the primary purpose of each of these books of the Bible, enable you to read them for greater insight and application? What effect does this knowledge have on how you might teach from these works?

6. What a text says and what a text does (its content and function) are intimately con-

nected. What happens when content and function are separated? What if Proverbs were read as a law code? What if Revelation were read as prediction of the distant future instead of as apocalyptic literature? Think of other examples you would like to examine.

7. What distinctions are the authors making between the Gospels as biography or theology? Do you think this distinction undermines the historical value of the events recorded in these books? What distinct theological perspective does each of the Gospels present?

8. How does knowing the theological perspective of each Gospel affect the following: Answering why there are four different Gospels. Reading, applying, and teaching the message of each Gospel.

9. How does the authors' explanation of how to read Law allow these texts to take on new meaning for believers today? Give a few examples. What insights have you gained about the nature of God from this discussion on the Law?

10. Many people remember the stories of the Bible from Sunday School or Vacation Bible School. We also use Bible stories to make moral conclusions or specific applications for daily living. How does the authors' retelling of the story differ from the way you have frequently heard them told? Are these differences significant? What do you learn from this retelling?

For Reflection & Prayer:

1. Read Hebrews 8:6-13 and 9:15. Review the authors' discussion on cult and covenant in the chapter. Share the insights that come

from these texts when you apply what the authors have said.

2. If you were asked to teach an overview of the entire Bible to a seventh grade class on Wednesday nights at your church, what insights from this chapter would you use to help them understand Scripture?

3. Reflect on how the material from this chapter might potentially change the way your church does Bible study. What effect do you think these changes might have on your personal life of study?

4. Spend time in prayer about both your church and home Bible study.

Chapter 6

For Study & Analysis:

1. In what ways do you think Scripture connects to the deepest aspirations and hopes of human beings? Describe specific examples of times you have made these kinds of connections.

2. How does it help readers to know that much of the material in the prophets is arranged thematically rather than chronologically? Why is this understanding helpful in recovering the theology of each book?

3. According to the authors, what three major concerns primarily occupy the writings of the prophets? How are these issues still pertinent to believers today? What effect does this understanding have on how we read the prophets?

4. Describe how understanding the various types of poetry in the Psalms helps readers

use them in worship. How has their collection into a larger whole (the Psalter) benefitted believers? What effect does looking at the larger context of the Psalter have on the reading of each individual psalm?

5. What specific value does Wisdom Literature contribute to a life of faith? What challenges or discoveries might result from reading Proverbs? Job? Ecclesiastes?

6. Why are apocalypses difficult to read and understand? What benefits would readers gain from a better understanding of the purpose of these works?

7. Why is knowledge of the nature of ancient letters helpful in reading the epistles? How does an understanding of the specific occasion of each letter affect its impact? What larger concerns become evident when reading the epistles? What is the relationship between the Christian message given to the early church and the message of the *Torah* (pp. 150-1)?

8. It is often said that Psalm 88 contains no hope. Is such a psalm ever appropriate for the work and ministry of the church? If so, how and when? If not, why not? What is lost when imprecatory psalms (psalms that display frustration toward God) are not utilized in the life of the church?

For Reflection & Prayer:

1. What happens to believers when we pay attention to the multiple voices of Scripture? How does this attention point to one cardinal Truth?

2. Reflect on how Scripture brings us a vision of the consummation of the ages. How are

you challenged to grow spiritually from this reflection?

3. Spend time in prayer about your personal and communal study of God's Word.

Chapter 7

For Study & Analysis:

1. What four reasons do the authors cite as to why Scripture can be difficult to understand? Which of these reasons is most challenging to you and why?

2. Eastern European Churches ask Western Churches to justify their disregard for a direct command concerning the holy kiss (Rom. 16:16; 1 Pet. 5:14; 1 Thess. 5:26; 1 Cor. 16: 20; 2 Cor. 13:12). How do you respond to the assertion that rules for one church may not apply to other churches?

3. Why do you think it is important to determine what the author of each book of the Bible actually wrote? What effect does this question have on how you read and use Scripture?

4. What did you find most useful in the authors' discussion about translations? Read Luke 2:1-14 in at least three types of translations. Find and discuss the differences in each translation. What did you learn from this exercise? How does this verify or challenge the statement "translation is interpretation"?

5. What challenges face a reader who tries to determine the intention of a biblical author? Why should readers be especially cautious in this pursuit?

6. List the "rules of thumb" given in the chapter that help readers of the Bible determine the place of culture in specific texts. Which of these do you find most enlightening and why? Read 1 Timothy 2:9-12 about women's apparel. Apply the rules to this verse and determine what you think is cultural and what is not.

7. How should congregations handle matters of biblical silence? Do you think silence in the Bible about a certain activity points toward permission or prohibition of that activity? Why or why not? Distinguish among the hermeneutical, theological, and pastoral tasks that leaders face on issues of silence (p. 182).

8. Read Galatians 4:10-11, Colossians 2:16, and Romans 14:5-6. How have churches used these passages to determine what can or cannot be done on Easter? How do you discern the tension among these texts? In what ways do these texts apply to church practices today?

For Reflection & Prayer:

1. How does the authors' distinction between a prototype and an archetype (pp. 184-5) help you deal with the diversity found in Scripture? Cite specific beliefs or practices you think the church needs to re-examine.

2. How have the insights from this chapter enhanced or hindered your understanding of and ability to do biblical interpretation?

3. Reflect on the strengths and weaknesses of your congregation's ability to do sound biblical interpretation. How does this compare to your own ability?

4. Spend time in prayer for greater insight and understanding of how to use and interpret God's Word.

Chapter 8

For Study & Analysis:

1. Describe ways that churches may have missed the theological message of Scripture. What are the possible results of this absence?

2. In your own words, define "theological reflection." Why is theological reflection important to the daily life of both individuals and the church? What is meant by the statement, "the search for the theological substance of a passage is both an art and a science" (p. 192)?

3. What do the authors mean when they talk about psychologizing or moralizing a biblical text? How common do you think these practices are? Why are we tempted to do either of them? Do you think they are dangerous practices or not? Explain your response.

4. When doing ethics, why is it important that the norm and the warrant be expressed together? In other words, what happens when people grow up only hearing "do's and don'ts?"

5. Review the five steps outlined for a process of individual discernment (pp. 203-9). Which of these practices are natural to your Christian walk and which ones are not? On a scale of 1 to 10 (1 = extremely effective, 10 = extremely ineffective), how would you evaluate these practices? Explain your rating.

6. Review the Ignatian Model (pp. 209-10) for community discernment. Which of these practices are natural to your Christian community and which ones are not? On a scale of 1 to 10 (1 = extremely effective, 10 = extremely ineffective), how would you evaluate these principles? Explain your rating.

7. Read Philippians 2:1-11. How do these verses form the theological center of this book? What would be lost if these verses were omitted from the epistle? What other passages in the letter are informed by these verses and to what extent?

For Reflection & Prayer:

1. What insights from this chapter have you found most meaningful and why?

2. What principles of theological reflection do you want to put into personal practice? Which dimensions of communal discernment are you most interested in implementing?

3. Reflect on your responses and pray about them.

Chapter 9

For Study & Analysis:

1. What is the difference between an excellent public reading and a performance? What can your congregation do to improve the public reading of Scripture in your services?

2. What else can your church do to enrich the use of Scripture in your public worship? What would it take to implement these changes?

3. What is catechesis? How has it been a lost dimension of the church's ministry? What

could be done to improve our biblical instruction to the children of the church?

4. How could adult Bible classes be improved? What would a curriculum for maturing Christians consist of? How can the Bible teachers in your congregation be better equipped for this important service they perform?

5. What is theological literacy and why is it important? How can it be enhanced at your congregation?

6. In terms of adult Bible classes, what are the strengths and weaknesses of group discussion? Of lecturing? Do you think it is possible to provide for different learning styles within the church? Why is this consideration an important one?

For Exploration:

Divide into small groups and read 1 Cor. 5. Ask participants to share what they think is going on in Corinth based on this passage. Have them write down questions about the situation in Corinth that they cannot yet determine. Have them discuss how they would arrive at answers to these questions. Each group should write what they think the main point of this passage is. Instruct each group to develop application questions as if they were going to teach it. Invite each group to share with the larger class what they learned from this process.

For Reflection & Prayer:

1. Share ways that you have incorporated Scripture into your communal and personal life. Explore ways that you could do this even more.

2. In Chapter 1, you were asked to reflect on the ways the Bible is used or not used in your local congregation in each of the following contexts. After reading *God's Holy Fire*, describe how you have been challenged to make improvements in the use of Scripture in each of these areas: Children's classes; Adult classes; Worship; Congregational decision-making; Personal decisions.

3. Read Romans 16 and describe your theological understanding of the repeated command to "greet." How does that relate to the doctrine of acceptance in Rom. 14:1 and 15:7? Personalize the message by responding to the following statements: "One area of our community life that needs to change is..." "A brother or sister with whom I have some distance is..." "I am going to accept and greet this person in the Lord by...."

4. Reflect on your responses to questions 1 and 3 in this section. What do they say about how God is at work in your church through his Word?

5. Spend time in prayer about your reflection.

Introduction to Congregational Scenarios

Read the following scenarios (each is followed by a set of possible discussion questions). All of them are fictitious, but they represent congregational issues that many will find familiar. Their purpose is to draw learners into true-to-life situations that will assist in processing what they have read in *God's Holy Fire*. Remember that while none of these scenarios has a single conclusion or "answer," they provide opportunities for individuals to decide what they would do in these situations and to explore why they would make particular choices.

The main task of the teacher in using the four scenarios (as well as the biblical case study that follows) is to serve as a facilitator by fostering meaningful discussion, highlighting significant insights, and assisting in examining the ramifications of actions and attitudes. Preparation for teaching a scenario or case demands that the teacher assume a learning stance alongside class participants. More rather than less study, analysis, and preparation are required to teach a scenario or case effectively.

The first step in preparing to teach these congregational scenarios is to read the scenario thoroughly. The teacher may choose to list the central issues presented, the main characters portrayed, or the major events or dates indicated (any details that help "flesh out" the situation).

The second step involves exploring the various paths that a scenario or case might take—the outcomes that might result from these situations. The teacher decides on a possible direction and selects teaching tools (role playing, voting, small groups, etc.) that will best facilitate discussion. Teachers should develop questions that help to clarify details and frame the discussion and that involve the participants in the situation presented.

Finally, the teacher will want to prepare a wrap-up of the discussion. This task can include summarizing what participants have shared or asking them to list what they have learned. The leader may want to share personal insights to the scenario or case at this point, but must be careful not to trump the learning process or invalidate the contribution of others.

Scenario 1: "No Ordinary Sunday"

The Situation:

Teddy Jackson drove to work Thursday, September 13, 2001 as he had for the past seventeen years. The events of Tuesday still lingered in his thoughts. Last night's prayer service at the church and then again at the Civic Center had left him exhausted. Today would be his first day back in the office. He arrived shortly before 8 A.M., sat at his desk, and checked his messages.

By 10 A.M. he had yet to look at his calendar. It read, 9 A.M.–12 P.M.: finish sermon preparation. What would he preach? Sunday's coming, and he hadn't given it a thought. His mind raced for a moment. What could he possibly say at a time like this?

Teddy picked up the phone to call Jason. Jason had preached for the past fifteen years at a church just twenty miles down the road. Ever since Teddy moved to Northpark, Jason had proven to be a trusted friend and mentor. Teddy admired Jason's preaching ability and his dedication to study. More importantly, Teddy respected Jason's heart for people.

"Hello." Jason answered after one ring.

"Jason, it's Teddy. How's it going?"

Jason answered slowly, "I imagine it's going for me about like it's going for you. I've done more counseling in the past two days than I've done in any two months combined. How about you?"

"I thought I was handling everything pretty well—considering," Teddy responded. "But it just hit me a few minutes ago, I've got to preach on Sunday. Jason, I don't have a clue where to begin."

"It's tough," Jason began. "I've been giving the subject some thought myself. I just pulled a good book off my shelf from Abingdon Press called *Crisis Preaching*, by Joseph Jeter. Jeter suggests a passage like Jeremiah 8:14-22. Other passages he mentions are Mark 13:3-7; Psalm 120; Psalm 55:20-22; Isaiah 26:12; Ezekiel 13:8-16; and John 20:24-29. I found the Jeremiah passage to be especially powerful. I think I'll use it. But wait a minute, Teddy," Jason hesitated. "Don't you publish in your bulletin what you plan to preach each week? You've already announced a text, haven't you?"

"As you know, the worship committee and I plan out our services several months in advance. But I don't usually look at it again until the Tuesday of that week." Teddy paused. "A bad habit I guess." Teddy picked up his day planner. September 16th. "Here it is. I'm supposed to preach on the theme of God's forgiveness. We've been doing a series on famous passages from Paul and this week is 1 Timothy 1:17."

"There you go," Jason answered. "I would stick with the announced text and see how Paul's words to Timothy apply to the week's events. Call me next week and tell me how it goes."

After a few more words of encouragement, Teddy and Jason promised to eat lunch together the next week.

The task for Thursday lay before him. It was obvious that he would need the rest of the afternoon to finish. Teddy picked up his Bible and began to read 1 Timothy. What could he possibly say that would make any difference?

For Discussion:

1. Given this situation, do you think Teddy should stick with the announced text or choose a different one? Explain the rationale you would use for making this decision. If you choose another text, which one would you select? Why?

2. Take the text you have selected (whether 1 Timothy or another one) and sketch out the process necessary for Teddy to move from text to sermon.

3. What was the original occasion of this text?

4. Discern the primary and secondary messages in the passage.

5. What specifics in this passage are analogous to situations in your local community? What is analogous with the events of September 11?

6. What different groups within the congregation will be present to hear this Scripture? What messages do each of these need to hear in this sermon?

7. What are the applications and implications from your selected text that the sermon should stress? Why do you think these are important?

For Exploration:

Assume that you have more time to write this sermon. A sermon team meets every week to help the minister write the sermon. This process is sometimes called a "feed-in" sermon group. Divide the class into groups of 5-7. After brainstorming together for 20 minutes, the teams are to report their initial feelings, experiences, impressions, or discernments regarding their selected text and what they believe should be the main message of the sermon. After each group has reported, have the class evaluate the strengths and weaknesses of each potential sermon for meeting the needs of the church after traumatic events like the terrorist attacks of September 11, 2001.

Scenario 2: "Remember Your Creator in the Days of Your Youth"

The Situation:

Jake and Brenda Blake sat across the kitchen table from each other, intermittently writing furiously on the legal pads in front of them or staring blankly at each other. Even with all the pages of notes they had written, neither of them had any real idea how to go about meeting the challenge laid before them at the last elders' meeting of the Pecan Hill Church.

Although they had worked with the young people at Pecan Hill for the past five years, they had only been asked to meet with the elders a couple of other times, ususally for a blessing and prayer session. They had been surprised when Peter Simmons called in the middle of the school year to ask them to meet with the elders on a matter of "real importance." Admittedly, both of them had been a bit anxious about the meeting.

"Simply put," Peter Simmons, the elder most engaged with the youth, said, "the survey of parents and teens at this church indicate that neither group is very satisfied with our current classes or youth programs."

"That doesn't mean they don't love the two of you!" Hal Ramsey quickly inserted. "You both got real high marks from all parts of the congregation. That's why we called you in tonight. We want you to put your heads together and figure out a way to turn this level of dissatisfaction around."

"What most families indicated," Peter added, "is that they want more in-depth Bible study in our youth classes and more spiritually-maturing materials for most of our programs. Somehow, folks seem to think we're selling our young people short and that many of them have stopped coming because things are too shallow. They've been attending youth functions at various other churches. We thought the spring youth retreat coming up would be a good place to get started."

The elders had proceeded to give Jake and Brenda the challenge of putting together a spiritually-nourishing retreat, outlining Bible classes for the youth for the next quarter, and making plans for how they would encourage the teens and their families to become personally involved in Scripture in the next three months.

For Discussion:

You have been asked to serve on a task force with the Blakes to determine how to make the youth program more biblically and spiritually mature. Use the following questions as an agenda for an imaginary meeting and prepare a report that you would give to the elders about your meeting.

1. What steps would you take to make the spring retreat more spiritually refreshing and biblically based?

2. Outline a program for the retreat. What would you include? What would you exclude? Why would you make these decisions?

3. What materials and speakers would you use to ensure that the teens become committed to the process?

4. Determine what measures might be taken to enrich the young people's personal and family involvement in Scripture for the next three months. What steps would you take to encourage participation? How would you go about developing materials and following up on their use?

5. Develop a sketch of a family action plan that might be used by various individuals and families. What would be the most important aspects in this plan? Why? How would this plan help to encourage involvement?

For Exploration:

1. Brainstorm several possible Bible classes that might interest the youth for the next quarter. Discuss the strengths and weaknesses of each suggestion. Develop a proposal that you would like to present to the teens, parents, and elders outlining the text, materials, and activities you might want to use.

2. Present your retreat program, Bible class proposal, and family action plan to the larger group. Evaluate the strengths and weaknesses of each. What have you learned in this process? Are there specific ideas that have surfaced that you might want to incorporate into the life of your church? What has this experience showed you that needs more attention and prayer?

Scenario 3: "Lesson III"

The Situation:

Taylor Scott Jackson left Mikhail Bialostosky's apartment exhausted. As Taylor walked the streets of Kiev, he replayed the Bible study with Mikhail over and over again in his head. He had used the same set of lessons for more than a decade on the mission field, but today the focus of Lesson III sounded empty. Taylor questioned whether even he believed the material he had just taught. He whispered to himself, "Surely I believe the Old Testament should be part of the Bible. Did I just tell someone it didn't count? Why have I not seen this before?" How could he expect Mikhail to accept as truth a concept that he himself doubted more and more?

As Taylor walked, he reflected on his tenure in the mission field that began soon after his graduation from college. He had completed internships the previous summers in the former Yugoslavia with missionaries his home congregation sponsored. Furthermore, these missionaries mentored him for two years before he left for the Ukraine. Although congregations in the States recognized the patience necessary for mission work in the former Soviet Union, Taylor believed he had exceeded all their expectations. Until today, he believed his mentors had prepared him well for working with both small group and one-on-one evangelism. Although he had modified the basic lesson plans somewhat, the primary sequence of the studies remained intact. Through the years, these lessons had proved invaluable to him for leading prospects to Christ.

285

As Taylor quickened his pace he thought, "Mikhail had no problem with what he was hearing. I used Lesson III the same way I always do. I stayed on topic and didn't do anything different. The same words and the same results." But deep down, Taylor knew there was indeed a difference. In the last few weeks, Taylor had come to realize that all of his life he had dismissed the Old Testament as a real source for discovering God's revelation. The Old Testament for him had merely been a stockroom for background materials, illustrations, and examples.

Lesson III on the nature of covenants had never tripped him up before. It seemed like such a straightforward study. As Taylor reached for the door of his apartment, he heard himself say aloud, "You must have a clear distinction between the Old and New Testaments in order to have pure New Testament Christianity!" As he slumped in his chair, his thoughts raced: "What was it I was reading that has jumbled all this up for me anyway?"

He glanced over to his kitchen table and saw the book *God's Holy Fire* in the same place he had left it the day before. The connection between Lesson III and his doubts stared at him back across the room. Was it as simple as using some verses out of context? Maybe he had misapplied Colossians 2:14 and 2 Timothy 2:15. But if that were true, then why had this study been so successful for years? Something else nagged at the edges of his thoughts as well. The authors seemed to understand the entire nature of the Old Testament differently than Lesson III did.

For Discussion:

1. In mission and evangelistic settings, do you think Lesson III is needed or not? Why? What would be lost if Lesson III were omitted? What would be some of the reasons

evangelists and missionaries in the past would include lessons on the distinctive nature of the two covenants? Why do you think Taylor is re-examining something he felt confident about previously?

2. Imagine yourself in a church meeting where one of the leaders makes the following statement: "If you undermine the clear demarcation between the testaments, you undermine the authority of the New Testament. If the Old Testament is allowed to give voice to doctrinal issues in the church, then false teachings concerning instrumental music, Sabbath, and infant baptism (just to name a few) would infiltrate our ranks." Do you agree with the concerns expressed in this statement? Why or why not?

3. What effect should these ideas have on how we teach about the Old and New Testaments?

4. "Unpack" the last line of the above scenario: "The authors seemed to understand the entire nature of the Old Testament differently than Lesson III." In what ways do the authors of *God's Holy Fire* see the Old Testament differently? What would your local congregation gain or lose if this understanding of the Old Testament were fully incorporated?

5. Examine the passages used in Lesson III again. What are these texts teaching in their original context?

6. What do these texts (especially the passages in Hebrews) teach about the relationship of the New Testament with the Old Testament?

7. Assume that Matthew 5:17 should be a primary text that interprets other texts (using the

principle "scripture interprets scripture"). How does this text confirm or modify your answers to the above questions?

For Exploration:

Rewrite Lesson III from the perspective of *God's Holy Fire* in a way that would be appropriate for a missions context.

Introduction to Biblical Case Study & Teaching Notes

Read the case below based upon Paul's letter to the church at Rome. This case helps readers understand that Paul was facing a real historical situation and that Christians then inevitably struggled with both interpreting and applying his teachings. Although some of the characters are fictitious, they represent the kind of people who might have been part of the church at Rome. Two of the characters, Phoebe and Asyncritus—as well as the households of Priscilla and Aquila and of Nereus—were people Paul knew (Rom. 16). The dialogue in the case is meant to flesh out the difficulties Paul's teachings in Romans 14 and 15 would have presented for the various house churches in Rome. It will be advantageous to read and be familiar with these chapters in Romans before reading the case. This case is an adaptation of "The Righteousness of God and Pauline Polity" by Stanley P. Saunders (Columbia Theological Seminary, The Case Study Institute, 1995; distributed by the Case Clearing House, Yale Divinity School Library, New Haven, CT 06511).

Following the case are suggested teaching notes that may help in preparing it for presentation. Also, re-examine the guidelines given in the directions before the congregational scenarios for helpful suggestions on how to maximize teaching effectiveness.

Biblical Case Study: "The Strong Ought to Bear With the Weak"

Eunice gave a hard look at the young woman, Phoebe, who now stood before the congregation meeting in the household of Eunice and her husband, Asyncritus. Phoebe, a servant in the church at Cenchreae, had traveled to Rome with the party that brought from Paul a most remarkable and troubling letter.

Eunice and Asyncritus had grown close to Paul after their conversions and were active in advancing the church in Rome as well as supporting Paul in his other missionary endeavors. They found Paul's teaching thought-provoking, but Eunice could not remember an occasion, prior to this letter, when Paul had been so forceful and detailed in laying out the implications of his "gospel of the righteousness of God." She began to worry about how members of the other Christian households in Rome would respond to his ideas. Paul had sent the letter in order to prepare the Roman Christians for his intended visit, and she knew that he hoped to use the Roman church as a base for mission activity to the west. But what kind of preparation was this?

Phoebe had been invited to meet with their household in an attempt to answer, on behalf of Paul, some serious questions about the letter. The correspondence began and ended with teachings that were intended to shape a new understanding of the gospel—a foundation for relationships—among the divided factions of the Roman church. Like many of Paul's congregations, the diverse peoples and households that made up the church at Rome had brought with them many ideas and practices that were rooted deeply in their spiritual convictions. These differences often bumped up against each other and threatened the unity of the Roman Christians. The division especially pressed these house churches when influential Jewish Christians tried to bind on the Gentiles the Jewish understandings of circumcision, special days, and food laws.

Many of the other household congregations were looking to the household of Asyncritus and Eunice for leadership. They questioned whether or not to continue table fellowship with one particular household, whose patron, Artemis, had continued, even after his conversion, to maintain strong connections with the synagogue. He argued that conversion to Christ in no way nullified the Law of Moses and that Gentiles needed to conform their teachings and practices in order to be sound in the faith.

Asyncritus was now challenging Phoebe to defend the logic of Paul's argument that different religious ideas and practices were permissible within the church: "I have a difficult time going as far as Brother Paul when he suggests that it is all right for some Christians to eat meat that is unclean, while others' consciences do not permit this, or that some Christians might observe holy days while others do not. These are not mere trifles, but matters that are rooted in the foundations of our identity as the people of God. The commandments of Moses expressly forbid such practices and command us to keep the Sabbath holy. Does our brother really believe that any and all behavior is permissible as long as we call ourselves Christians?"

"Brother Asyncritus," Phoebe replied, "I understand that Paul's argument seems new and disconcerting. But the commandment to love our neighbors as ourselves is the commandment that fulfills all the rest of the commandments—even the central prohibitions in the Ten Commandments. It is the fulfillment even of the prohibitions not to steal and not to kill. Remember, Paul was not the first one to say this, but our Lord Jesus."

"So even thieves and murderers are now permitted to join us at table?" Asyncritus countered.

"Not because they are thieves and murderers, but because they are now God's children, ransomed by the blood of our Lord. You have high standards, Asyncritus, and so you want to hold others to them. But I am wondering, brother, on what grounds you regard yourself fit to judge others? You are not their master, but a fellow slave of Jesus Christ. Do you now think yourself so righteous that you no longer need to rely on the mercy and righteousness of our God? You are called to build up the household of God, not to tear it down with your own righteousness."

Eunice turned away this challenge to her husband with her own question. "I understand Paul to be saying that we can continue to be one, even when our religious practices and beliefs are different, and that we should continue to eat with each other even when we disagree. I have no dispute with this. But where do we draw lines? If we are so different, where is our oneness? How will those who do not yet know the Lord recognize us? And how will we know who our real sisters and brothers are?"

"Yes, that is my real question." Asyncritus returned to the fray. "We know that we are not to do things that the pagans find dishonorable, but we know, too, that our righteousness is to exceed that of the pagans. Our Lord taught us that our righteousness is to exceed even that of the Pharisees. From our Father Abraham until now, we have been taught well to mark the differences between those who are righteous and those who are not. It is by observing and preserving these differences that we know we are God's children. Our distinction is clearest when we align ourselves with our Jewish brothers and sisters who are so well versed in the Law."

Phoebe spoke again. "But Asyncritus, how is this way of seeing the world different at all from the pagans? Do they not also have their standards of honor? Do they not also despise the weak and shameful? Is not their sense of glory and honor dependent on their judgments against the poor and the slaves? Are you not doing the very same things as the pagans you condemn?"

"But we are the household of God, not the household of Caesar," Asyncritus returned. "How can the household of God not pass judgment on the household of Caesar? The members of my household know they are 'of Asyncritus' and this means that they are not 'of Stephanus' or 'of Andronicus.' And we know that when we are in the marketplace, we will contest for our livelihood with the members of those houses. And now, above all, we also know that through our baptism into Christ Jesus that we are 'of God.' Does this not mean that we must guard our boundaries against those who are 'of Caesar,' and that we must struggle against those who are of the flesh? Brother Paul himself has said as much. Is this not how we know that we continue to stand in God's honor and grace?"

"You are right, Asyncritus, when you say that we are no longer slaves of the flesh but slaves to Jesus Christ. We know that Caesar no longer rules our spirits." Phoebe paused to collect her thoughts. "But is the matter simply a question of having a different master? Do we still look at our neighbors and our enemies as we did before, but only as if we had changed households? Does it make any difference to those of us who call upon the Lord that our master, our God, is impartial and does not look upon the face of things? I think Paul means that God does not share our interests in distinctions and boundaries. And if God looks past our differences, how can we not do the same with our brothers and sisters?"

"But Paul himself begins his letter by describing in no uncertain terms those sinners against whom God's wrath will descend on the Day of Judgment," Asyncritus replied. "Let me give you a concrete example of what I am talking about. Paul describes those who exchange the relations that are natural between men and women for lustful passion with members of the same sex. Our ancestors have always said that God will condemn these people, for their sinful desires, and their darkened minds are the results of their idolatry. They do these unnatural things because they have turned their backs on God, and so God has abandoned them to their own debased desires. Now Paul says, on the one hand, that we should continue to be at table with those who eat meat offered to idols, but he also says that God will condemn idolaters. Are we not then also to condemn such idolatrous acts? I ask you, how are we to reconcile such ideas? How can we be part of God's household and *not* condemn

293

brothers and sisters who do such things? Tell me, would you consider someone who has sex with a member of the same sex a brother or sister? Is this person not an idolater? Would you accept this individual and the members of his household at table? Would you want to live in a household where such a man was the patron? Phoebe, would you or Paul submit to the authority of such a person? I say you would not.

"Therefore," Asyncritus raised himself to make his final point. "Therefore, my dear sister, in the same way we preserve our sacred table by obeying *all* the food laws found in Moses and held dear by our Jewish brothers and sisters. There is our true righteousness."

"Asyncritus, you are confusing the issues," Phoebe replied, "Paul is not saying that everything is acceptable. You are right in looking closely at his teachings about morality; he is not encouraging us to abandon the sexual purity that is central to the life lived in Christ. But what Paul acknowledges is that there are matters of faith that are disputable—not central to the cross but matters of opinion. On these issues, we must be careful not to play God because that would be but another form of idolatry. If Paul were here, he would insist that it is not our privilege as servants of Jesus Christ to judge our brothers and sisters on matters of opinion. To do so would be to claim our own righteousness over theirs, and to claim our righteousness before God. Asyncritus, you know that it is God's love and mercy, and this alone, that has set us free from the bondage of our own sinful idolatry and brokenness. God has loved us when we did not deserve it. Even when we were sinners, unable to see God because of our idolatry, Jesus Christ died for us. And because of this we now are free, reconciled to God and to one another. We are the same as the people we might judge, except that God has revealed grace and mercy to us in Jesus Christ. If God has loved us, how can we not love these brothers and sisters? Is not judging them a sign that we trust in our own righteousness rather than God's? That is why Paul said, 'Christ is the end of the Law.' Not that the Law is dead, but that the Law has completed its purpose. The Law was never intended to make us righteous. We are declared righteous by God because of our faith."

Phoebe paused a moment, then continued. "Brothers and sisters, when Paul sent you this letter he knew that you would find many things in it deeply disturbing. But he is convinced in the Lord that we will never become one in Christ as long as we continue to judge one another. He is appealing especially to you in this household, and those of Priscilla and Aquila and of Nereus, to set an example for the others. He believes that if we continue to judge one another and draw close lines of fellowship, the result will be more and more divisions. If we are to be one, if we are to continue to live in God's spirit of reconciliation, we must trust God's love and grace, not our own merit. I appeal to you in the name of our brother, Paul, to trust God's grace and faithfulness. Only by trusting God can we resolve differences and live as one people. I beg you, keep the table of our Lord open, especially to those who are weak."

There was a long moment of silence in the house. Eunice herself had been silent for a long time and now felt many eyes turning toward her, as if waiting for what she would say. She remembered how difficult it had been for Jews and Gentiles at first to sit down together at the Lord's table—something she could never have imagined before her call to follow Jesus Christ. She understood Paul now to be calling the Christian households of Rome to continue their walk down that same road, placing their trust in the same faithful God. But where would it all lead? How could they continue to preserve their unity when the differences were so real and so deep? What were these Christians to do with Paul and his ideas?

Teaching Notes: "The Strong Ought to Bear With the Weak"

Preparation:

Before addressing the issues of this case, read the following passages: Acts 26–28; Romans 1:14–16; Romans 15; Romans 16.

Goals:

This case presents a fictitious account of a dialogue among Christians at Rome (Phoebe and Asyncritus are mentioned in Romans 16:1 and 10b. Eunice is the fictitious wife of Asyncritus). Their discussion is based on Paul's teachings to the church from chapters fourteen and fifteen on how to handle disputable matters, such as eating meat and observing holy days. The goals of studying this case are:

1) To enter the historical world of the New Testament;

2) To discuss matters of the interpretation and application of the biblical text from the perspective of ancient Christians;

3) To discern whether or not difficult issues facing the church (then and now) are matters of gospel or matters of spiritual maturity (see pp. 62-7);

4) To determine what task—the hermeneutical, the theological, or the pastoral (see p. 182)—the church should use in addressing issues when the Bible is silent.

Preliminary Activities:

1. Describe the main characters:

Phoebe: a deaconess/servant from the church in Cenchreae, sent to Rome with the letter from Paul (Rom. 16:1).

Asyncritus: a friend of Paul and house church leader in Rome (Rom. 16:10b).

Eunice: fictitious wife of Asyncritus.

2. Describe the minor characters:

Artemis: fictitious patron of a house church in Rome who argues for continued association with the Law of Moses.

Priscilla and *Aquila*: cohosts of a house church in Rome and fellow workers with Paul (Rom. 16:3-4; Acts 18:2-3).

Nereus: patron of a house church in Rome (Rom. 16:11b).

3. Identify the main characters' interests.

4. Identify the main characters' feelings.

Detailed Questions & Activities:

1. Has Paul ever used similar arguments to address different issues? If so, where?

2. What do you think are the main characters' interests? What are their feelings? What is at stake for each of them in this discussion?

3. Compare 1 Corinthians 8-10 with Acts 26-28 and Romans 1:14-16. Note the difference between the trouble caused by meat offered to idols at Corinth and the Jewish food laws that caused problems for the Christians at Rome.

4. How would you describe what Paul means by the "strong" in Romans 14 and 15? Who are the "weak" in this context? What do these terms have to do with spiritual maturity?

5. How do the roles of strong and weak play out in the case?

6. Why do you think Paul finds it necessary to write about these matters? What relationship do they have to the gospel?

Making Applications:

1. In *God's Holy Fire*, the authors talk about three tasks that face the church on matters of silence: the hermeneutical task, the theological task, and the pastoral task (see p. 182). How would you use *each* of these to deal with the case? What effect do you think each would have in this situation? How would they help the leaders in this context decide what to do?

2. Which issues facing the church today are matters of silence in relation to the biblical text but are of utmost importance in the practice of the church?

3. Why do you think these issues are so significant? What interests or feelings lie behind each issue?

4. Do you see individuals in positions of strength or weakness on these issues? Why do you think these individuals fit in that particular

category? What relationship do these issues have with the gospel?

5. Examine the hermeneutical, theological, and pastoral tasks that you might use to address these issues. Which task would you choose in addressing the controversial issue presented in this case? Why?

6. Pray for the local and worldwide church as it deals with disputable matters.

Recommended Reading

The authors recommend the following books and articles for further reading. Although we do not fully endorse everything they say, we have found them to be useful conversation partners in some of the topics discussed in this book.

Scripture

Braaten, Carl E. and Robert W. Jenson, eds. *Reclaiming the Bible for the Church*. Grand Rapids: Eerdmans, 1995.

Burgess, John P. *Why Scripture Matters: Reading the Bible in a Time of Church Conflict*. Louisville: Westminster John Knox, 1998.

Hauerwas, Stanley. *Unleashing Scripture: Freeing the Bible from Captivity in America*. Nashville: Abingdon, 1993.

Inspiration

Achtemeier, Paul. *Inspiration and Authority*. Peabody, MA: Hendrickson, 1999.

Dunn, James D. G. *The Living Word*. Philadelphia: Fortress, 1987.

Interpretation

Eagleton, Terry. *Literary Theory: An Introduction*. Minneapolis: University of Minnesota Press, 1983.

Fee, Gordon D. and Douglas Stuart. *How to Read the Bible for All Its Worth*. 2nd ed. Grand Rapids: Zondervan, 1993.

Hays, Richard B. *The Moral Vision of the New Testament: A Contemporary Introduction to New Testament Ethics*. New York: HarperCollins, 1996.

Hirsch, E. D. *Validity in Interpretation*. New Haven: Yale University Press, 1967.

Sheeley, Steven M. and Robert N. Nash, Jr. *The Bible in English Translation: An Essential Guide*. Nashville: Abingdon, 1997.

Theological Reflection

Johnson, Luke Timothy. *Scripture and Discernment: Decision-Making in the Church*. Nashville: Abingdon, 1996.

Morris, Danny E. and Charles M. Olsen. *Discerning God's Will Together: A Spiritual Practice for the Church*. Bethesda, MD: Alban, 1997.

Stone, Howard W. and James D. Duke. *How to Think Theologically*. Minneapolis: Fortress, 1996.

Use of Scripture in Worship

McComiskey, Thomas Edward. *Reading Scripture in Public: A Guide for Preachers and Lay Readers.* Grand Rapids: Baker, 1991.

The Revised Common Lectionary: Consultation on Common Texts. Nashville: Abingdon, 1992.

Teaching Scripture

Hestenes, Roberta. *Using the Bible in Groups.* Philadelphia: Westminster, 1983.

Devotional Works

Foster, Richard and James Bryan Smith, eds. *Devotional Classics: Selected Readings for Individuals and Groups.* New York: HarperSan Francisco, 1993.

Hawkins, Peter and Paula Carlson, eds. *Listening for God: Contemporary Literature and the Life of Faith.* Minneapolis: Augsburg Fortress, 1994.

Peterson, Eugene. *Take and Read: Spiritual Readings: An Annotated List.* Grand Rapids: Eerdmans, 1996.

Tippens, Darryl, Stephen Weathers, and Jack Welch, eds. *Shadow and Light: Literature and the Life of Faith.* Abilene, TX: ACU Press, 1997.